The GOSSIP Family Handbook

BY THE SAME AUTHOR

GOSSIP:
A History of High Society from 1920 to 1970

INTERNATIONAL GOSSIP:
A History of High Society from 1970 to 1980

THE FLESH IS WEAK:
An Intimate History of The Church of England

The GOSSIP Family Handbook

Andrew Barrow

HAMISH HAMILTON
LONDON

Design by Craig Dodd

First published in Great Britain 1983
by Hamish Hamilton Ltd
Garden House, 57–59 Long Acre,
London WC2E 8JZ

British Library Cataloguing in Publication Data

Barrow, Andrew
The gossip family handbook.
1. Upper classes—Great Britain—History
—20th century
2. Great Britain—Social Life and customs
—20th century
I. Title
941.082′0880621 DA566.4

ISBN 0–241–11097–1

Filmset by Northumberland Press Ltd
Gateshead, Tyne and Wear
Printed in Great Britain by
Fletcher & Son Ltd, Norwich

Contents

Sources of the Illustrations

The illustrations are reproduced by kind permission of the following: Lady Katharine Asquith p. 51; Associated Newspapers Ltd., p. 100; BBC Hulton Picture Library, pp. 7, 8, 14, 17, 18 top, 23, 24 top & bottom, 31, 36, 47, 48, 53, 55, 56, 58, 60, 62, 65, 66, 72, 74, 76, 78, 81, 83, 89, 91, 93, 94, 101 & 102; Camera Press London, pp. 1 & 43 (Patrick Lichfield), 27 (Jean Desaundis), 63 (Michael Blackman) & 88 (Godfrey Argent); André Deutsch, p. 69; Angel Gorgas, p. 50; Keystone Press Agency Ltd., p. 5, 11, 13, 38, 45, 71, 82, 87, 99 & 103; Tim Mercer, *Harpers & Queen*, p. 75; Popperfoto, pp. 18 bottom, 20, 33, 39, 40, 77 & 100; Rex Features Ltd., p. 35 (Richard Young) & 84; Robert Rosen, p. 49; Sport & General Press Agency Ltd., p. 97.

The photographs on the jacket are reproduced by kind permission of the BBC Hulton Picture Library; Camera Press (Lord Snowdon, Karsh of Ottawa, Peter Abbey, *The Times*); and Express Newspapers.

Introduction

This book consists of one big family tree spread over more than a hundred pages.

Unlike the conventional family tree, it goes *sideways* rather than backwards, linking people together through their brothers-in-law, step-mothers and first wives rather than through a common ancestor. Everyone in this book is connected with everyone else but, as often as not, there is no actual blood relationship.

I hope that readers will soon master the simple format. As shown in the key at the end of this introduction, a double ruled line indicates a marriage, an arrow indicates the parent-child relationship and a single ruled line means a siblingship.

It should be noted here that half-brothers and half-sisters are shown in the same way as full brothers and sisters and that a broken marriage is treated in the same way as an on-going marriage. Another feature of this format is that it is only possible to identify one parent of each child, although both parents may appear on the page: in no case is there any suggestion that the child is illegitimate.

While the book can claim to cover a variety of people and families, many of them far from aristocratic, it is also very selective. I have concentrated on people in the public eye or at least well known to readers of the gossip columns. Not all the husbands or wives of a much married person will necessarily be shown and I have tried to keep the names of less well-known people who sometimes link the famous together to a minimum. Inevitably, some famous names have been omitted. This is usually because of reasons of space or because too many 'dull' names were required to link them to the whole.

It will be seen that the book divides into a number of over-lapping sections: I must emphasise that this is only a very loose grouping. Some very unathletic types crop up in the Sporting section, some very untheatrical types appear in the Show Biz group and not everyone in the Jewish section necessarily has even a drop of Jewish blood. A few names appear more than once: Lord Weidenfeld, for example, appears in the International group, the Media group and the Jewish section, while the late David Tennant crops up no less than six times. Certain widespread families re-occur constantly throughout the book.

Some readers may be confused by my rather slap-dash approach to titles, ranks and nicknames. The general rule I have tried to follow is to give people the names by which they are best known. Thus, some titles have been dropped altogether. I have called the present Viscountess Rothermere 'Bubbles Rothermere' as this seems to be the name by which she is generally known. On the other hand, I have given Colin Tennant and Michael Pearson their courtesy title 'Hon.' because this is how they usually appear in the newspapers. For the same reason, Captain Mark Phillips has been given his rank while many far more senior officers go unidentified as such. I have only broken this general rule where there is a line of remarkable sisters. In this case I have used their maiden names to emphasise the siblingship, although they are probably better known by their married names.

I will leave it to others to draw conclusions from the closely knit network that follows and I will not comment here on the incestuousness of public life, the survival of old boy networks or the new fluidity of the contemporary class system. This is partly laziness, partly because I am sure that *everyone has connections* if one took the trouble to find out. There are, I hope, enough surprising names here to make any analysis of the text a complicated task.

Many people have helped me complete this book. Firstly, I must acknowledge my debt to Hugo Vickers who five years ago introduced me to the amusing possibilities of lateral genealogy and has permitted me to go on developing what was originally his idea. Others who have made invaluable contributions include Peter Townend, Charles Kidd, David Williamson, Patrick Montague-Smith, Mary Killon, Ann Barr, Piers Dixon, Nicholas Phipps, Tom Hartman, Tim de Lisle, Anthony Blond, Felix Hope-Nicholson, Christopher Moorsom, John Gross, Hugh Montgomery-Massingberd, Meredith Etherington-Smith and Zygmunt Zamoyski. The fact that many of these people themselves appear in the book is my own affair and no reflection of any self-importance or vanity on their part. Any erro that may have survived to the final version are c course entirely my own responsibility.

I would also like to thank Caroline Tonson Ry of Hamish Hamilton, who worked on this boo from the start, Willie Landels for publishin several early extracts in *Harpers & Queen*, Crai Dodd for coping with the complicated design prob lems and my agent Gillon Aitken for his advice an encouragement.

Finally, I hope it may be possible to produce new and updated version of this book some time i the future and I would therefore be delighted t hear from anyone who has anything to add to i Families are always changing and the pages th follow could look quite different in a few year time.

Key

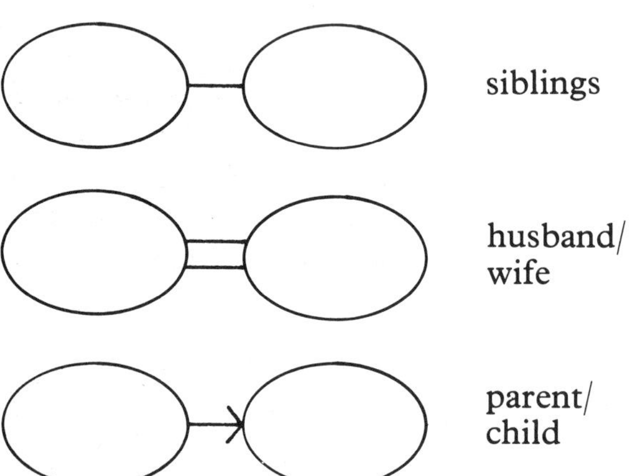
siblings
husband/wife
parent/child

Barbara Cartland (b 1901) turned down an invitation to t wedding of the Prince and Princess of Wales. She watched t ceremony on television dressed in her uniform as a Dame the St John's Ambulance Brigade.

The Princess of Wales (b 1961). Before her marriage s lived briefly at 60 Coleherne Court, Old Brompton Roa SW5, and had her telephone number listed in the Londo directory.

Earl Spencer (b 1924) drives a bronze Rolls-Royce.

Mrs Meyrick (d 1933). Nightclub proprietor. She was d scribed as 'the most inveterate law-breaker with regard licensing matters that the police have ever dealt with in t metropolis' and was several times imprisoned.

Lord de Clifford (d 1982). The last peer to be tried by t House of Lords. He was acquitted on a manslaughter charge 1935.

4th Earl of Craven drowned at Cowes in 1921 when he fe from his yacht in full evening dress.

Lord Dulverton (d 1956). President of the Imperial Tobacc Company.

Robin Douglas-Home (d 1968) worked in the grocery d partment at Selfridges and played the piano at the Berkel Hotel, Piccadilly.

Mrs Wynne-Morgan ran a tea-shop at Harrow-on-the-Hi which was popular among Harrovians during the 1960s.

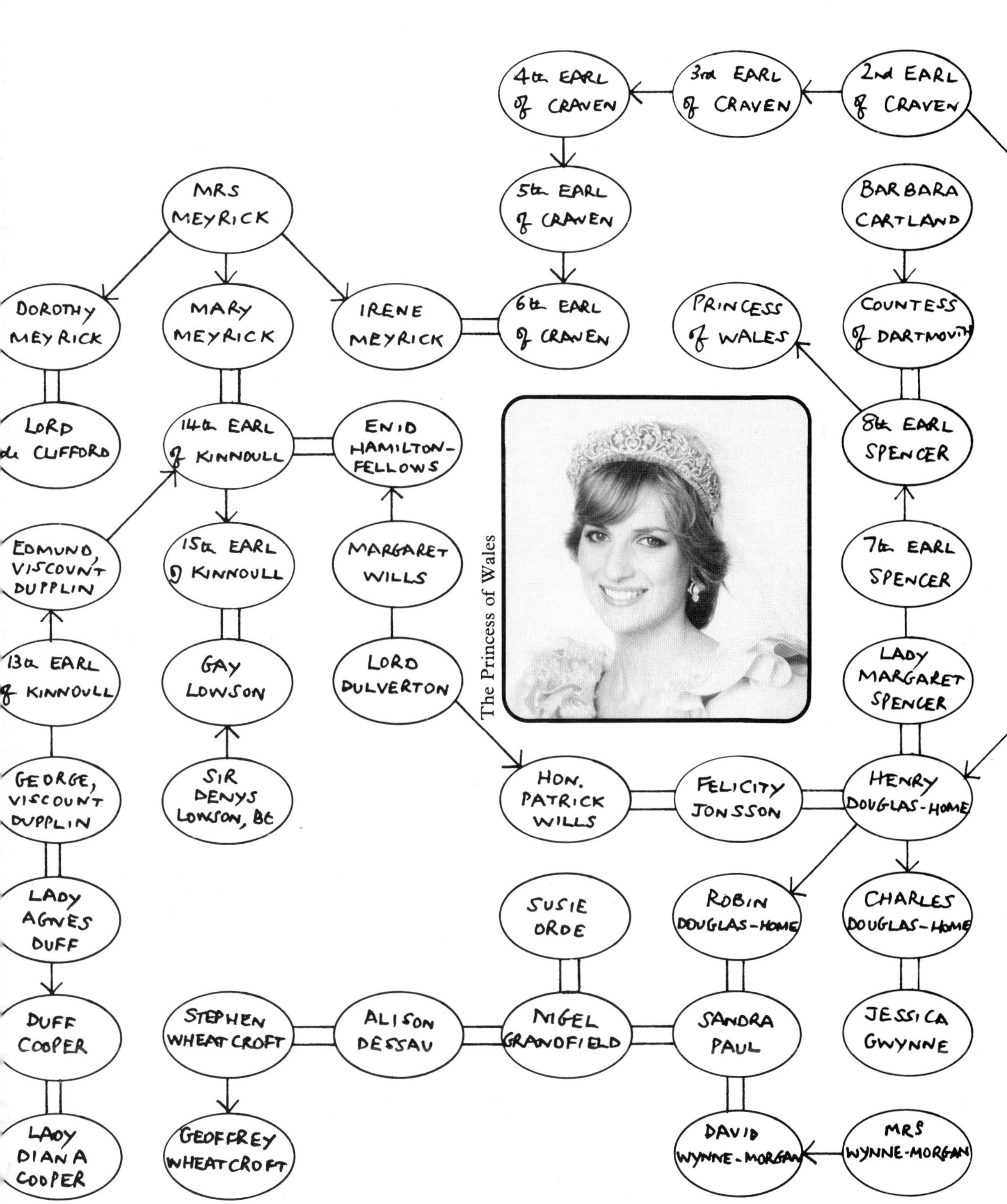
4th EARL of CRAVEN
3rd EARL of CRAVEN
2nd EARL of CRAVEN
MRS MEYRICK
5th EARL of CRAVEN
BARBARA CARTLAND
DOROTHY MEYRICK
MARY MEYRICK
IRENE MEYRICK
6th EARL of CRAVEN
PRINCESS of WALES
COUNTESS of DARTMOUTH
LORD de CLIFFORD
14th EARL of KINNOULL
ENID HAMILTON-FELLOWS
8th EARL SPENCER
EDMUND, VISCOUNT DUPPLIN
15th EARL of KINNOULL
MARGARET WILLS
7th EARL SPENCER
13th EARL of KINNOULL
GAY LOWSON
LORD DULVERTON
LADY MARGARET SPENCER
GEORGE, VISCOUNT DUPPLIN
SIR DENYS LOWSON, Bt
HON. PATRICK WILLS
FELICITY JONSSON
HENRY DOUGLAS-HOME
LADY AGNES DUFF
SUSIE ORDE
ROBIN DOUGLAS-HOME
CHARLES DOUGLAS-HOME
DUFF COOPER
STEPHEN WHEATCROFT
ALISON DESSAU
NIGEL GRANDFIELD
SANDRA PAUL
JESSICA GWYNNE
LADY DIANA COOPER
GEOFFREY WHEATCROFT
DAVID WYNNE-MORGAN
MRS WYNNE-MORGAN

The Princess of Wales

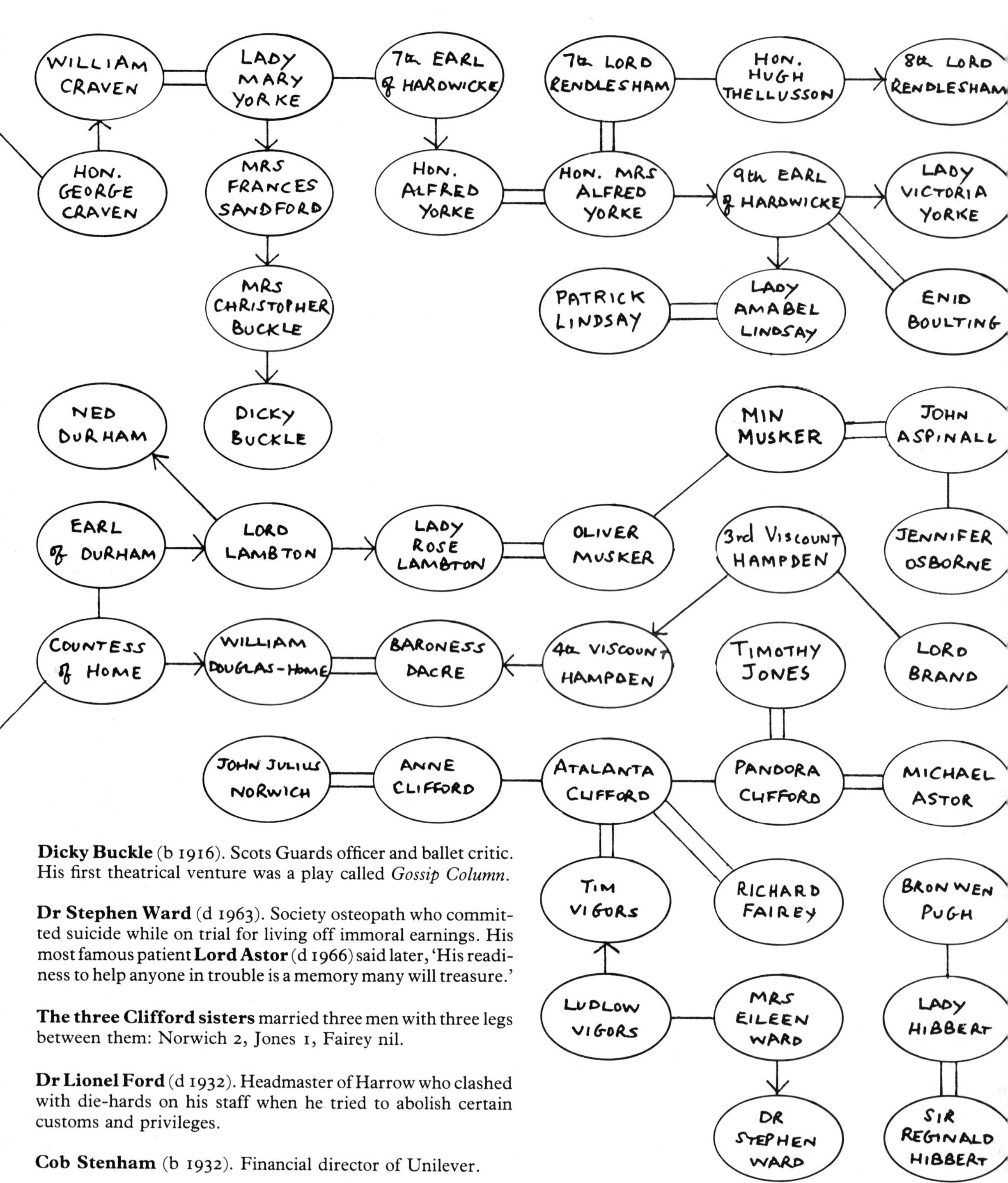
WILLIAM CRAVEN
LADY MARY YORKE
7th EARL of HARDWICKE
7th LORD RENDLESHAM
HON. HUGH THELLUSSON
8th LORD RENDLESHAM
HON. GEORGE CRAVEN
MRS FRANCES SANDFORD
HON. ALFRED YORKE
HON. MRS ALFRED YORKE
9th EARL of HARDWICKE
LADY VICTORIA YORKE
MRS CHRISTOPHER BUCKLE
PATRICK LINDSAY
LADY AMABEL LINDSAY
ENID BOULTING
NED DURHAM
DICKY BUCKLE
MIN MUSKER
JOHN ASPINALL
EARL of DURHAM
LORD LAMBTON
LADY ROSE LAMBTON
OLIVER MUSKER
3rd VISCOUNT HAMPDEN
JENNIFER OSBORNE
COUNTESS of HOME
WILLIAM DOUGLAS-HOME
BARONESS DACRE
4th VISCOUNT HAMPDEN
TIMOTHY JONES
LORD BRAND
JOHN JULIUS NORWICH
ANNE CLIFFORD
ATALANTA CLIFFORD
PANDORA CLIFFORD
MICHAEL ASTOR
TIM VIGORS
RICHARD FAIREY
BRONWEN PUGH
LUDLOW VIGORS
MRS EILEEN WARD
LADY HIBBERT
DR STEPHEN WARD
SIR REGINALD HIBBERT

Dicky Buckle (b 1916). Scots Guards officer and ballet critic. His first theatrical venture was a play called *Gossip Column*.

Dr Stephen Ward (d 1963). Society osteopath who committed suicide while on trial for living off immoral earnings. His most famous patient **Lord Astor** (d 1966) said later, 'His readiness to help anyone in trouble is a memory many will treasure.'

The three Clifford sisters married three men with three legs between them: Norwich 2, Jones 1, Fairey nil.

Dr Lionel Ford (d 1932). Headmaster of Harrow who clashed with die-hards on his staff when he tried to abolish certain customs and privileges.

Cob Stenham (b 1932). Financial director of Unilever.

Claire Rendlesham is manager of the Yves St Laurent shops in London.

Ken Lane is a jeweller with shops in Burlington Arcade and elsewhere.

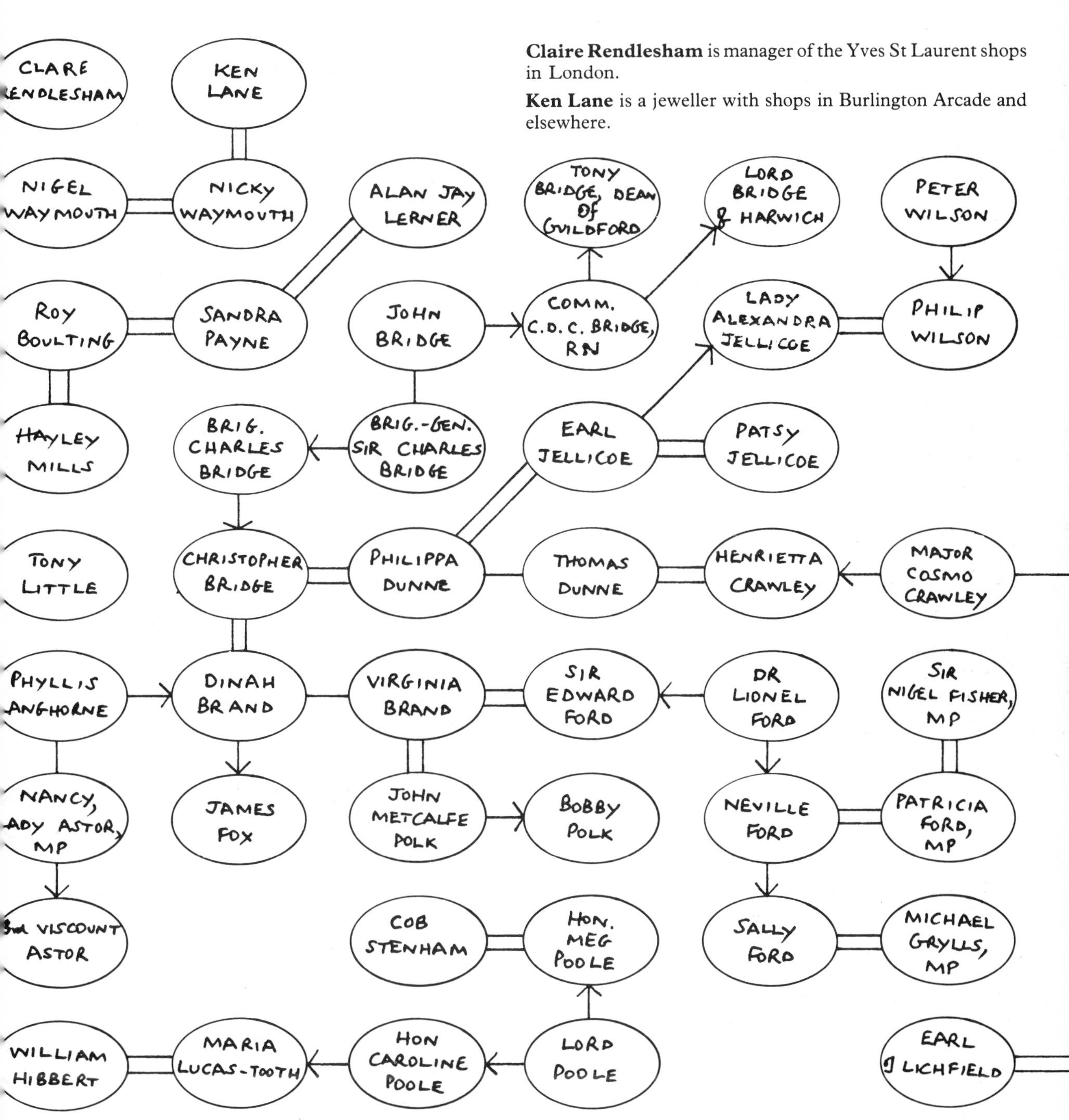
CLARE
RENDLESHAM
KEN
LANE
NIGEL
WAYMOUTH
NICKY
WAYMOUTH
ALAN JAY
LERNER
TONY
BRIDGE, DEAN
OF
GUILDFORD
LORD
BRIDGE
OF HARWICH
PETER
WILSON
ROY
BOULTING
SANDRA
PAYNE
JOHN
BRIDGE
COMM.
C.D.C. BRIDGE,
RN
LADY
ALEXANDRA
JELLICOE
PHILIP
WILSON
HAYLEY
MILLS
BRIG.
CHARLES
BRIDGE
BRIG.-GEN.
SIR CHARLES
BRIDGE
EARL
JELLICOE
PATSY
JELLICOE
TONY
LITTLE
CHRISTOPHER
BRIDGE
PHILIPPA
DUNNE
THOMAS
DUNNE
HENRIETTA
CRAWLEY
MAJOR
COSMO
CRAWLEY
PHYLLIS
LANGHORNE
DINAH
BRAND
VIRGINIA
BRAND
SIR
EDWARD
FORD
DR
LIONEL
FORD
SIR
NIGEL FISHER,
MP
NANCY,
LADY ASTOR,
MP
JAMES
FOX
JOHN
METCALFE
POLK
BOBBY
POLK
NEVILLE
FORD
PATRICIA
FORD,
MP
3rd VISCOUNT
ASTOR
COB
STENHAM
HON.
MEG
POOLE
SALLY
FORD
MICHAEL
GRYLLS,
MP
WILLIAM
HIBBERT
MARIA
LUCAS-TOOTH
HON
CAROLINE
POOLE
LORD
POOLE
EARL
OF LICHFIELD

ony Bridge (b 1914) was formerly Vicar of Christ Church, ancaster Gate. During the Profumo Crisis he asked his congregation to pray for Christine Keeler and Mandy Rice-Davies. When several people walked out, he said, 'Now let's pray for all those people who walked out.'

James Fox (b 1945). Author of *White Mischief* and an important article on 'the Lucan set'.

Jennifer Osborne and **Tony Little** founded the King's Road wallpaper shop bearing their names.

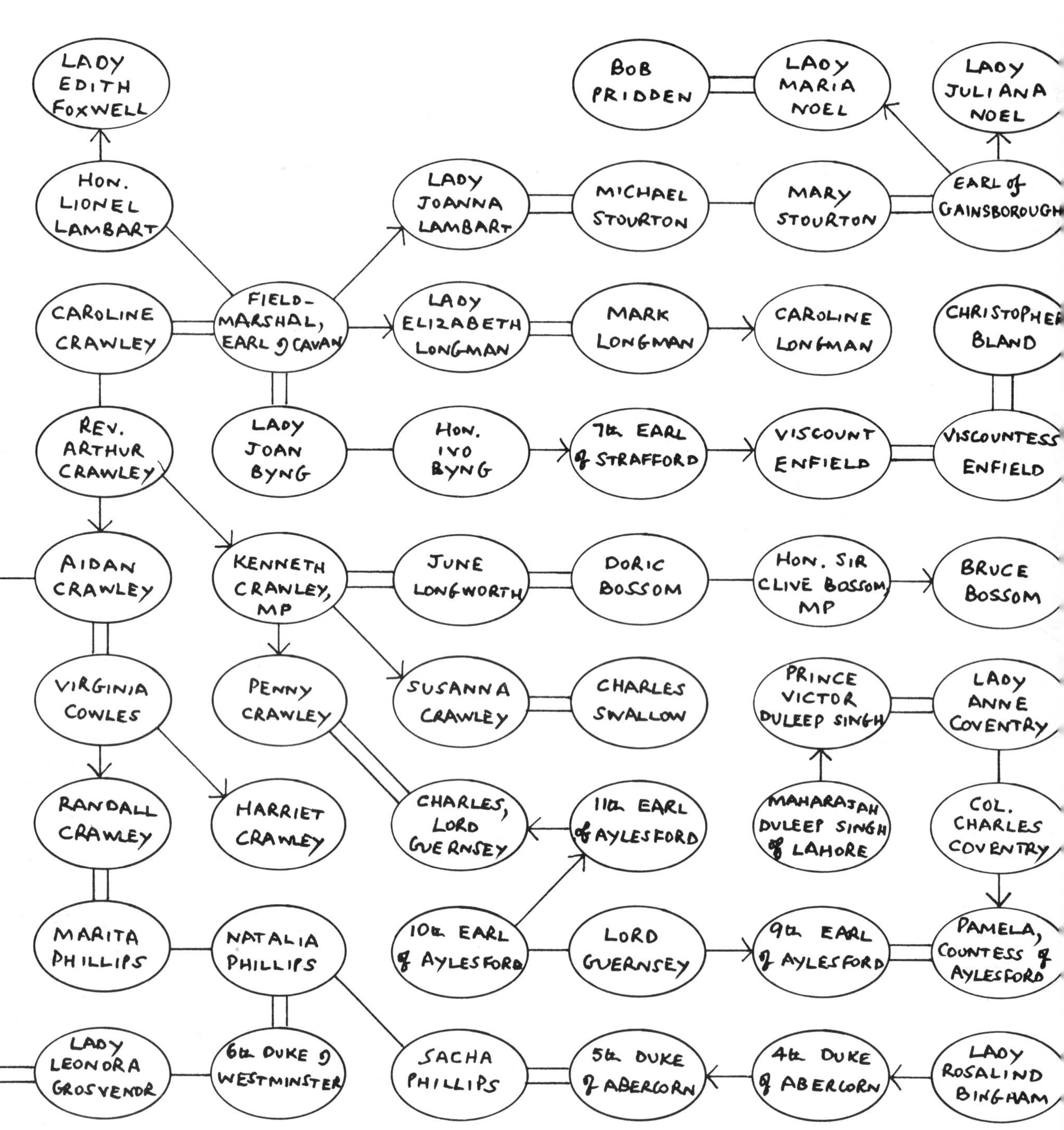
LADY EDITH FOXWELL
HON. LIONEL LAMBART
LADY JOANNA LAMBART
MICHAEL STOURTON
MARY STOURTON
EARL of GAINSBOROUGH
BOB PRIDDEN
LADY MARIA NOEL
LADY JULIANA NOEL
CAROLINE CRAWLEY
FIELD-MARSHAL, EARL of CAVAN
LADY ELIZABETH LONGMAN
MARK LONGMAN
CAROLINE LONGMAN
CHRISTOPHER BLAND
REV. ARTHUR CRAWLEY
LADY JOAN BYNG
HON. IVO BYNG
7th EARL of STRAFFORD
VISCOUNT ENFIELD
VISCOUNTESS ENFIELD
AIDAN CRAWLEY
KENNETH CRAWLEY, MP
JUNE LONGWORTH
DORIC BOSSOM
HON. SIR CLIVE BOSSOM, MP
BRUCE BOSSOM
VIRGINIA COWLES
PENNY CRAWLEY
SUSANNA CRAWLEY
CHARLES SWALLOW
PRINCE VICTOR DULEEP SINGH
LADY ANNE COVENTRY
RANDALL CRAWLEY
HARRIET CRAWLEY
CHARLES, LORD GUERNSEY
11th EARL of AYLESFORD
MAHARAJAH DULEEP SINGH of LAHORE
COL. CHARLES COVENTRY
MARITA PHILLIPS
NATALIA PHILLIPS
10th EARL of AYLESFORD
LORD GUERNSEY
9th EARL of AYLESFORD
PAMELA, COUNTESS of AYLESFORD
LADY LEONORA GROSVENOR
6th DUKE of WESTMINSTER
SACHA PHILLIPS
5th DUKE of ABERCORN
4th DUKE of ABERCORN
LADY ROSALIND BINGHAM

Lady Edith Foxwell (b 1918). High-spirited and beautiful patroness of the Embassy Club, Bond Street.

Lady Juliana Noel (b 1949) gave her name to Britain's best known mobile discothèque.

7th Earl of Lucan (b 1934) disappeared in 1974 following upheaval at his house in Upper Belgrave Street during whi his children's nursemaid was murdered.

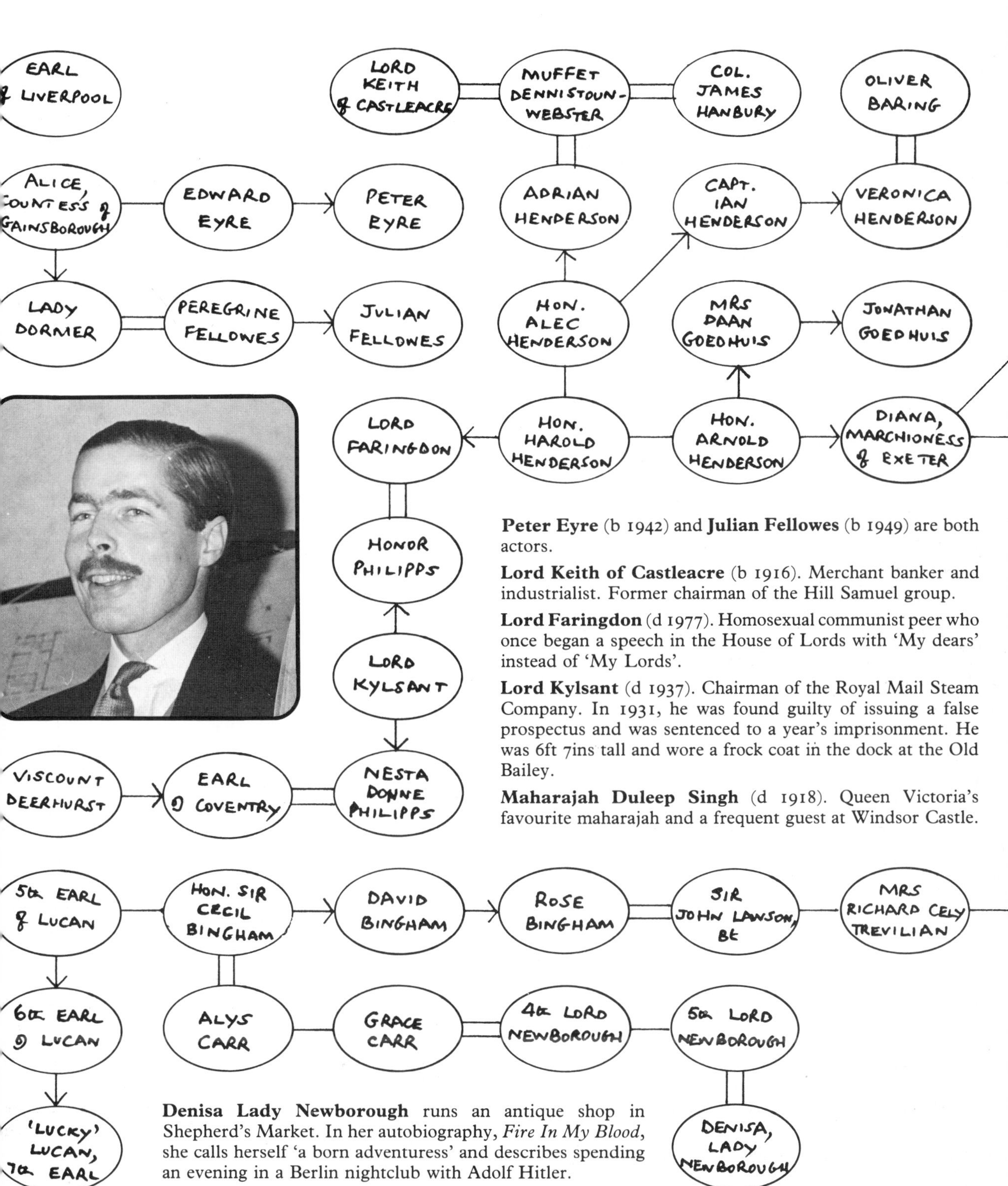
EARL of LIVERPOOL
LORD KEITH of CASTLEACRE
MUFFET DENNISTOUN-WEBSTER
COL. JAMES HANBURY
OLIVER BARING
ALICE, COUNTESS of GAINSBOROUGH
EDWARD EYRE
PETER EYRE
ADRIAN HENDERSON
CAPT. IAN HENDERSON
VERONICA HENDERSON
LADY DORMER
PEREGRINE FELLOWES
JULIAN FELLOWES
HON. ALEC HENDERSON
MRS DAAN GOEDHUIS
JONATHAN GOEDHUIS
LORD FARINGDON
HON. HAROLD HENDERSON
HON. ARNOLD HENDERSON
DIANA, MARCHIONESS of EXETER
HONOR PHILIPPS
LORD KYLSANT
VISCOUNT DEERHURST
EARL of COVENTRY
NESTA DONNE PHILIPPS
5th EARL of LUCAN
HON. SIR CECIL BINGHAM
DAVID BINGHAM
ROSE BINGHAM
SIR JOHN LAWSON, Bt
MRS RICHARD CELY TREVILIAN
6th EARL of LUCAN
ALYS CARR
GRACE CARR
4th LORD NEWBOROUGH
5th LORD NEWBOROUGH
'LUCKY' LUCAN, 7th EARL
DENISA, LADY NEWBOROUGH

Peter Eyre (b 1942) and **Julian Fellowes** (b 1949) are both actors.

Lord Keith of Castleacre (b 1916). Merchant banker and industrialist. Former chairman of the Hill Samuel group.

Lord Faringdon (d 1977). Homosexual communist peer who once began a speech in the House of Lords with 'My dears' instead of 'My Lords'.

Lord Kylsant (d 1937). Chairman of the Royal Mail Steam Company. In 1931, he was found guilty of issuing a false prospectus and was sentenced to a year's imprisonment. He was 6ft 7ins tall and wore a frock coat in the dock at the Old Bailey.

Maharajah Duleep Singh (d 1918). Queen Victoria's favourite maharajah and a frequent guest at Windsor Castle.

Denisa Lady Newborough runs an antique shop in Shepherd's Market. In her autobiography, *Fire In My Blood*, she calls herself 'a born adventuress' and describes spending an evening in a Berlin nightclub with Adolf Hitler.

Robin Leigh-Pemberton (b 1927). Governor of the Bank of England since 1982.

Nancy Cunard (d 1965) wore ivory bangles on her arms which 'rattled and clicked like balls on a billiard table'.

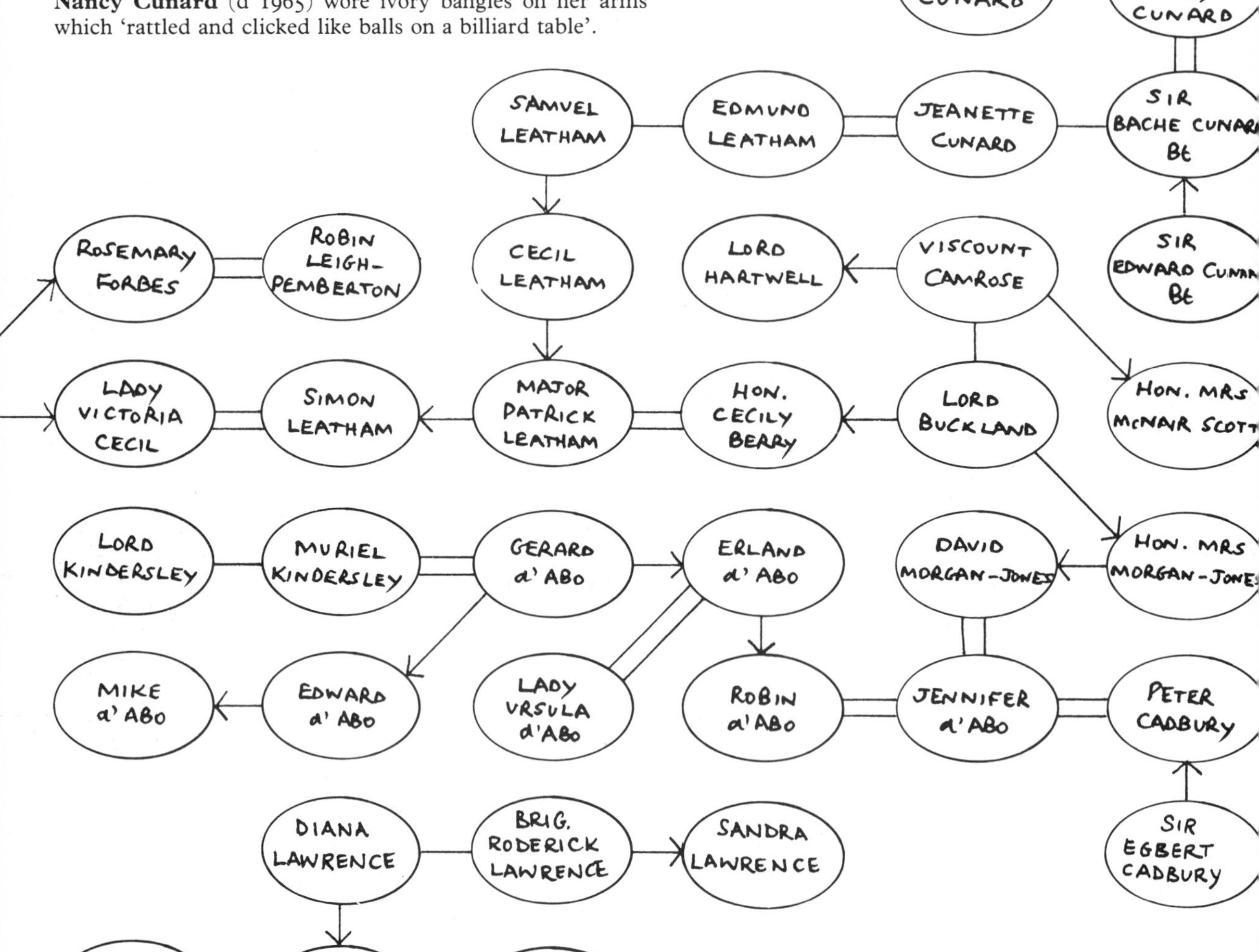
NANCY CUNARD
EMERALD, LADY CUNARD
SAMUEL LEATHAM
EDMUND LEATHAM
JEANETTE CUNARD
SIR BACHE CUNARD Bt
ROSEMARY FORBES
ROBIN LEIGH-PEMBERTON
CECIL LEATHAM
LORD HARTWELL
VISCOUNT CAMROSE
SIR EDWARD CUNARD Bt
LADY VICTORIA CECIL
SIMON LEATHAM
MAJOR PATRICK LEATHAM
HON. CECILY BERRY
LORD BUCKLAND
HON. MRS McNAIR SCOTT
LORD KINDERSLEY
MURIEL KINDERSLEY
GERARD d'ABO
ERLAND d'ABO
DAVID MORGAN-JONES
HON. MRS MORGAN-JONES
MIKE d'ABO
EDWARD d'ABO
LADY URSULA d'ABO
ROBIN d'ABO
JENNIFER d'ABO
PETER CADBURY
DIANA LAWRENCE
BRIG. RODERICK LAWRENCE
SANDRA LAWRENCE
SIR EGBERT CADBURY
SUSANNA CELY TREVILIAN
JEREMY PILCHER
MEREDITH ETHERINGTON-SMITH

Lord Hartwell (b 1911). Owner of the *Daily Telegraph* and *Sunday Telegraph*.

Mike d'Abo (b 1944). Former lead singer with the Manfred Mann pop group.

Jennifer d'Abo (b 1944). Self-made tycoon who purchased the Ryman's chain of office supply shops for just under £3 million. 'I was a duffer at school—no good at anything really. I still can't add up.'

Sir Adrian Cadbury (b 1929). Chairman of Cadbu Schweppes and director of the Bank of England.

Mavis Wheeler (d 1970). Famous beauty who in 1954 sh her lover Lord Vivian and served six months for malicio wounding.

Horace de Vere Cole (d 1936). Famous Old Etonian pra tical joker who once ran through the streets of London with cow's udder hanging out of his fly-buttons.

Geoffrey Dawson (d 1944). Editor of *The Times* and apos of appeasement. Made sure that nothing appeared in his new paper which 'would offend Mr. Hitler'.

Earl of Longford (b 1905). Banker and publisher. On bei appointed chief executive of Sidgwick & Jackson, he declare 'We want all the best books by all the best authors'.

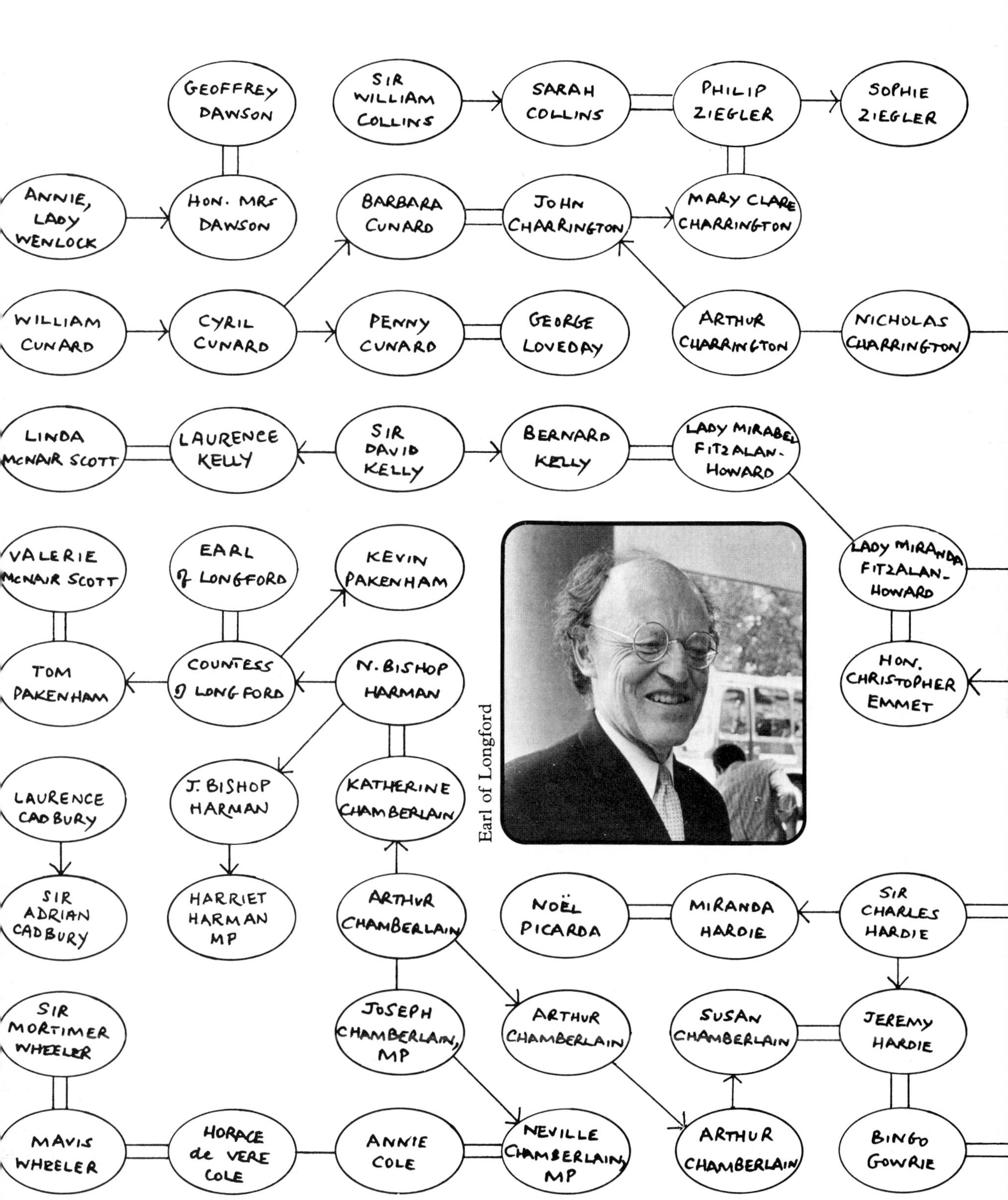
GEOFFREY DAWSON
SIR WILLIAM COLLINS
SARAH COLLINS
PHILIP ZIEGLER
SOPHIE ZIEGLER
ANNIE, LADY WENLOCK
HON. MRS DAWSON
BARBARA CUNARD
JOHN CHARRINGTON
MARY CLARE CHARRINGTON
WILLIAM CUNARD
CYRIL CUNARD
PENNY CUNARD
GEORGE LOVEDAY
ARTHUR CHARRINGTON
NICHOLAS CHARRINGTON
LINDA McNAIR SCOTT
LAURENCE KELLY
SIR DAVID KELLY
BERNARD KELLY
LADY MIRABEL FITZALAN-HOWARD
VALERIE McNAIR SCOTT
EARL of LONGFORD
KEVIN PAKENHAM
LADY MIRANDA FITZALAN-HOWARD
TOM PAKENHAM
COUNTESS of LONGFORD
N. BISHOP HARMAN
HON. CHRISTOPHER EMMET
LAURENCE CADBURY
J. BISHOP HARMAN
KATHERINE CHAMBERLAIN
SIR ADRIAN CADBURY
HARRIET HARMAN MP
ARTHUR CHAMBERLAIN
NOËL PICARDA
MIRANDA HARDIE
SIR CHARLES HARDIE
SIR MORTIMER WHEELER
JOSEPH CHAMBERLAIN, MP
ARTHUR CHAMBERLAIN
SUSAN CHAMBERLAIN
JEREMY HARDIE
MAVIS WHEELER
HORACE de VERE COLE
ANNIE COLE
NEVILLE CHAMBERLAIN, MP
ARTHUR CHAMBERLAIN
BINGO GOWRIE
Earl of Longford

Olga Deterding (d 1979) abandoned the high life to work as nurse in Dr Albert Schweitzer's leper colony. She later lived in a triplex penthouse overlooking Green Park.

Sir Henri Deterding (d 1939). One of the founders of Roy Dutch Petroleum Company.

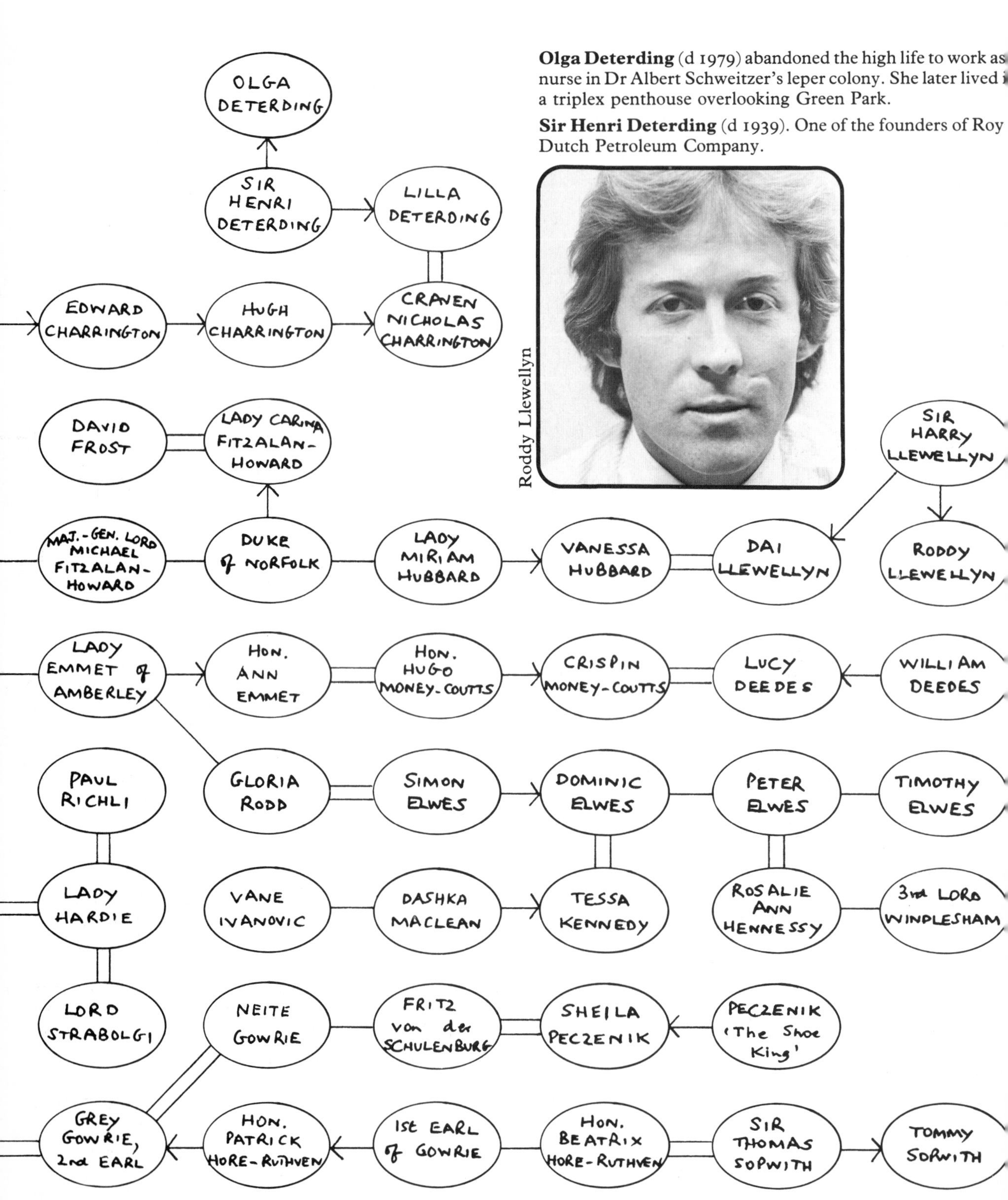
OLGA DETERDING
SIR HENRI DETERDING
LILLA DETERDING
EDWARD CHARRINGTON
HUGH CHARRINGTON
CRAVEN NICHOLAS CHARRINGTON
DAVID FROST
LADY CARINA FITZALAN-HOWARD
SIR HARRY LLEWELLYN
MAJ.-GEN. LORD MICHAEL FITZALAN-HOWARD
DUKE of NORFOLK
LADY MIRIAM HUBBARD
VANESSA HUBBARD
DAI LLEWELLYN
RODDY LLEWELLYN
LADY EMMET of AMBERLEY
HON. ANN EMMET
HON. HUGO MONEY-COUTTS
CRISPIN MONEY-COUTTS
LUCY DEEDES
WILLIAM DEEDES
PAUL RICHLI
GLORIA RODD
SIMON ELWES
DOMINIC ELWES
PETER ELWES
TIMOTHY ELWES
LADY HARDIE
VANE IVANOVIC
DASHKA MACLEAN
TESSA KENNEDY
ROSALIE ANN HENNESSY
3rd LORD WINDLESHAM
LORD STRABOLGI
NEITE GOWRIE
FRITZ von der SCHULENBURG
SHEILA PECZENIK
PECZENIK 'The Shoe King'
GREY GOWRIE, 2nd EARL
HON. PATRICK HORE-RUTHVEN
1st EARL of GOWRIE
HON. BEATRIX HORE-RUTHVEN
SIR THOMAS SOPWITH
TOMMY SOPWITH

Roddy Llewellyn

David Frost (b 1939) has recently moved from Egerton Crescent to Carlisle Square, SW3.

Dai Llewellyn (b 1946). Playboy and nightclub 'greeter' who sold his memoirs to the *News of the World*.

William Deedes (b 1913). Editor of the *Daily Telegraph* noted for his odd voice.

Janet Lyle (b 1944). Founder of the Annacat shop.

2nd Earl of Gowrie (b 1939). Minister for the Arts noted for his black 'afro' hairstyle.

Dominic Elwes (d 1975). Playboy and raconteur 'to whom even Peter Ustinov was said to bow a knee'. His elopement with **Tessa Kennedy** filled the newspapers in 1958. He later committed suicide.

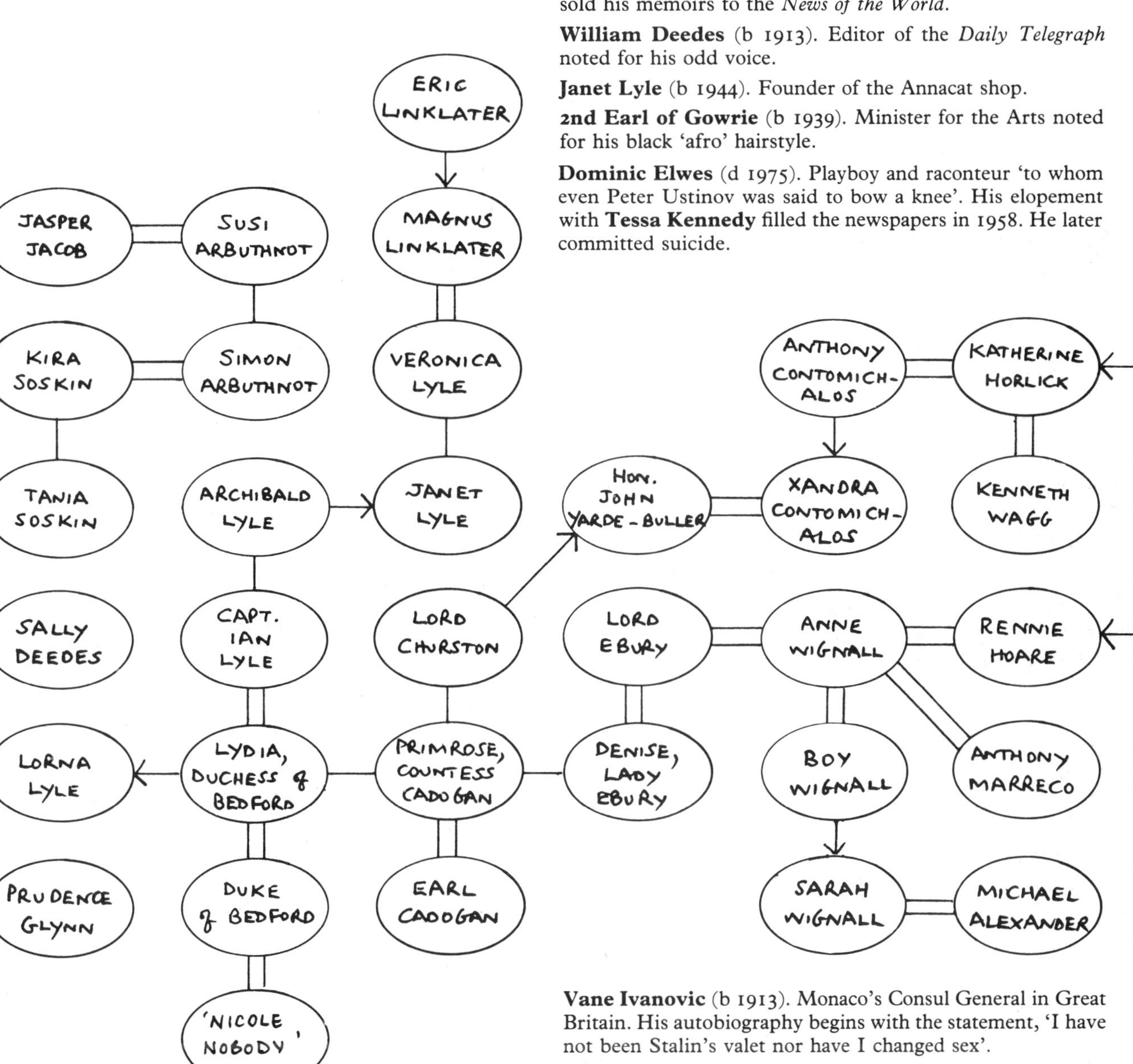
ERIC LINKLATER
JASPER JACOB
SUSI ARBUTHNOT
MAGNUS LINKLATER
KIRA SOSKIN
SIMON ARBUTHNOT
VERONICA LYLE
ANTHONY CONTOMICHALOS
KATHERINE HORLICK
TANIA SOSKIN
ARCHIBALD LYLE
JANET LYLE
HON. JOHN YARDE-BULLER
XANDRA CONTOMICHALOS
KENNETH WAGG
SALLY DEEDES
CAPT. IAN LYLE
LORD CHURSTON
LORD EBURY
ANNE WIGNALL
RENNIE HOARE
LORNA LYLE
LYDIA, DUCHESS OF BEDFORD
PRIMROSE, COUNTESS CADOGAN
DENISE, LADY EBURY
BOY WIGNALL
ANTHONY MARRECO
PRUDENCE GLYNN
DUKE OF BEDFORD
EARL CADOGAN
SARAH WIGNALL
MICHAEL ALEXANDER
'NICOLE NOBODY'

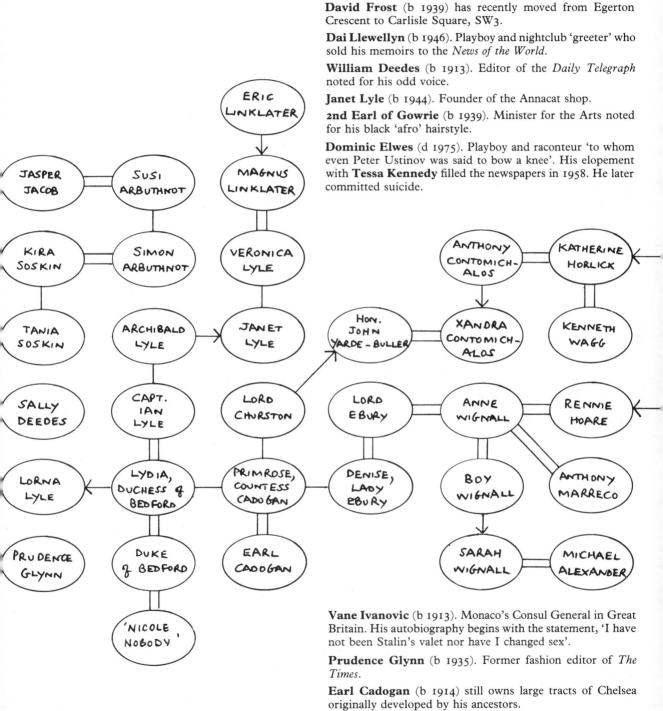

Vane Ivanovic (b 1913). Monaco's Consul General in Great Britain. His autobiography begins with the statement, 'I have not been Stalin's valet nor have I changed sex'.

Prudence Glynn (b 1935). Former fashion editor of *The Times*.

Earl Cadogan (b 1914) still owns large tracts of Chelsea originally developed by his ancestors.

Michael Alexander (b 1920). Author, restaurant owner and one of the founders of the Chelsea Set.

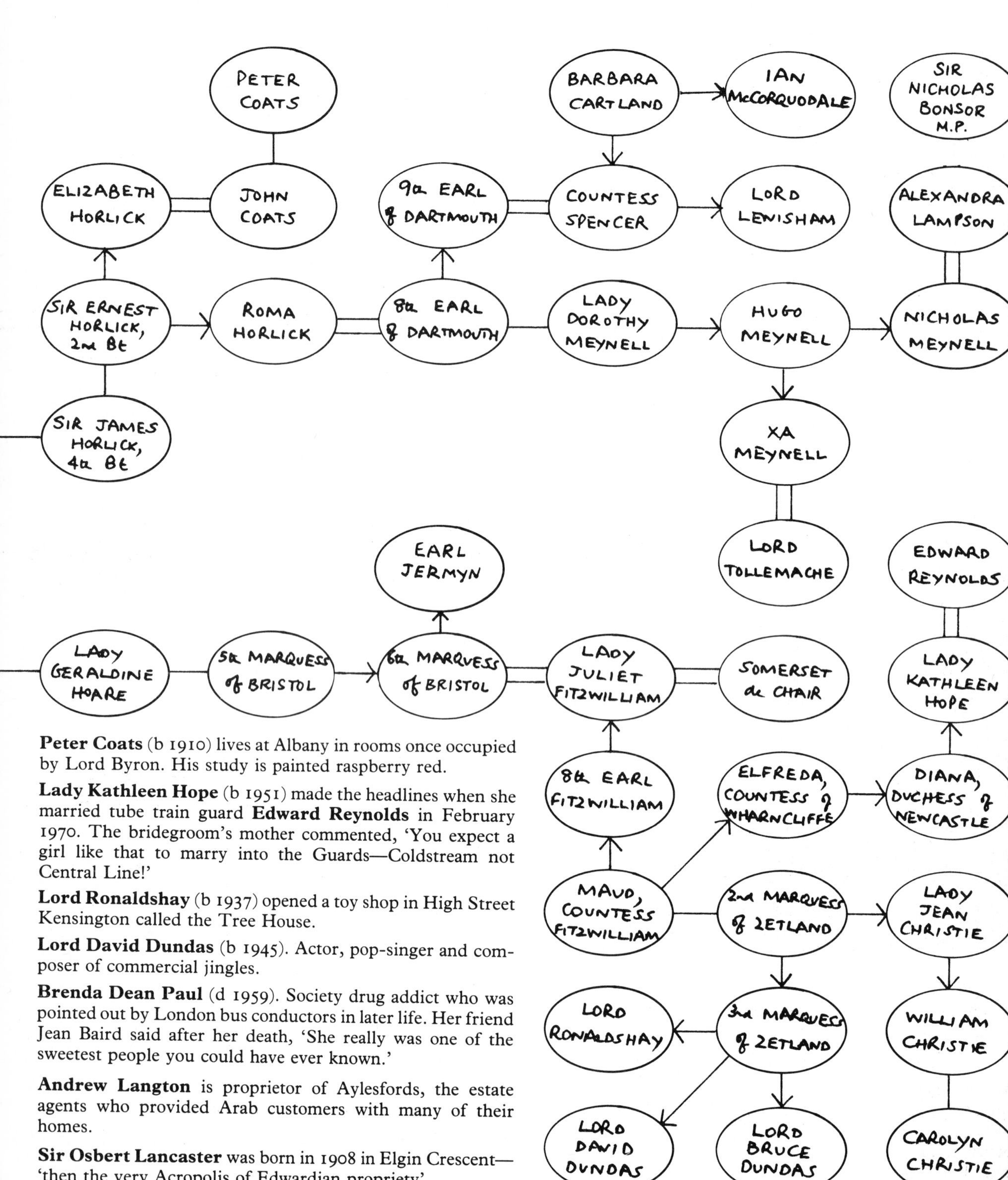

PETER COATS
BARBARA CARTLAND
IAN McCORQUODALE
SIR NICHOLAS BONSOR M.P.
ELIZABETH HORLICK
JOHN COATS
9th EARL of DARTMOUTH
COUNTESS SPENCER
LORD LEWISHAM
ALEXANDRA LAMPSON
SIR ERNEST HORLICK, 2nd Bt
ROMA HORLICK
8th EARL of DARTMOUTH
LADY DOROTHY MEYNELL
HUGO MEYNELL
NICHOLAS MEYNELL
SIR JAMES HORLICK, 4th Bt
XA MEYNELL
LORD TOLLEMACHE
EARL JERMYN
EDWARD REYNOLDS
LADY GERALDINE HOARE
5th MARQUESS of BRISTOL
6th MARQUESS of BRISTOL
LADY JULIET FITZWILLIAM
SOMERSET de CHAIR
LADY KATHLEEN HOPE
8th EARL FITZWILLIAM
ELFREDA, COUNTESS of WHARNCLIFFE
DIANA, DUCHESS of NEWCASTLE
MAUD, COUNTESS FITZWILLIAM
2nd MARQUESS of ZETLAND
LADY JEAN CHRISTIE
LORD RONALDSHAY
3rd MARQUESS of ZETLAND
WILLIAM CHRISTIE
LORD DAVID DUNDAS
LORD BRUCE DUNDAS
CAROLYN CHRISTIE

Peter Coats (b 1910) lives at Albany in rooms once occupied by Lord Byron. His study is painted raspberry red.

Lady Kathleen Hope (b 1951) made the headlines when she married tube train guard **Edward Reynolds** in February 1970. The bridegroom's mother commented, 'You expect a girl like that to marry into the Guards—Coldstream not Central Line!'

Lord Ronaldshay (b 1937) opened a toy shop in High Street Kensington called the Tree House.

Lord David Dundas (b 1945). Actor, pop-singer and composer of commercial jingles.

Brenda Dean Paul (d 1959). Society drug addict who was pointed out by London bus conductors in later life. Her friend Jean Baird said after her death, 'She really was one of the sweetest people you could have ever known.'

Andrew Langton is proprietor of Aylesfords, the estate agents who provided Arab customers with many of their homes.

Sir Osbert Lancaster was born in 1908 in Elgin Crescent—'then the very Acropolis of Edwardian propriety'.

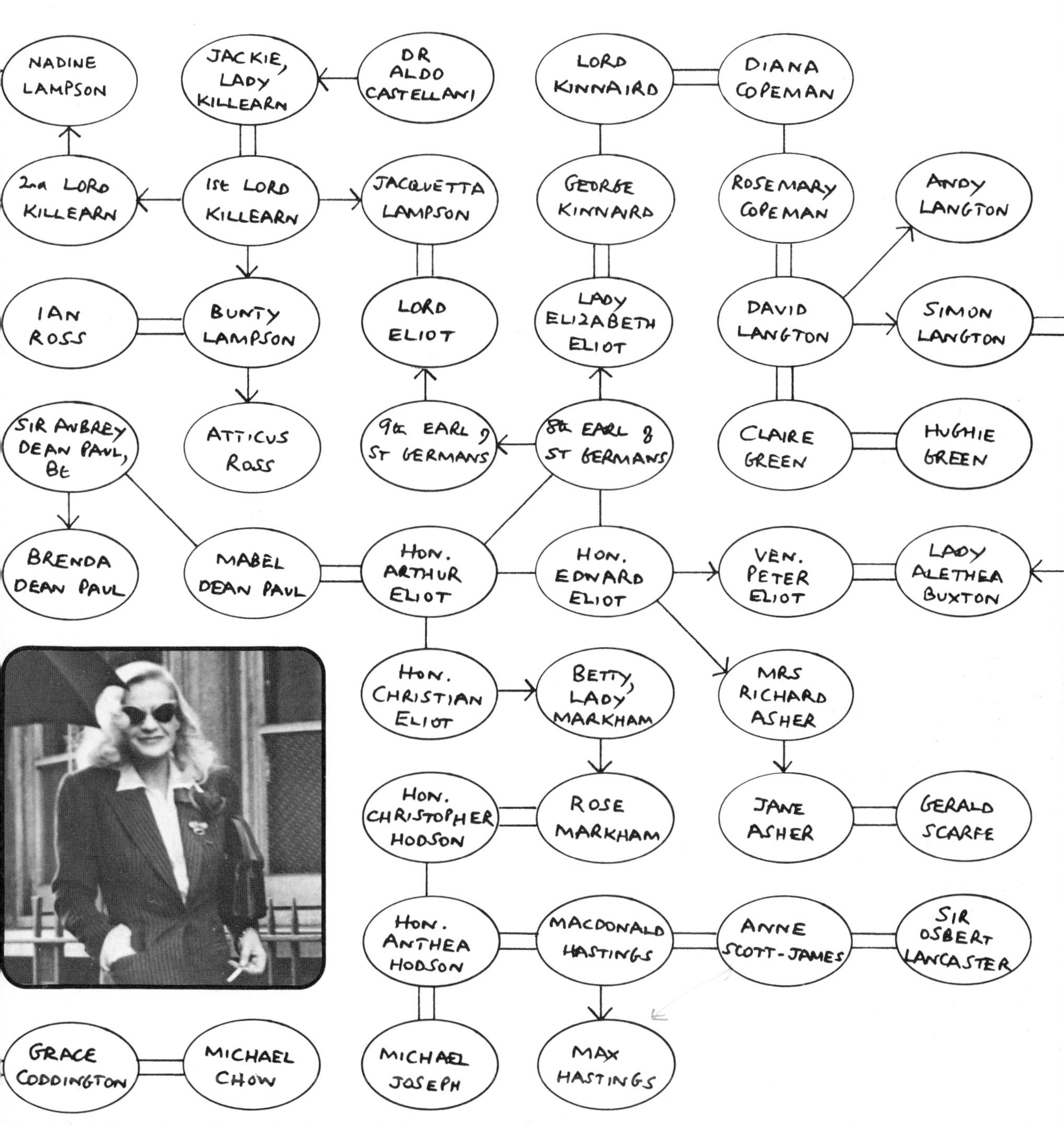
NADINE LAMPSON
JACKIE, LADY KILLEARN
DR ALDO CASTELLANI
LORD KINNAIRD
DIANA COPEMAN
2nd LORD KILLEARN
1st LORD KILLEARN
JACQUETTA LAMPSON
GEORGE KINNAIRD
ROSEMARY COPEMAN
ANDY LANGTON
IAN ROSS
BUNTY LAMPSON
LORD ELIOT
LADY ELIZABETH ELIOT
DAVID LANGTON
SIMON LANGTON
SIR AUBREY DEAN PAUL, Bt
ATTICUS ROSS
9th EARL of ST GERMANS
8th EARL of ST GERMANS
CLAIRE GREEN
HUGHIE GREEN
BRENDA DEAN PAUL
MABEL DEAN PAUL
HON. ARTHUR ELIOT
HON. EDWARD ELIOT
VEN. PETER ELIOT
LADY ALETHEA BUXTON
HON. CHRISTIAN ELIOT
BETTY, LADY MARKHAM
MRS RICHARD ASHER
HON. CHRISTOPHER HODSON
ROSE MARKHAM
JANE ASHER
GERALD SCARFE
HON. ANTHEA HODSON
MACDONALD HASTINGS
ANNE SCOTT-JAMES
SIR OSBERT LANCASTER
GRACE CODDINGTON
MICHAEL CHOW
MICHAEL JOSEPH
MAX HASTINGS

Macdonald Hastings (d 1982). Distinguished war correspondent during the 2nd World War. His son **Max Hastings** (b 1945) reported on the Falklands conflict and was the first person to enter Port Stanley. 'It was like liberating a surburban golf club.'

Michael Chow is proprietor of the Mr Chow restaurants in London, New York and Beverly Hills.

Hughie Green (b 1920). TV personality and chairman of *Opportunity Knocks*.

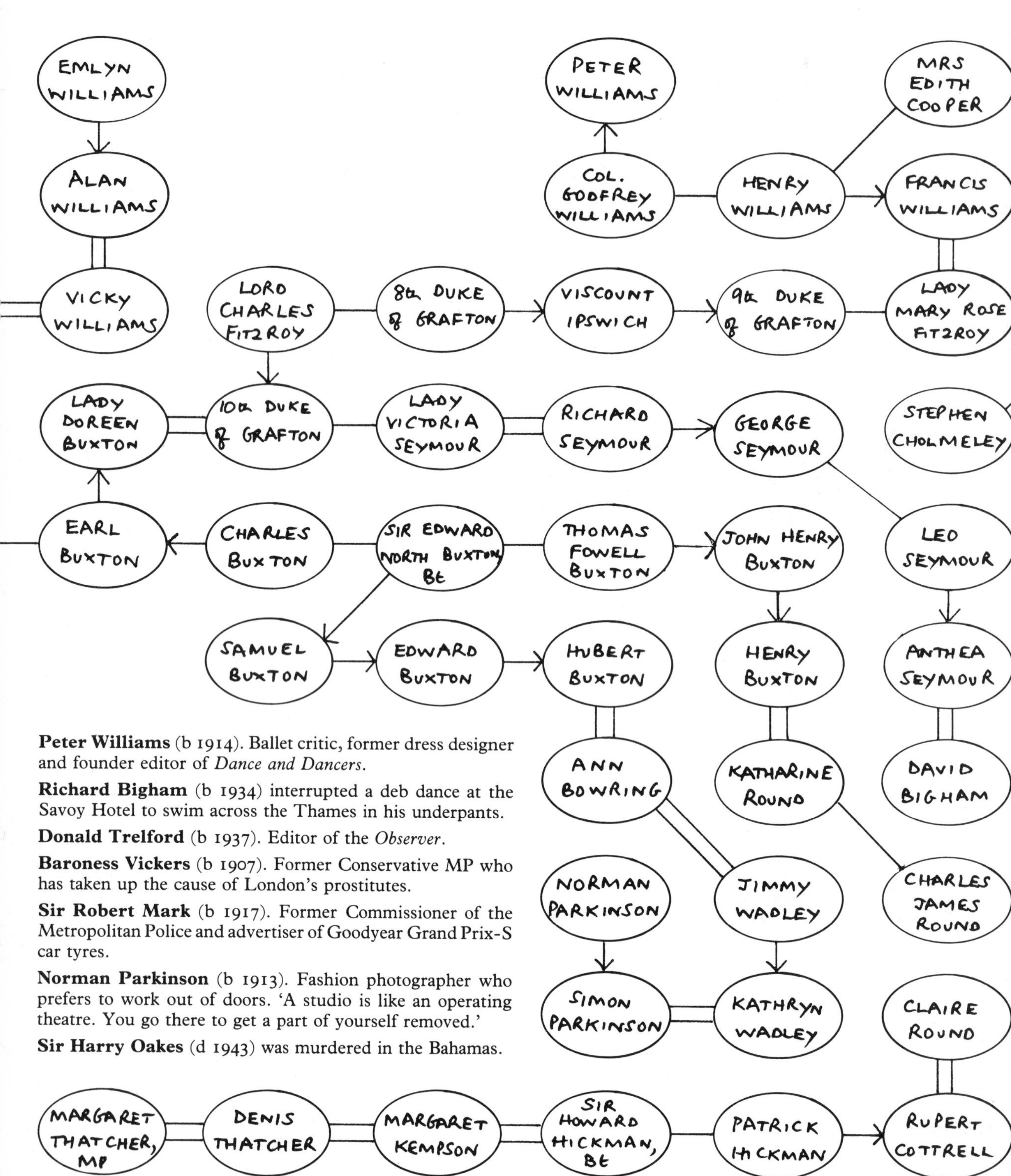
EMLYN WILLIAMS
ALAN WILLIAMS
VICKY WILLIAMS
PETER WILLIAMS
COL. GODFREY WILLIAMS
HENRY WILLIAMS
MRS EDITH COOPER
FRANCIS WILLIAMS
LORD CHARLES FITZROY
8th DUKE of GRAFTON
VISCOUNT IPSWICH
9th DUKE of GRAFTON
LADY MARY ROSE FITZROY
LADY DOREEN BUXTON
10th DUKE of GRAFTON
LADY VICTORIA SEYMOUR
RICHARD SEYMOUR
GEORGE SEYMOUR
STEPHEN CHOLMELEY
EARL BUXTON
CHARLES BUXTON
SIR EDWARD NORTH BUXTON Bt
THOMAS FOWELL BUXTON
JOHN HENRY BUXTON
LEO SEYMOUR
SAMUEL BUXTON
EDWARD BUXTON
HUBERT BUXTON
HENRY BUXTON
ANTHEA SEYMOUR
ANN BOWRING
KATHARINE ROUND
DAVID BIGHAM
NORMAN PARKINSON
JIMMY WADLEY
CHARLES JAMES ROUND
SIMON PARKINSON
KATHRYN WADLEY
CLAIRE ROUND
MARGARET THATCHER, MP
DENIS THATCHER
MARGARET KEMPSON
SIR HOWARD HICKMAN, Bt
PATRICK HICKMAN
RUPERT COTTRELL

Peter Williams (b 1914). Ballet critic, former dress designer and founder editor of *Dance and Dancers*.

Richard Bigham (b 1934) interrupted a deb dance at the Savoy Hotel to swim across the Thames in his underpants.

Donald Trelford (b 1937). Editor of the *Observer*.

Baroness Vickers (b 1907). Former Conservative MP who has taken up the cause of London's prostitutes.

Sir Robert Mark (b 1917). Former Commissioner of the Metropolitan Police and advertiser of Goodyear Grand Prix-S car tyres.

Norman Parkinson (b 1913). Fashion photographer who prefers to work out of doors. 'A studio is like an operating theatre. You go there to get a part of yourself removed.'

Sir Harry Oakes (d 1943) was murdered in the Bahamas.

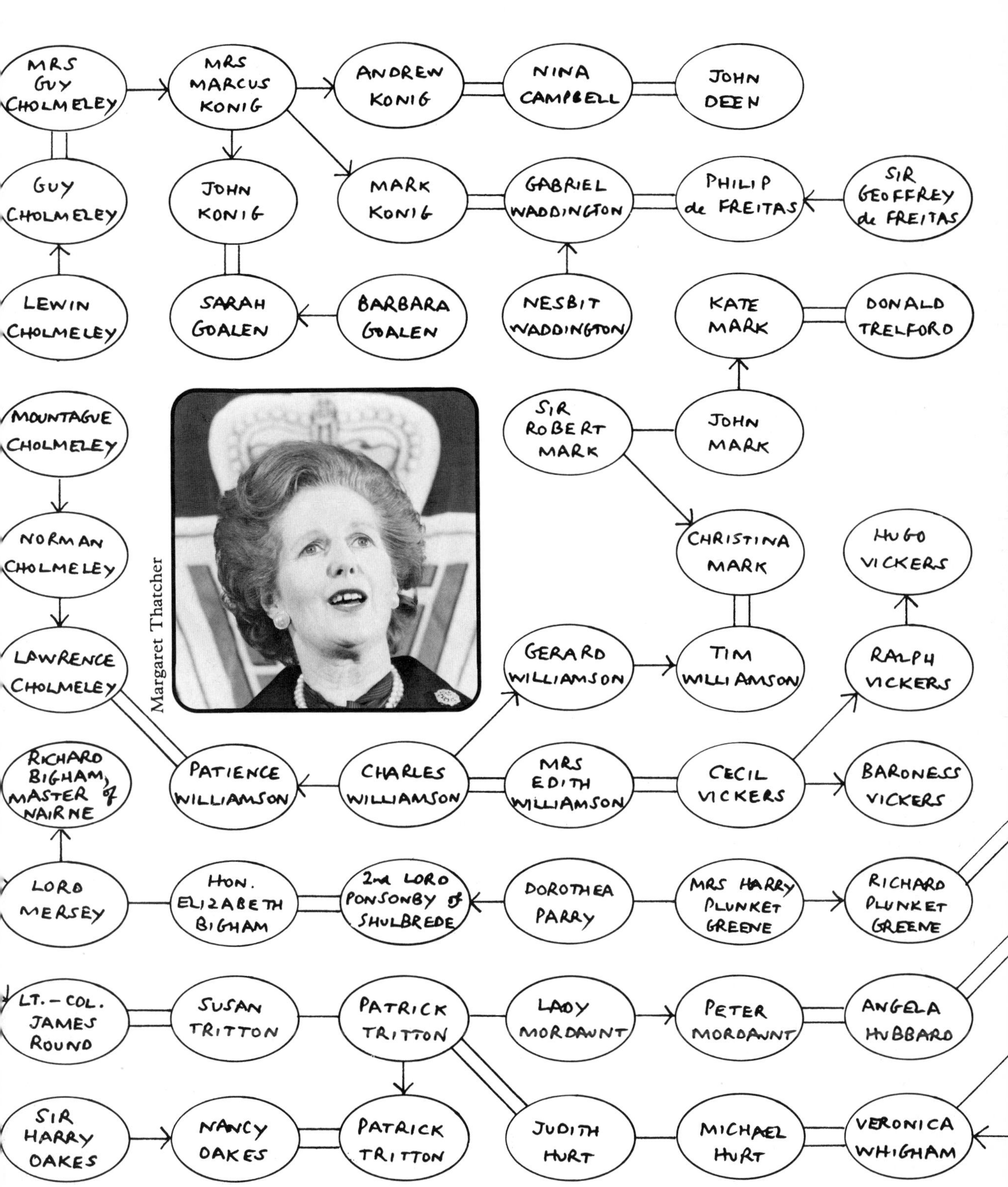
MRS GUY CHOLMELEY
MRS MARCUS KONIG
ANDREW KONIG
NINA CAMPBELL
JOHN DEEN
GUY CHOLMELEY
JOHN KONIG
MARK KONIG
GABRIEL WADDINGTON
PHILIP de FREITAS
SIR GEOFFREY de FREITAS
LEWIN CHOLMELEY
SARAH GOALEN
BARBARA GOALEN
NESBIT WADDINGTON
KATE MARK
DONALD TRELFORD
MOUNTAGUE CHOLMELEY
SIR ROBERT MARK
JOHN MARK
NORMAN CHOLMELEY
CHRISTINA MARK
HUGO VICKERS
LAWRENCE CHOLMELEY
GERARD WILLIAMSON
TIM WILLIAMSON
RALPH VICKERS
RICHARD BIGHAM, MASTER of NAIRNE
PATIENCE WILLIAMSON
CHARLES WILLIAMSON
MRS EDITH WILLIAMSON
CECIL VICKERS
BARONESS VICKERS
LORD MERSEY
HON. ELIZABETH BIGHAM
2nd LORD PONSONBY of SHULBREDE
DOROTHEA PARRY
MRS HARRY PLUNKET GREENE
RICHARD PLUNKET GREENE
LT.-COL. JAMES ROUND
SUSAN TRITTON
PATRICK TRITTON
LADY MORDAUNT
PETER MORDAUNT
ANGELA HUBBARD
SIR HARRY OAKES
NANCY OAKES
PATRICK TRITTON
JUDITH HURT
MICHAEL HURT
VERONICA WHIGHAM

Margaret Thatcher

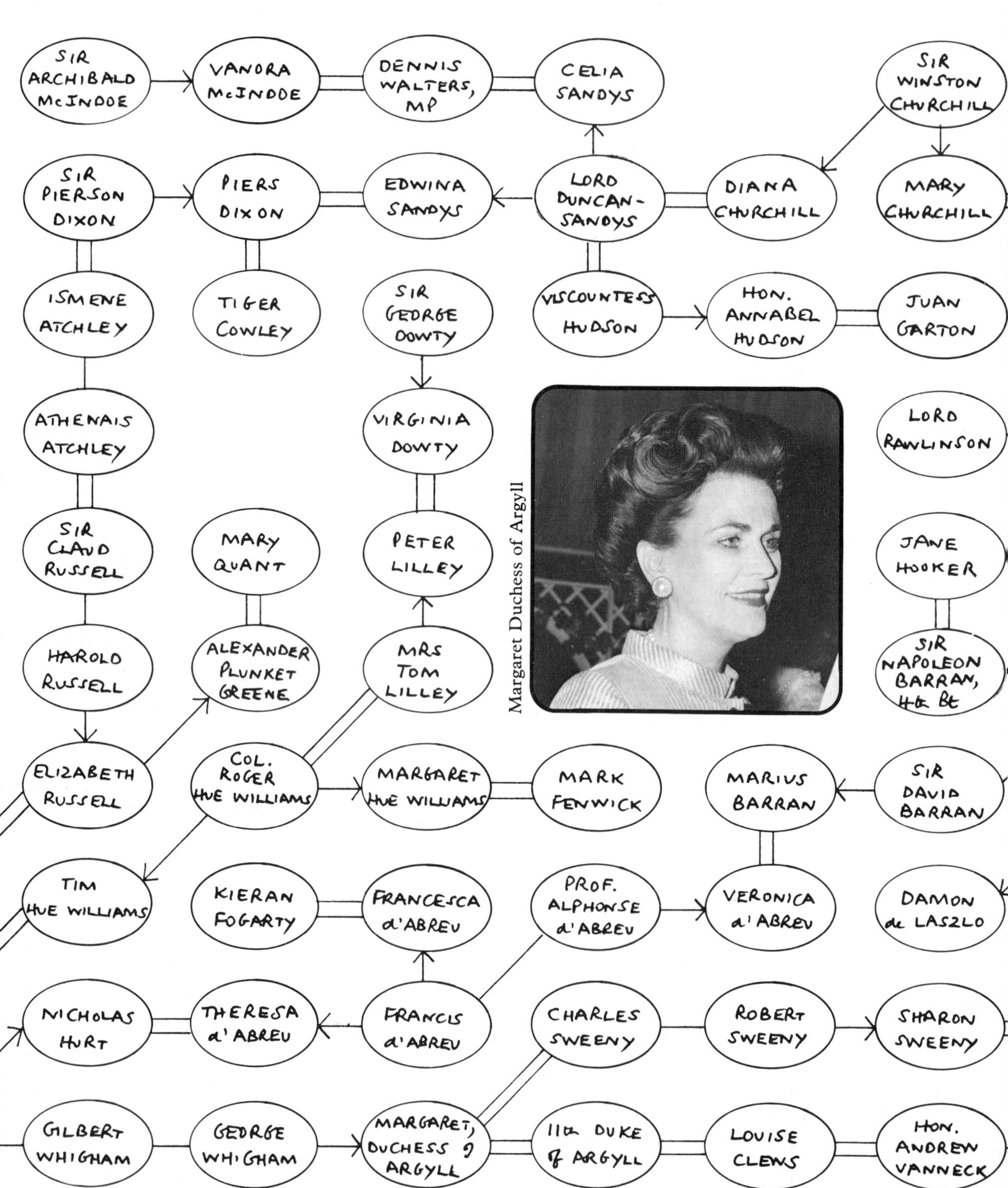
SIR ARCHIBALD McINDOE
VANORA McINDOE
DENNIS WALTERS, MP
CELIA SANDYS
SIR WINSTON CHURCHILL
SIR PIERSON DIXON
PIERS DIXON
EDWINA SANDYS
LORD DUNCAN-SANDYS
DIANA CHURCHILL
MARY CHURCHILL
ISMENE ATCHLEY
TIGER COWLEY
SIR GEORGE DOWTY
VISCOUNTESS HUDSON
HON. ANNABEL HUDSON
JUAN GARTON
ATHENAIS ATCHLEY
VIRGINIA DOWTY
LORD RAWLINSON
SIR CLAUD RUSSELL
MARY QUANT
PETER LILLEY
JANE HOOKER
HAROLD RUSSELL
ALEXANDER PLUNKET GREENE
MRS TOM LILLEY
SIR NAPOLEON BARRAN, 4th Bt
ELIZABETH RUSSELL
COL. ROGER HUE WILLIAMS
MARGARET HUE WILLIAMS
MARK FENWICK
MARIUS BARRAN
SIR DAVID BARRAN
TIM HUE WILLIAMS
KIERAN FOGARTY
FRANCESCA d'ABREU
PROF. ALPHONSE d'ABREU
VERONICA d'ABREU
DAMON de LASZLO
NICHOLAS HURT
THERESA d'ABREU
FRANCIS d'ABREU
CHARLES SWEENY
ROBERT SWEENY
SHARON SWEENY
GILBERT WHIGHAM
GEORGE WHIGHAM
MARGARET, DUCHESS of ARGYLL
11th DUKE of ARGYLL
LOUISE CLEWS
HON. ANDREW VANNECK

Margaret Duchess of Argyll

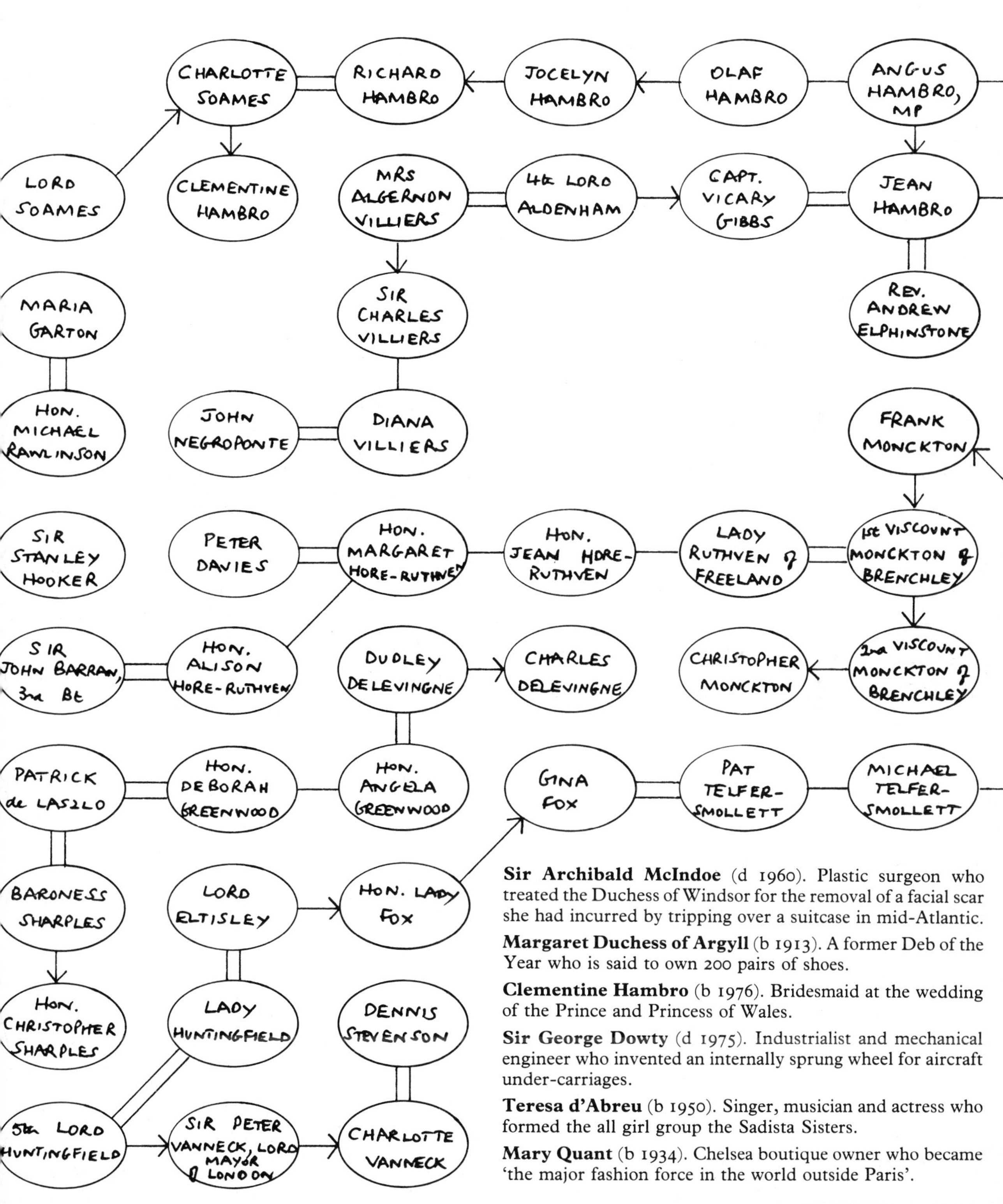
CHARLOTTE SOAMES
RICHARD HAMBRO
JOCELYN HAMBRO
OLAF HAMBRO
ANGUS HAMBRO, MP
LORD SOAMES
CLEMENTINE HAMBRO
MRS ALGERNON VILLIERS
4th LORD ALDENHAM
CAPT. VICARY GIBBS
JEAN HAMBRO
MARIA GARTON
SIR CHARLES VILLIERS
REV. ANDREW ELPHINSTONE
HON. MICHAEL RAWLINSON
JOHN NEGROPONTE
DIANA VILLIERS
FRANK MONCKTON
SIR STANLEY HOOKER
PETER DAVIES
HON. MARGARET HORE-RUTHVEN
HON. JEAN HORE-RUTHVEN
LADY RUTHVEN of FREELAND
1st VISCOUNT MONCKTON of BRENCHLEY
SIR JOHN BARRAN, 3rd Bt
HON. ALISON HORE-RUTHVEN
DUDLEY DELEVINGNE
CHARLES DELEVINGNE
CHRISTOPHER MONCKTON
2nd VISCOUNT MONCKTON of BRENCHLEY
PATRICK de LASZLO
HON. DEBORAH GREENWOOD
HON. ANGELA GREENWOOD
GINA FOX
PAT TELFER-SMOLLETT
MICHAEL TELFER-SMOLLETT
BARONESS SHARPLES
LORD ELTISLEY
HON. LADY FOX
HON. CHRISTOPHER SHARPLES
LADY HUNTINGFIELD
DENNIS STEVENSON
5th LORD HUNTINGFIELD
SIR PETER VANNECK, LORD MAYOR of LONDON
CHARLOTTE VANNECK

Sir Archibald McIndoe (d 1960). Plastic surgeon who treated the Duchess of Windsor for the removal of a facial scar she had incurred by tripping over a suitcase in mid-Atlantic.

Margaret Duchess of Argyll (b 1913). A former Deb of the Year who is said to own 200 pairs of shoes.

Clementine Hambro (b 1976). Bridesmaid at the wedding of the Prince and Princess of Wales.

Sir George Dowty (d 1975). Industrialist and mechanical engineer who invented an internally sprung wheel for aircraft under-carriages.

Teresa d'Abreu (b 1950). Singer, musician and actress who formed the all girl group the Sadista Sisters.

Mary Quant (b 1934). Chelsea boutique owner who became 'the major fashion force in the world outside Paris'.

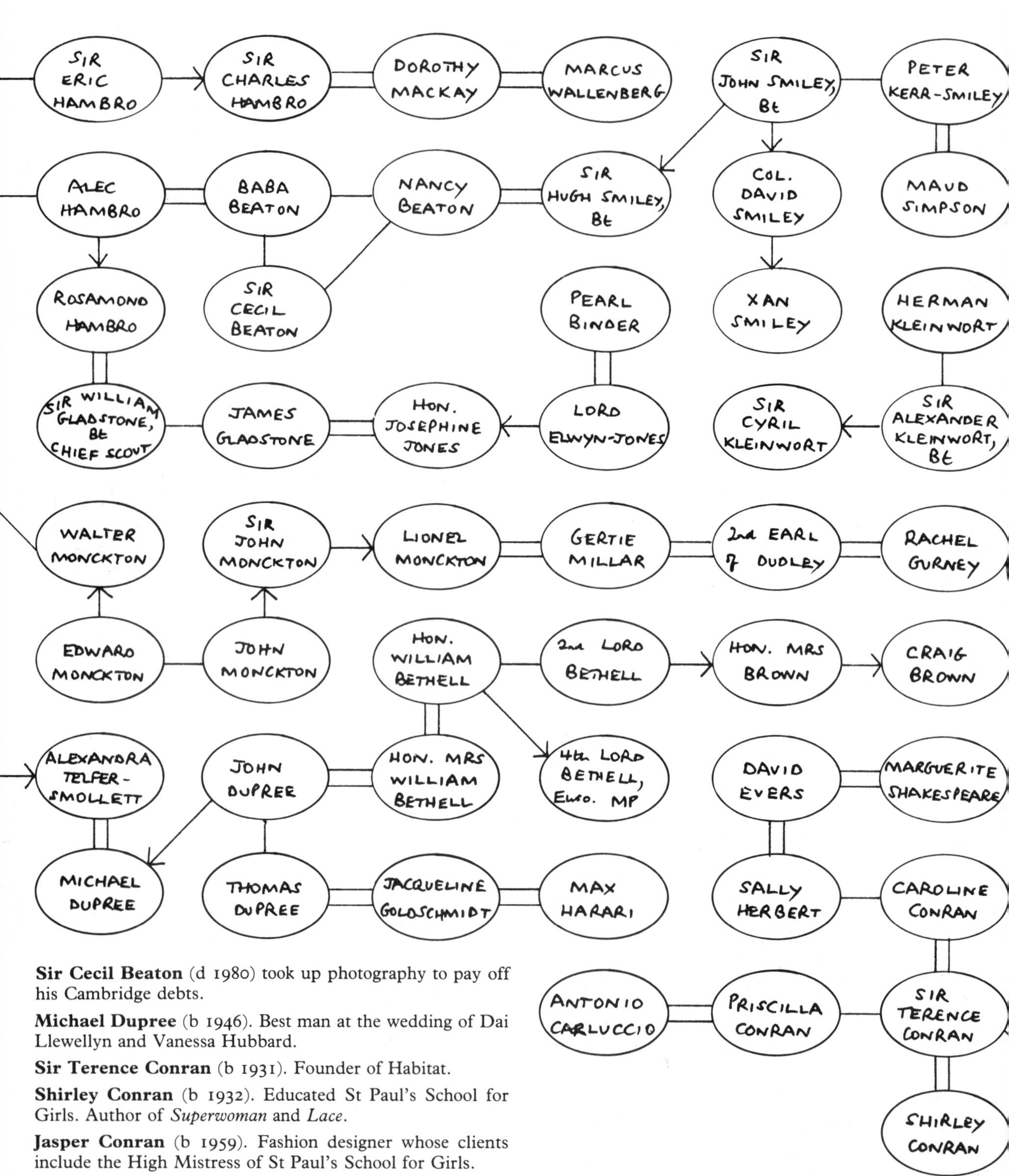

SIR ERIC HAMBRO
SIR CHARLES HAMBRO
DOROTHY MACKAY
MARCUS WALLENBERG
SIR JOHN SMILEY, Bt
PETER KERR-SMILEY
ALEC HAMBRO
BABA BEATON
NANCY BEATON
SIR HUGH SMILEY, Bt
COL. DAVID SMILEY
MAUD SIMPSON
ROSAMOND HAMBRO
SIR CECIL BEATON
PEARL BINDER
XAN SMILEY
HERMAN KLEINWORT
SIR WILLIAM GLADSTONE, Bt CHIEF SCOUT
JAMES GLADSTONE
HON. JOSEPHINE JONES
LORD ELWYN-JONES
SIR CYRIL KLEINWORT
SIR ALEXANDER KLEINWORT, Bt
WALTER MONCKTON
SIR JOHN MONCKTON
LIONEL MONCKTON
GERTIE MILLAR
2nd EARL of DUDLEY
RACHEL GURNEY
EDWARD MONCKTON
JOHN MONCKTON
HON. WILLIAM BETHELL
2nd LORD BETHELL
HON. MRS BROWN
CRAIG BROWN
ALEXANDRA TELFER-SMOLLETT
JOHN DUPREE
HON. MRS WILLIAM BETHELL
4th LORD BETHELL, Euro. MP
DAVID EVERS
MARGUERITE SHAKESPEARE
MICHAEL DUPREE
THOMAS DUPREE
JACQUELINE GOLDSCHMIDT
MAX HARARI
SALLY HERBERT
CAROLINE CONRAN
ANTONIO CARLUCCIO
PRISCILLA CONRAN
SIR TERENCE CONRAN
SHIRLEY CONRAN

Sir Cecil Beaton (d 1980) took up photography to pay off his Cambridge debts.

Michael Dupree (b 1946). Best man at the wedding of Dai Llewellyn and Vanessa Hubbard.

Sir Terence Conran (b 1931). Founder of Habitat.

Shirley Conran (b 1932). Educated St Paul's School for Girls. Author of *Superwoman* and *Lace*.

Jasper Conran (b 1959). Fashion designer whose clients include the High Mistress of St Paul's School for Girls.

dmiral Sir Ernest Troubridge (d 1926) caused a sen-
ıtion when he sued his wife Una for divorce, naming lesbian
ıthoress Radclyffe Hall as co-respondent.

Felix Hope-Nicholson (b 1921). Lord of the Manor of Tite Street, Chelsea, where he lives in a house bought by his grandmother, **Mrs Adrian Hope,** in the 1890s.

Dirk Bogarde (b 1921) began his theatrical career cleaning lavatories at the Q Theatre.

Georgi Markov (d 1978). Bulgarian defector who died after being stabbed by a poisoned umbrella on Waterloo Bridge.

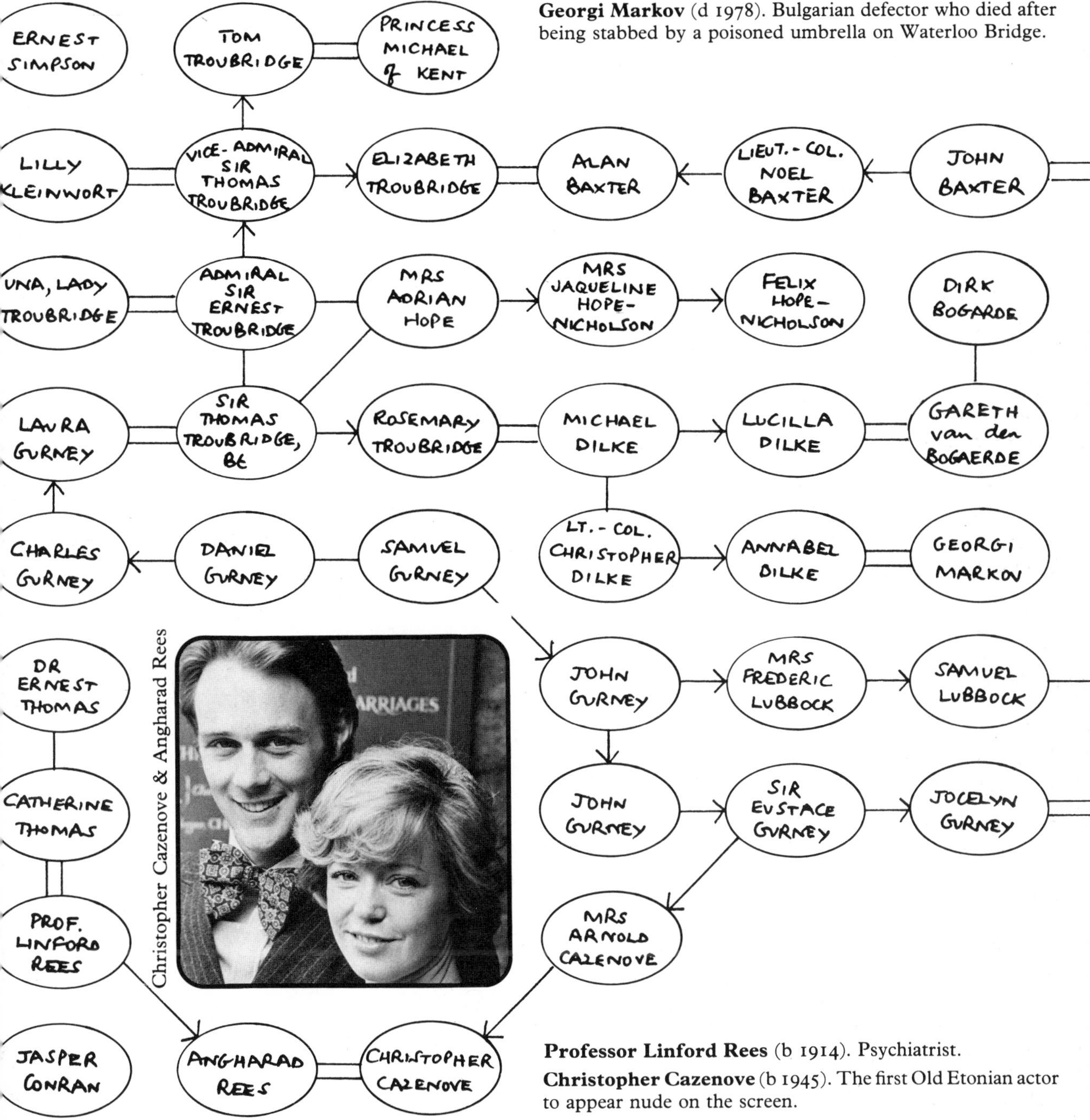
ERNEST SIMPSON
TOM TROUBRIDGE
PRINCESS MICHAEL of KENT
LILLY KLEINWORT
VICE-ADMIRAL SIR THOMAS TROUBRIDGE
ELIZABETH TROUBRIDGE
ALAN BAXTER
LIEUT.-COL. NOEL BAXTER
JOHN BAXTER
UNA, LADY TROUBRIDGE
ADMIRAL SIR ERNEST TROUBRIDGE
MRS ADRIAN HOPE
MRS JAQUELINE HOPE-NICHOLSON
FELIX HOPE-NICHOLSON
DIRK BOGARDE
LAURA GURNEY
SIR THOMAS TROUBRIDGE, BT
ROSEMARY TROUBRIDGE
MICHAEL DILKE
LUCILLA DILKE
GARETH van den BOGAERDE
CHARLES GURNEY
DANIEL GURNEY
SAMUEL GURNEY
LT.-COL. CHRISTOPHER DILKE
ANNABEL DILKE
GEORGI MARKOV
DR ERNEST THOMAS
JOHN GURNEY
MRS FREDERIC LUBBOCK
SAMUEL LUBBOCK
CATHERINE THOMAS
JOHN GURNEY
SIR EUSTACE GURNEY
JOCELYN GURNEY
PROF. LINFORD REES
MRS ARNOLD CAZENOVE
JASPER CONRAN
ANGHARAD REES
CHRISTOPHER CAZENOVE

Christopher Cazenove & Angharad Rees

Professor Linford Rees (b 1914). Psychiatrist.

Christopher Cazenove (b 1945). The first Old Etonian actor to appear nude on the screen.

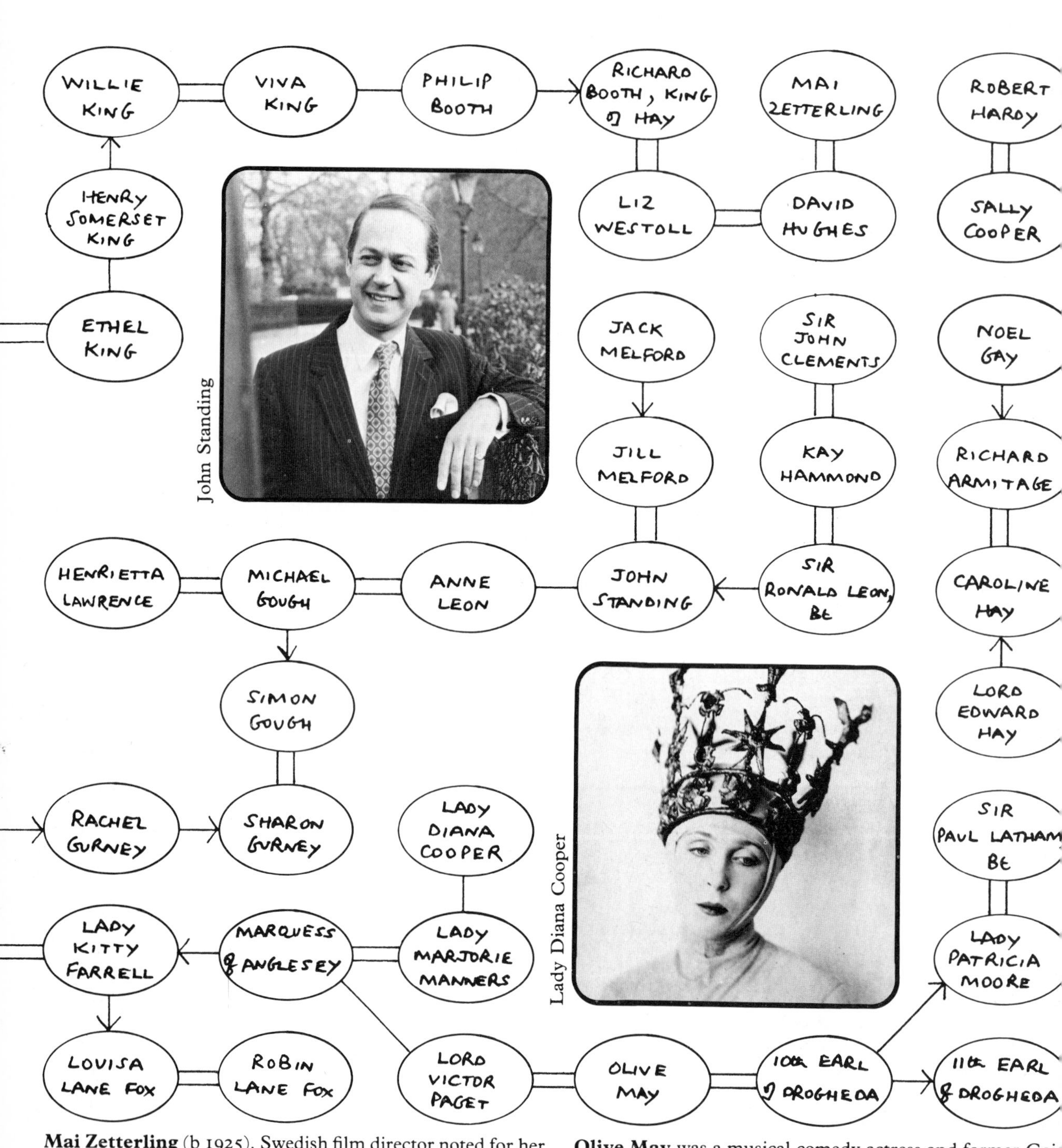
WILLIE KING
VIVA KING
PHILIP BOOTH
RICHARD BOOTH, KING OF HAY
MAI ZETTERLING
ROBERT HARDY
HENRY SOMERSET KING
LIZ WESTOLL
DAVID HUGHES
SALLY COOPER
ETHEL KING
JACK MELFORD
SIR JOHN CLEMENTS
NOEL GAY
JILL MELFORD
KAY HAMMOND
RICHARD ARMITAGE
HENRIETTA LAWRENCE
MICHAEL GOUGH
ANNE LEON
JOHN STANDING
SIR RONALD LEON, BT
CAROLINE HAY
SIMON GOUGH
LORD EDWARD HAY
RACHEL GURNEY
SHARON GURNEY
LADY DIANA COOPER
SIR PAUL LATHAM BT
LADY KITTY FARRELL
MARQUESS OF ANGLESEY
LADY MARJORIE MANNERS
LADY PATRICIA MOORE
LOUISA LANE FOX
ROBIN LANE FOX
LORD VICTOR PAGET
OLIVE MAY
10th EARL OF DROGHEDA
11th EARL OF DROGHEDA

John Standing

Lady Diana Cooper

Mai Zetterling (b 1925). Swedish film director noted for her *Loving Couples* and *Night Games*.

Lady Diana Cooper (b 1892) took the leading part in Max Reinhardt's play *The Miracle*. In 1983, aged 90, she drove herself to see Richard Attenborough's film *Gandhi*.

Olive May was a musical comedy actress and former Gai Girl.

10th Earl of Drogheda (d 1957). Chairman of the Cinemat graph Films Council and of the Films Selection Board.

Gladys Cooper (d 1971). Edwardian beauty who first appeared on stage in 1905 as Bluebell in *Bluebell in Fairyland* at the Theatre Royal, Colchester. A few months before her death she appeared in a revival of *The Chalk Garden* at the Haymarket.

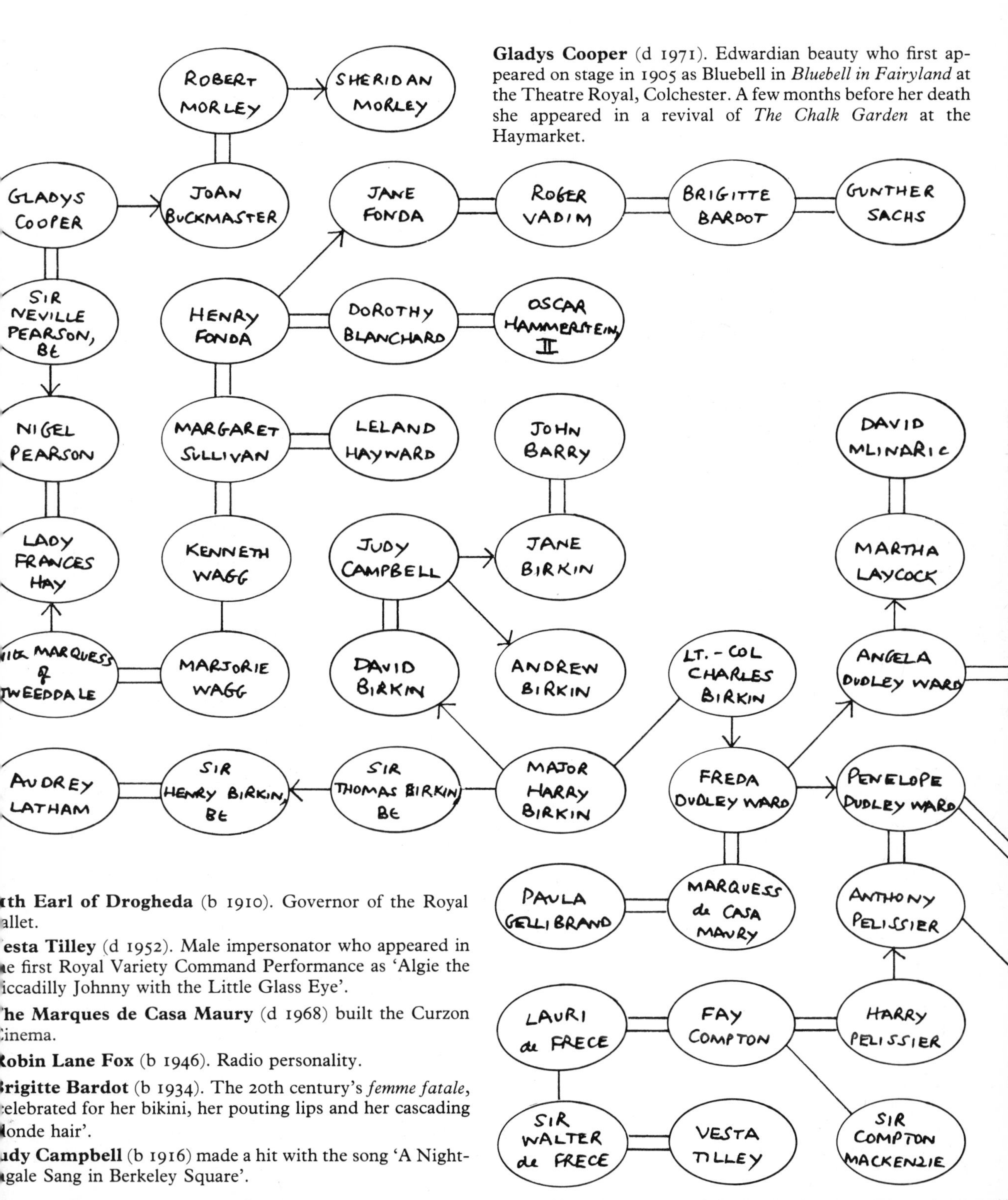
ROBERT MORLEY
SHERIDAN MORLEY
GLADYS COOPER
JOAN BUCKMASTER
JANE FONDA
ROGER VADIM
BRIGITTE BARDOT
GUNTHER SACHS
SIR NEVILLE PEARSON, Bt
HENRY FONDA
DOROTHY BLANCHARD
OSCAR HAMMERSTEIN II
NIGEL PEARSON
MARGARET SULLIVAN
LELAND HAYWARD
JOHN BARRY
DAVID MLINARIC
LADY FRANCES HAY
KENNETH WAGG
JUDY CAMPBELL
JANE BIRKIN
MARTHA LAYCOCK
MARQUESS of TWEEDDALE
MARJORIE WAGG
DAVID BIRKIN
ANDREW BIRKIN
LT.-COL CHARLES BIRKIN
ANGELA DUDLEY WARD
AUDREY LATHAM
SIR HENRY BIRKIN, Bt
SIR THOMAS BIRKIN Bt
MAJOR HARRY BIRKIN
FREDA DUDLEY WARD
PENELOPE DUDLEY WARD
PAULA GELLIBRAND
MARQUESS de CASA MAURY
ANTHONY PELISSIER
LAURI de FRECE
FAY COMPTON
HARRY PELISSIER
SIR WALTER de FRECE
VESTA TILLEY
SIR COMPTON MACKENZIE

th Earl of Drogheda (b 1910). Governor of the Royal allet.

esta Tilley (d 1952). Male impersonator who appeared in e first Royal Variety Command Performance as 'Algie the iccadilly Johnny with the Little Glass Eye'.

he Marques de Casa Maury (d 1968) built the Curzon inema.

obin Lane Fox (b 1946). Radio personality.

rigitte Bardot (b 1934). The 20th century's *femme fatale*, elebrated for her bikini, her pouting lips and her cascading londe hair'.

udy Campbell (b 1916) made a hit with the song 'A Nightngale Sang in Berkeley Square'.

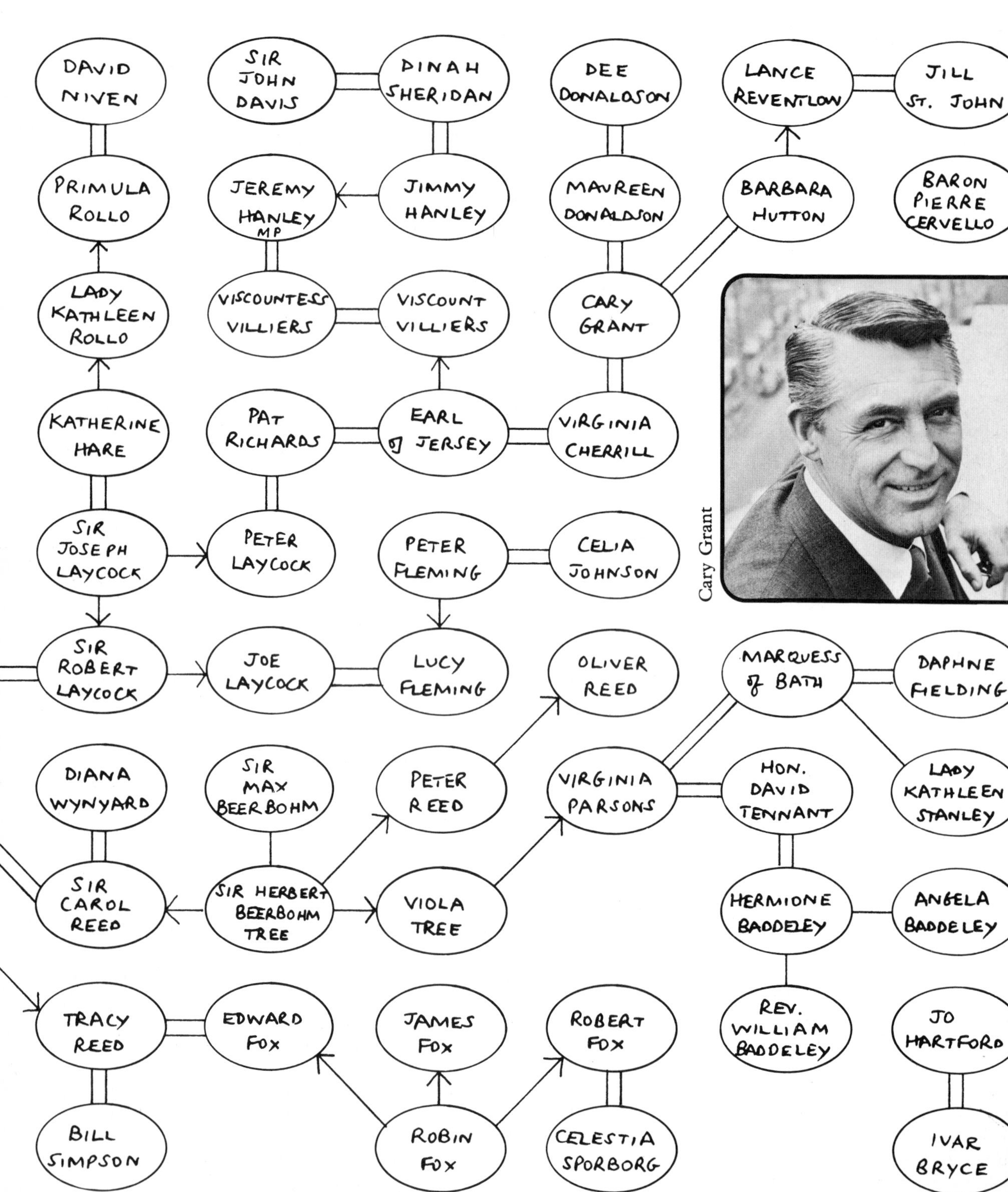
DAVID NIVEN
SIR JOHN DAVIS
DINAH SHERIDAN
DEE DONALDSON
LANCE REVENTLOW
JILL ST. JOHN
PRIMULA ROLLO
JEREMY HANLEY MP
JIMMY HANLEY
MAUREEN DONALDSON
BARBARA HUTTON
BARON PIERRE CERVELLO
LADY KATHLEEN ROLLO
VISCOUNTESS VILLIERS
VISCOUNT VILLIERS
CARY GRANT
KATHERINE HARE
PAT RICHARDS
EARL OF JERSEY
VIRGINIA CHERRILL
SIR JOSEPH LAYCOCK
PETER LAYCOCK
PETER FLEMING
CELIA JOHNSON
SIR ROBERT LAYCOCK
JOE LAYCOCK
LUCY FLEMING
OLIVER REED
MARQUESS OF BATH
DAPHNE FIELDING
DIANA WYNYARD
SIR MAX BEERBOHM
PETER REED
VIRGINIA PARSONS
HON. DAVID TENNANT
LADY KATHLEEN STANLEY
SIR CAROL REED
SIR HERBERT BEERBOHM TREE
VIOLA TREE
HERMIONE BADDELEY
ANGELA BADDELEY
TRACY REED
EDWARD FOX
JAMES FOX
ROBERT FOX
REV. WILLIAM BADDELEY
JO HARTFORD
BILL SIMPSON
ROBIN FOX
CELESTIA SPORBORG
IVAR BRYCE

Cary Grant

Baron Pierre Cervello was briefly engaged to Mandy Rice-Davies.

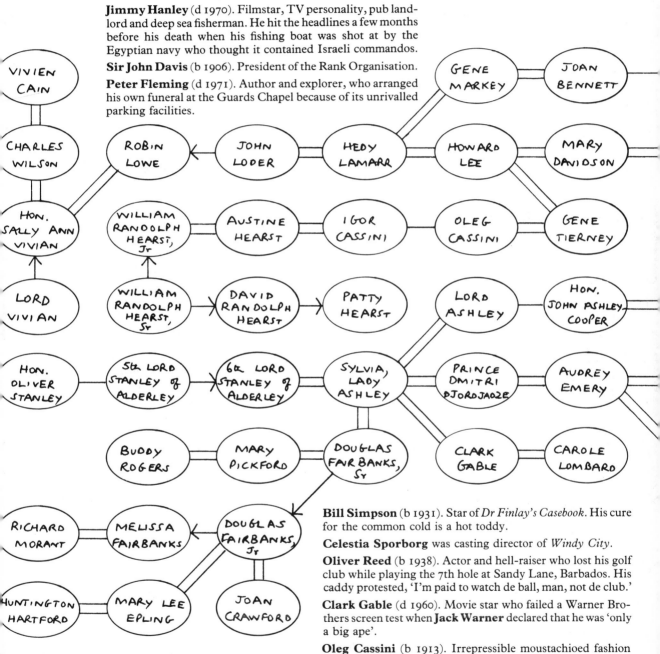

Jimmy Hanley (d 1970). Filmstar, TV personality, pub landlord and deep sea fisherman. He hit the headlines a few months before his death when his fishing boat was shot at by the Egyptian navy who thought it contained Israeli commandos.

Sir John Davis (b 1906). President of the Rank Organisation.

Peter Fleming (d 1971). Author and explorer, who arranged his own funeral at the Guards Chapel because of its unrivalled parking facilities.

VIVIEN CAIN
GENE MARKEY — JOAN BENNETT
CHARLES WILSON — ROBIN LOWE — JOHN LODER — HEDY LAMARR — HOWARD LEE — MARY DAVIDSON
HON. SALLY ANN VIVIAN — WILLIAM RANDOLPH HEARST, Jr — AUSTINE HEARST — IGOR CASSINI — OLEG CASSINI — GENE TIERNEY
LORD VIVIAN — WILLIAM RANDOLPH HEARST, Sr — DAVID RANDOLPH HEARST — PATTY HEARST — LORD ASHLEY — HON. JOHN ASHLEY-COOPER
HON. OLIVER STANLEY — 5th LORD STANLEY of ALDERLEY — 6th LORD STANLEY of ALDERLEY — SYLVIA, LADY ASHLEY — PRINCE DMITRI DJORDJADZE — AUDREY EMERY
BUDDY ROGERS — MARY PICKFORD — DOUGLAS FAIRBANKS, Sr — CLARK GABLE — CAROLE LOMBARD
RICHARD MORANT — MELISSA FAIRBANKS — DOUGLAS FAIRBANKS, Jr
HUNTINGTON HARTFORD — MARY LEE EPLING — JOAN CRAWFORD

ledy Lamarr (b 1914) was the first woman to appear naked n the screen.

ally Ann Vivian (b 1930). A former Deb of the Year who vorked at Fortnum and Mason.

Bill Simpson (b 1931). Star of *Dr Finlay's Casebook*. His cure for the common cold is a hot toddy.

Celestia Sporborg was casting director of *Windy City*.

Oliver Reed (b 1938). Actor and hell-raiser who lost his golf club while playing the 7th hole at Sandy Lane, Barbados. His caddy protested, 'I'm paid to watch de ball, man, not de club.'

Clark Gable (d 1960). Movie star who failed a Warner Brothers screen test when **Jack Warner** declared that he was 'only a big ape'.

Oleg Cassini (b 1913). Irrepressible moustachioed fashion designer. 'It is easy to be humble when things are going well for you. The trick is to be arrogant when you are a flop.'

Sir Robert Laycock (d 1968). One of the youths who threw the young Cecil Beaton into the river during a ball at Wilton.

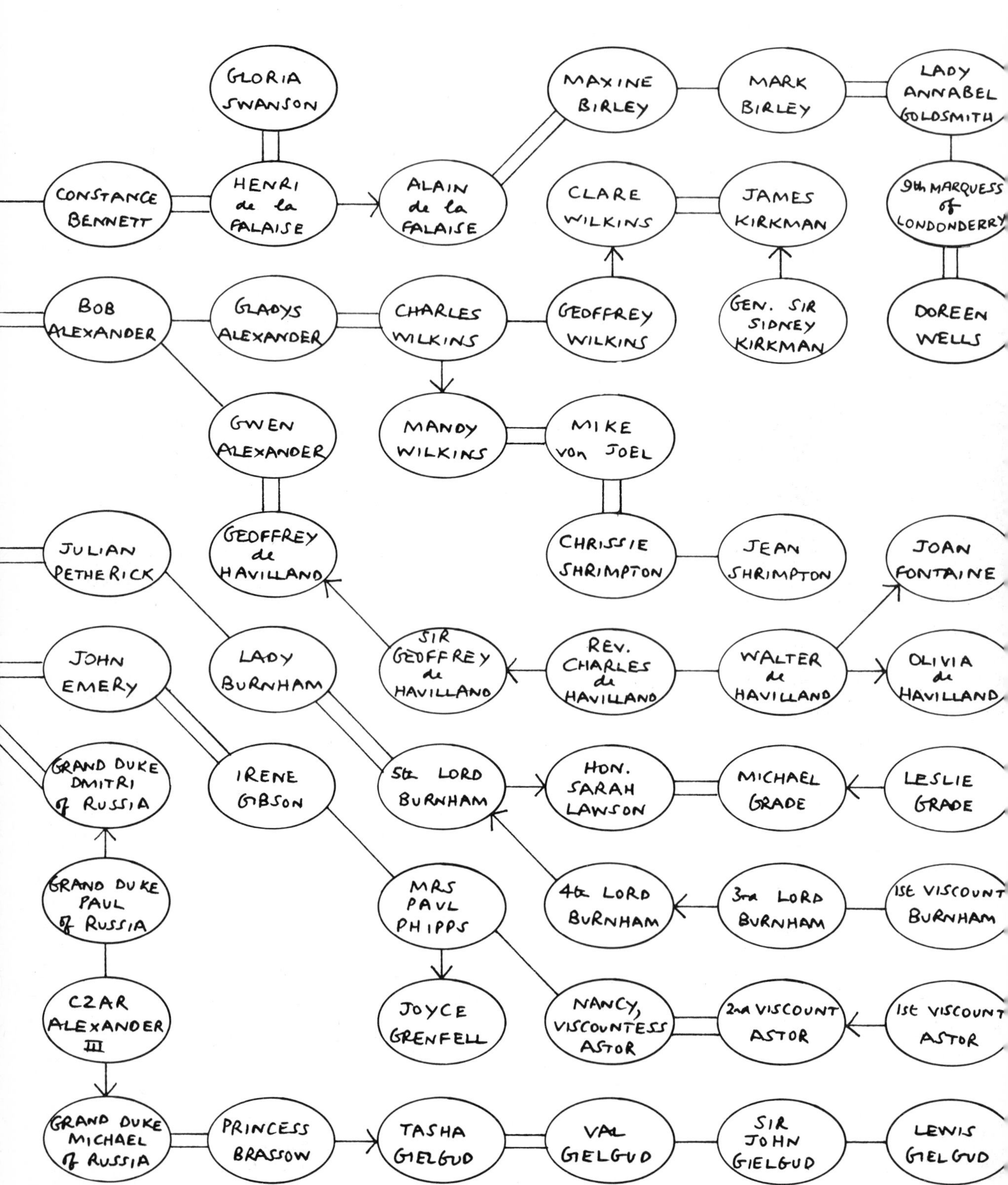
GLORIA SWANSON
MAXINE BIRLEY
MARK BIRLEY
LADY ANNABEL GOLDSMITH
CONSTANCE BENNETT
HENRI de la FALAISE
ALAIN de la FALAISE
CLARE WILKINS
JAMES KIRKMAN
9th MARQUESS of LONDONDERRY
BOB ALEXANDER
GLADYS ALEXANDER
CHARLES WILKINS
GEOFFREY WILKINS
GEN. SIR SIDNEY KIRKMAN
DOREEN WELLS
GWEN ALEXANDER
MANDY WILKINS
MIKE von JOEL
JULIAN PETHERICK
GEOFFREY de HAVILLAND
CHRISSIE SHRIMPTON
JEAN SHRIMPTON
JOAN FONTAINE
JOHN EMERY
LADY BURNHAM
SIR GEOFFREY de HAVILLAND
REV. CHARLES de HAVILLAND
WALTER de HAVILLAND
OLIVIA de HAVILLAND
GRAND DUKE DMITRI of RUSSIA
IRENE GIBSON
5th LORD BURNHAM
HON. SARAH LAWSON
MICHAEL GRADE
LESLIE GRADE
GRAND DUKE PAUL of RUSSIA
MRS PAUL PHIPPS
4th LORD BURNHAM
3rd LORD BURNHAM
1st VISCOUNT BURNHAM
CZAR ALEXANDER III
JOYCE GRENFELL
NANCY, VISCOUNTESS ASTOR
2nd VISCOUNT ASTOR
1st VISCOUNT ASTOR
GRAND DUKE MICHAEL of RUSSIA
PRINCESS BRASSOW
TASHA GIELGUD
VAL GIELGUD
SIR JOHN GIELGUD
LEWIS GIELGUD

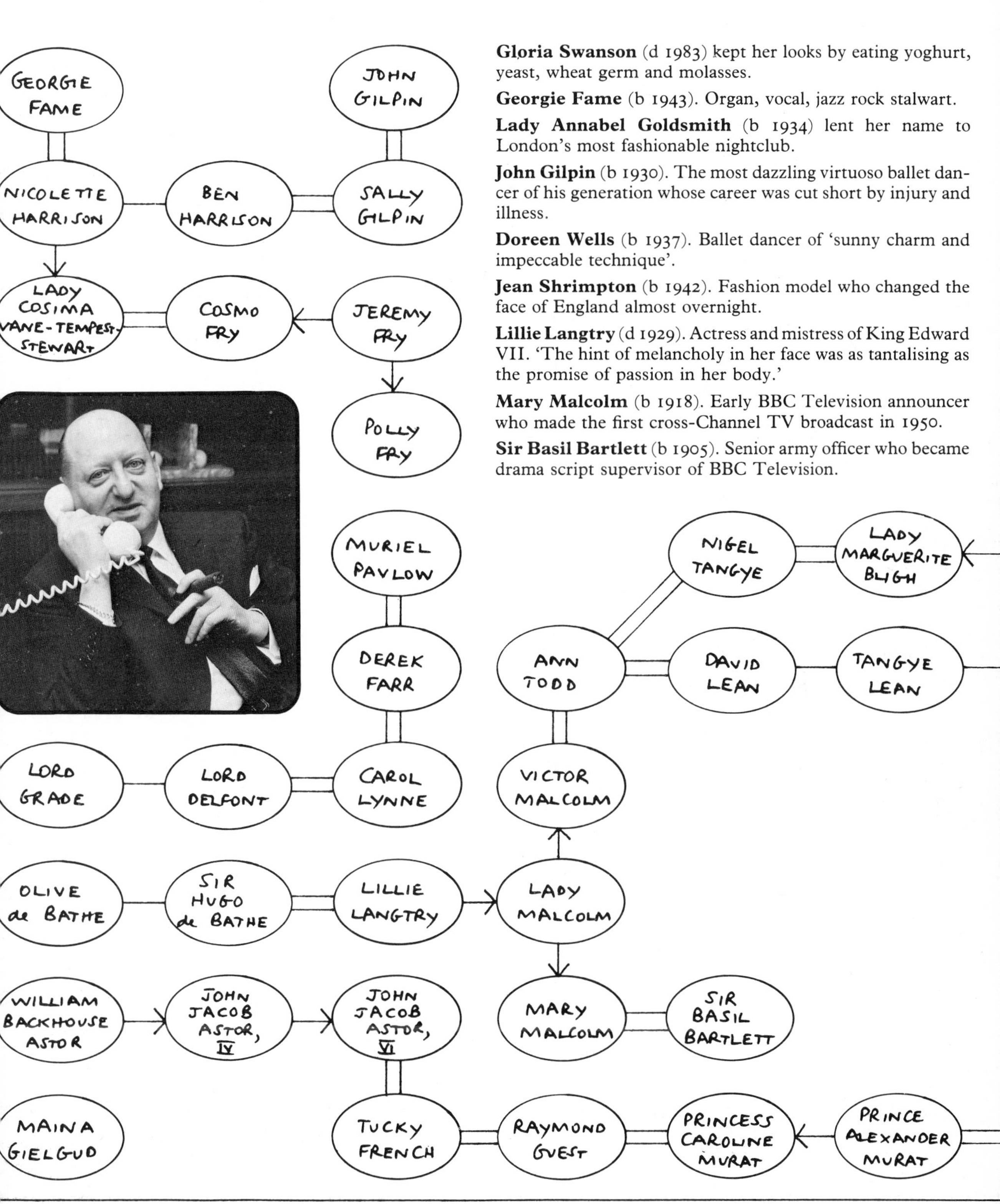
GEORGIE FAME
JOHN GILPIN
NICOLETTE HARRISON
BEN HARRISON
SALLY GILPIN
LADY COSIMA VANE-TEMPEST-STEWART
COSMO FRY
JEREMY FRY
POLLY FRY
MURIEL PAVLOW
DEREK FARR
NIGEL TANGYE
LADY MARGUERITE BLIGH
ANN TODD
DAVID LEAN
TANGYE LEAN
LORD GRADE
LORD DELFONT
CAROL LYNNE
VICTOR MALCOLM
OLIVE de BATHE
SIR HUGO de BATHE
LILLIE LANGTRY
LADY MALCOLM
WILLIAM BACKHOUSE ASTOR
JOHN JACOB ASTOR, IV
JOHN JACOB ASTOR, VI
MARY MALCOLM
SIR BASIL BARTLETT
MAINA GIELGUD
TUCKY FRENCH
RAYMOND GUEST
PRINCESS CAROLINE MURAT
PRINCE ALEXANDER MURAT

Gloria Swanson (d 1983) kept her looks by eating yoghurt, yeast, wheat germ and molasses.

Georgie Fame (b 1943). Organ, vocal, jazz rock stalwart.

Lady Annabel Goldsmith (b 1934) lent her name to London's most fashionable nightclub.

John Gilpin (b 1930). The most dazzling virtuoso ballet dancer of his generation whose career was cut short by injury and illness.

Doreen Wells (b 1937). Ballet dancer of 'sunny charm and impeccable technique'.

Jean Shrimpton (b 1942). Fashion model who changed the face of England almost overnight.

Lillie Langtry (d 1929). Actress and mistress of King Edward VII. 'The hint of melancholy in her face was as tantalising as the promise of passion in her body.'

Mary Malcolm (b 1918). Early BBC Television announcer who made the first cross-Channel TV broadcast in 1950.

Sir Basil Bartlett (b 1905). Senior army officer who became drama script supervisor of BBC Television.

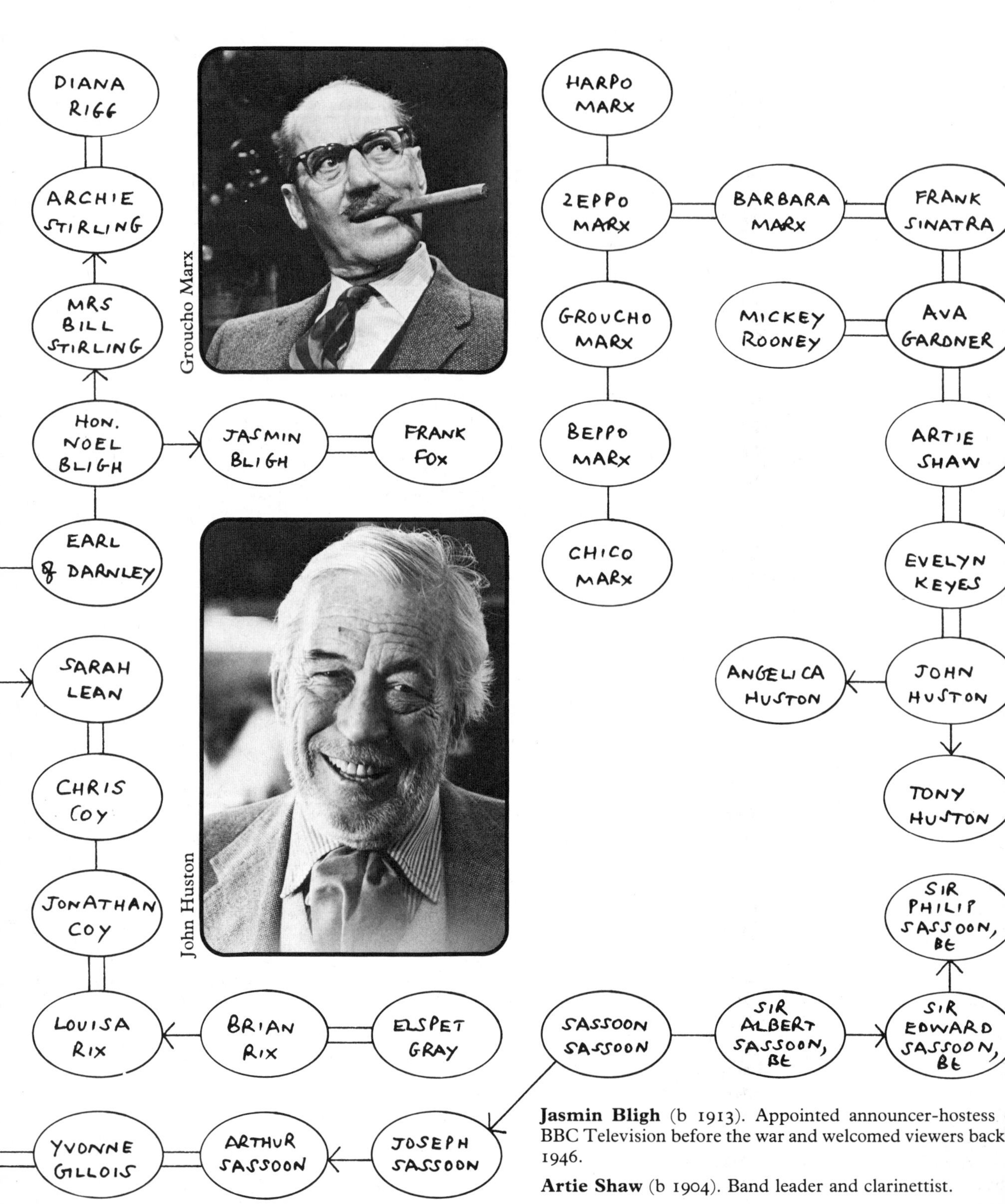
DIANA RIGG
ARCHIE STIRLING
MRS BILL STIRLING
HON. NOEL BLIGH
JASMIN BLIGH
FRANK FOX
EARL of DARNLEY
SARAH LEAN
CHRIS COY
JONATHAN COY
LOUISA RIX
BRIAN RIX
ELSPET GRAY
YVONNE GILLOIS
ARTHUR SASSOON
JOSEPH SASSOON
HARPO MARX
ZEPPO MARX
GROUCHO MARX
BEPPO MARX
CHICO MARX
BARBARA MARX
FRANK SINATRA
MICKEY ROONEY
AVA GARDNER
ARTIE SHAW
EVELYN KEYES
ANGELICA HUSTON
JOHN HUSTON
TONY HUSTON
SIR PHILIP SASSOON, Bt
SASSOON SASSOON
SIR ALBERT SASSOON, Bt
SIR EDWARD SASSOON, Bt

Groucho Marx

John Huston

Jasmin Bligh (b 1913). Appointed announcer-hostess c BBC Television before the war and welcomed viewers back 1946.

Artie Shaw (b 1904). Band leader and clarinettist.

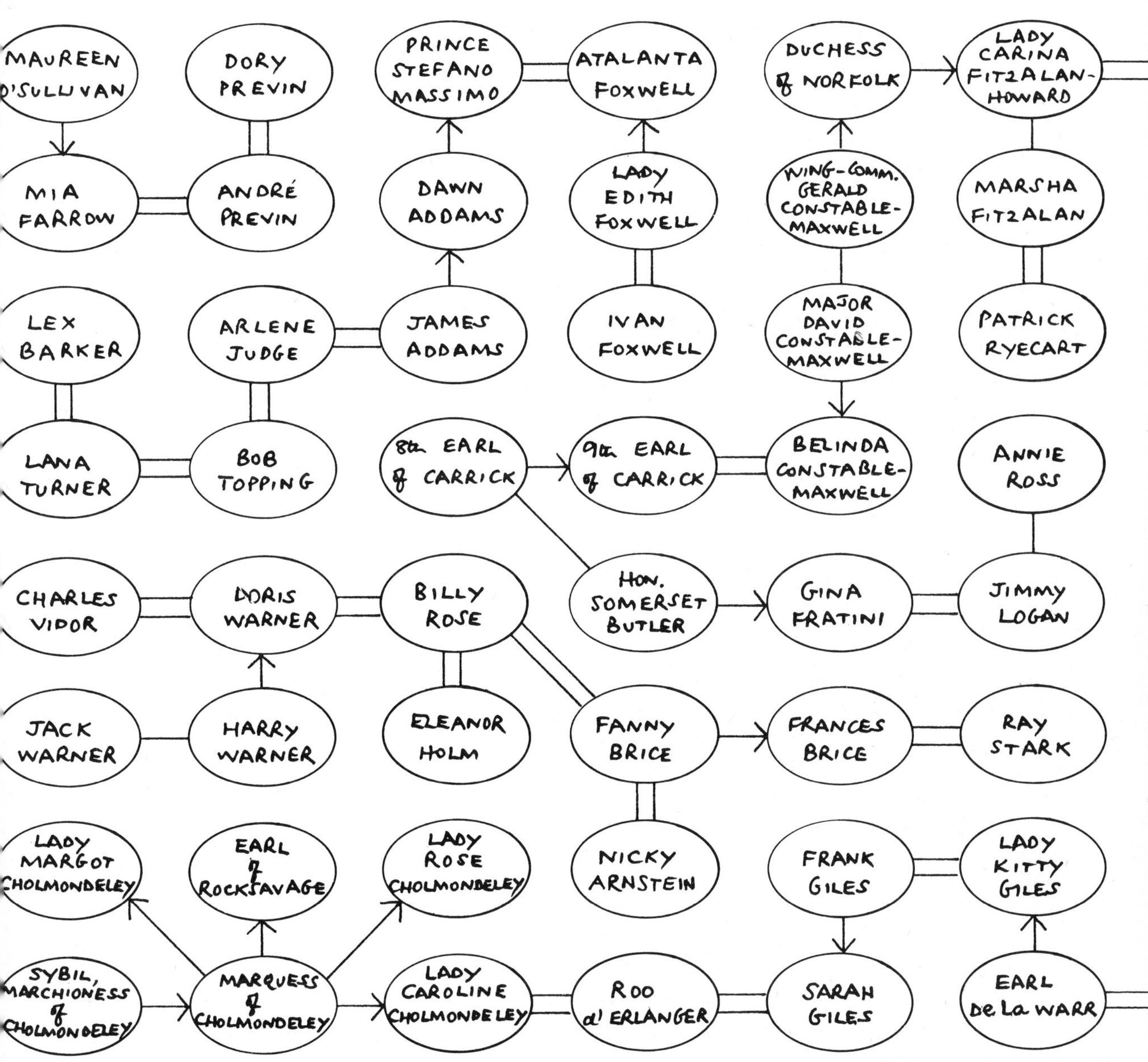
MAUREEN O'SULLIVAN
DORY PREVIN
PRINCE STEFANO MASSIMO
ATALANTA FOXWELL
DUCHESS of NORFOLK
LADY CARINA FITZALAN-HOWARD
MIA FARROW
ANDRÉ PREVIN
DAWN ADDAMS
LADY EDITH FOXWELL
WING-COMM. GERALD CONSTABLE-MAXWELL
MARSHA FITZALAN
LEX BARKER
ARLENE JUDGE
JAMES ADDAMS
IVAN FOXWELL
MAJOR DAVID CONSTABLE-MAXWELL
PATRICK RYECART
LANA TURNER
BOB TOPPING
8th EARL of CARRICK
9th EARL of CARRICK
BELINDA CONSTABLE-MAXWELL
ANNIE ROSS
CHARLES VIDOR
DORIS WARNER
BILLY ROSE
HON. SOMERSET BUTLER
GINA FRATINI
JIMMY LOGAN
JACK WARNER
HARRY WARNER
ELEANOR HOLM
FANNY BRICE
FRANCES BRICE
RAY STARK
LADY MARGOT CHOLMONDELEY
EARL of ROCKSAVAGE
LADY ROSE CHOLMONDELEY
NICKY ARNSTEIN
FRANK GILES
LADY KITTY GILES
SYBIL, MARCHIONESS of CHOLMONDELEY
MARQUESS of CHOLMONDELEY
LADY CAROLINE CHOLMONDELEY
ROO d'ERLANGER
SARAH GILES
EARL De La WARR

Sassoon Sassoon (d 1867) dropped dead in the foyer of the Langham Hotel while waiting for a cab to take him to the newly opened Victoria and Albert Museum.

Frank Sinatra (b 1915). Singer and actor with a deceptively lazy, inimitable voice. During the 1970s he won substantial damages from the BBC after a broadcast suggesting that he had a connection with the Mafia.

Mia Farrow (b 1945). Former *Peyton Place* star whose fans gasped when she cut her long blonde hair less than half an inch short.

Sir Philip Sassoon (d 1939). Politician, aesthete and social arbiter. One of the baths at his country home was sunk into a floor of black marble and surrounded by walls covered in zig-zagging red stripes.

Rose Cholmondeley (b 1948). Concert pianist.

Fanny Brice (d 1951). Jewish entertainer who made a virtue of her plainness. She made her début at an amateur night at Keeney's Theatre, Brooklyn, playing an alligator.

Frank Giles (b 1919) once described the study of the aristocracy as 'like eating too many cream cakes'.

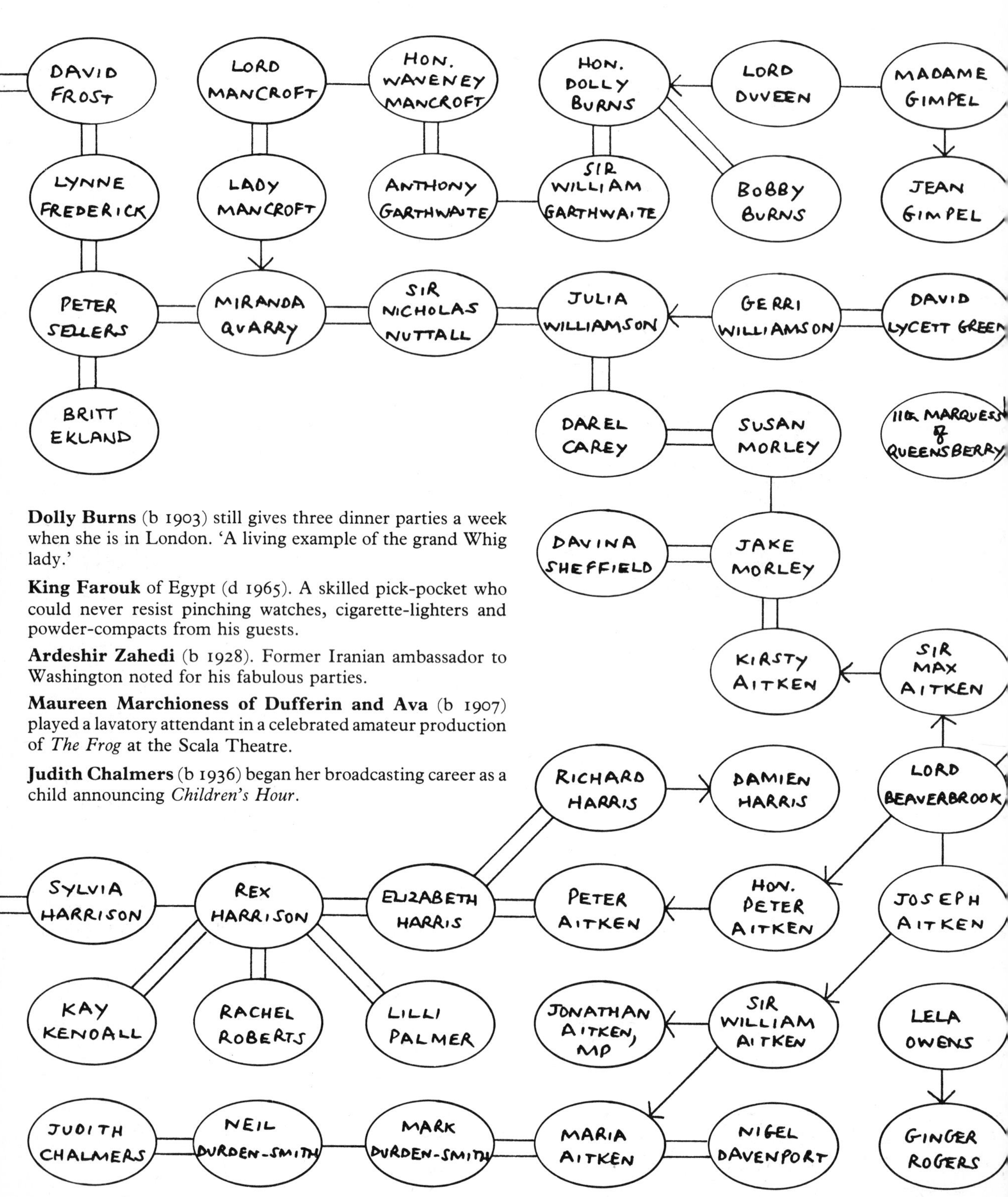

DAVID FROST
LORD MANCROFT
HON. WAVENEY MANCROFT
HON. DOLLY BURNS
LORD DUVEEN
MADAME GIMPEL
LYNNE FREDERICK
LADY MANCROFT
ANTHONY GARTHWAITE
SIR WILLIAM GARTHWAITE
BOBBY BURNS
JEAN GIMPEL
PETER SELLERS
MIRANDA QUARRY
SIR NICHOLAS NUTTALL
JULIA WILLIAMSON
GERRI WILLIAMSON
DAVID LYCETT GREEN
BRITT EKLAND
DAREL CAREY
SUSAN MORLEY
11th MARQUESS of QUEENSBERRY
DAVINA SHEFFIELD
JAKE MORLEY
KIRSTY AITKEN
SIR MAX AITKEN
RICHARD HARRIS
DAMIEN HARRIS
LORD BEAVERBROOK
SYLVIA HARRISON
REX HARRISON
ELIZABETH HARRIS
PETER AITKEN
HON. PETER AITKEN
JOSEPH AITKEN
KAY KENDALL
RACHEL ROBERTS
LILLI PALMER
JONATHAN AITKEN, MP
SIR WILLIAM AITKEN
LELA OWENS
JUDITH CHALMERS
NEIL DURDEN-SMITH
MARK DURDEN-SMITH
MARIA AITKEN
NIGEL DAVENPORT
GINGER ROGERS

Dolly Burns (b 1903) still gives three dinner parties a week when she is in London. 'A living example of the grand Whig lady.'

King Farouk of Egypt (d 1965). A skilled pick-pocket who could never resist pinching watches, cigarette-lighters and powder-compacts from his guests.

Ardeshir Zahedi (b 1928). Former Iranian ambassador to Washington noted for his fabulous parties.

Maureen Marchioness of Dufferin and Ava (b 1907) played a lavatory attendant in a celebrated amateur production of *The Frog* at the Scala Theatre.

Judith Chalmers (b 1936) began her broadcasting career as a child announcing *Children's Hour*.

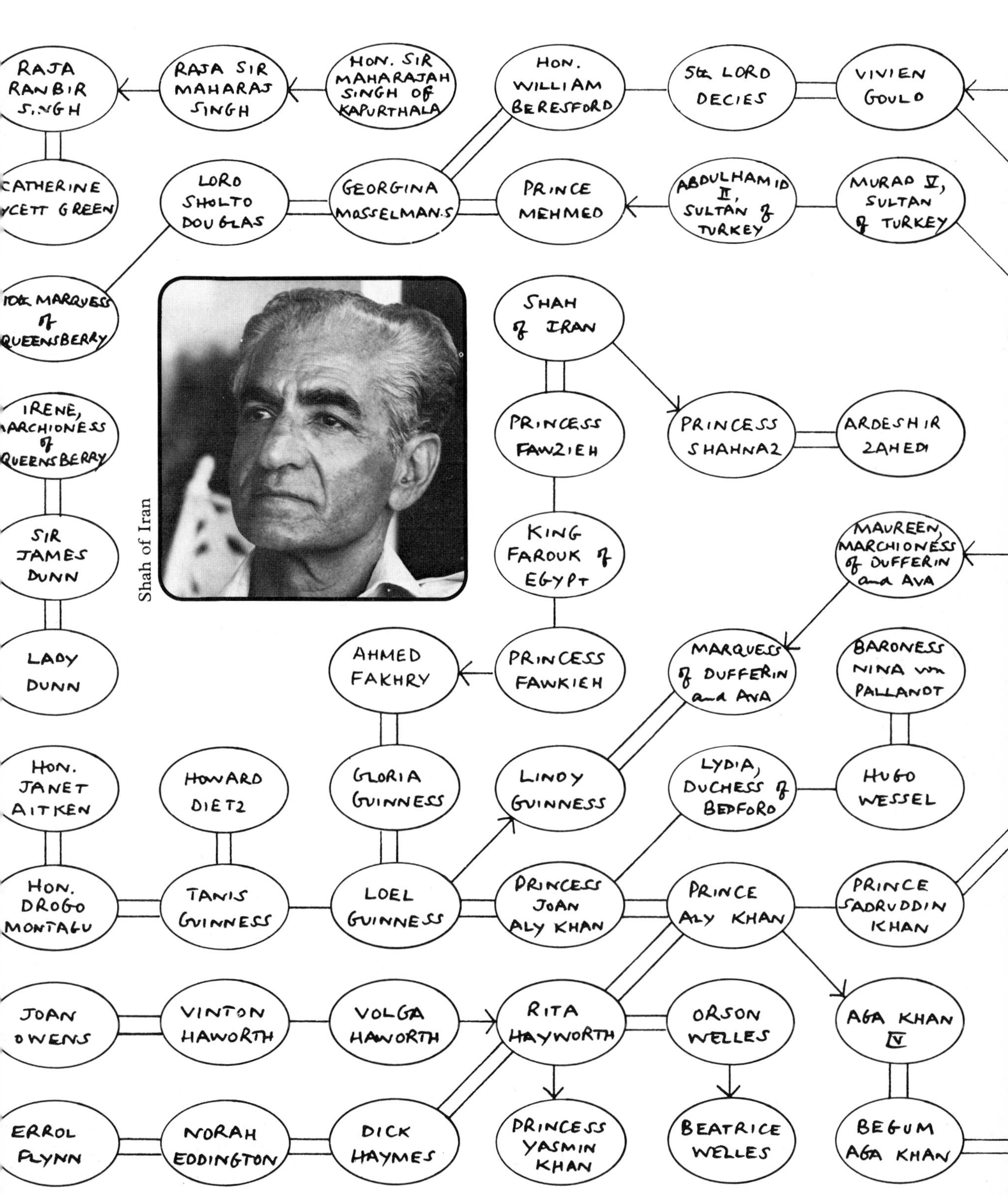
RAJA RANBIR SINGH
RAJA SIR MAHARAJ SINGH
HON. SIR MAHARAJAH SINGH OF KAPURTHALA
HON. WILLIAM BERESFORD
5th LORD DECIES
VIVIEN GOULD
CATHERINE LYCETT GREEN
LORD SHOLTO DOUGLAS
GEORGINA MOSSELMANS
PRINCE MEHMED
ABDULHAMID II, SULTAN of TURKEY
MURAD V, SULTAN of TURKEY
10th MARQUESS of QUEENSBERRY
SHAH of IRAN
IRENE, MARCHIONESS of QUEENSBERRY
PRINCESS FAWZIEH
PRINCESS SHAHNAZ
ARDESHIR ZAHEDI
SIR JAMES DUNN
KING FAROUK of EGYPT
MAUREEN, MARCHIONESS of DUFFERIN and AVA
LADY DUNN
AHMED FAKHRY
PRINCESS FAWKIEH
MARQUESS of DUFFERIN and AVA
BARONESS NINA von PALLANDT
HON. JANET AITKEN
HOWARD DIETZ
GLORIA GUINNESS
LINDY GUINNESS
LYDIA, DUCHESS of BEDFORD
HUGO WESSEL
HON. DROGO MONTAGU
TANIS GUINNESS
LOEL GUINNESS
PRINCESS JOAN ALY KHAN
PRINCE ALY KHAN
PRINCE SADRUDDIN KHAN
JOAN OWENS
VINTON HAWORTH
VOLGA HAWORTH
RITA HAYWORTH
ORSON WELLES
AGA KHAN IV
ERROL FLYNN
NORAH EDDINGTON
DICK HAYMES
PRINCESS YASMIN KHAN
BEATRICE WELLES
BEGUM AGA KHAN

Shah of Iran

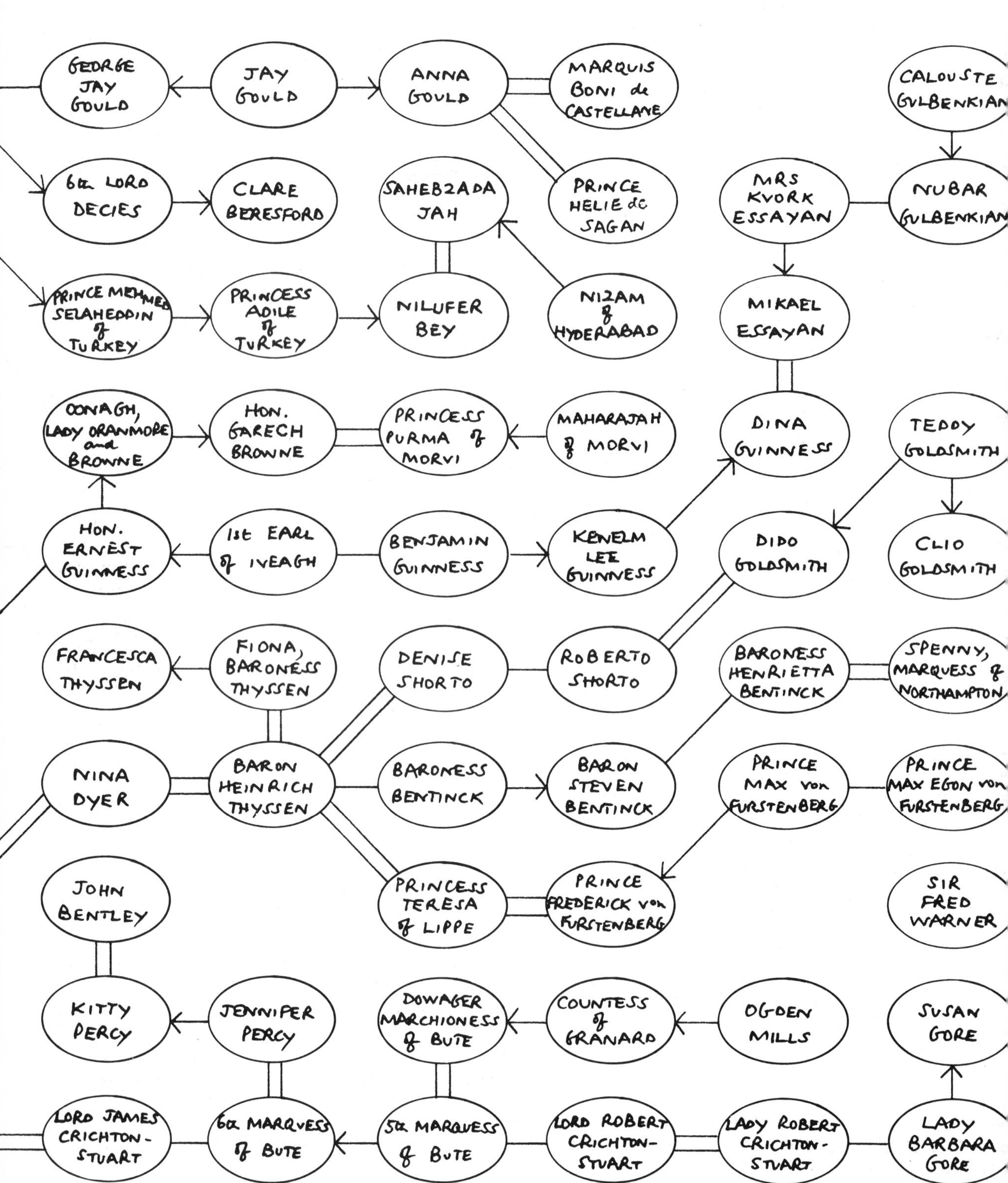

GEORGE JAY GOULD
JAY GOULD
ANNA GOULD
MARQUIS BONI de CASTELLANE
CALOUSTE GULBENKIAN
6th LORD DECIES
CLARE BERESFORD
SAHEBZADA JAH
PRINCE HELIE de SAGAN
MRS KVORK ESSAYAN
NUBAR GULBENKIAN
PRINCE MEHMED SELAHEDDIN of TURKEY
PRINCESS ADILE of TURKEY
NILUFER BEY
NIZAM of HYDERABAD
MIKAEL ESSAYAN
OONAGH, LADY ORANMORE and BROWNE
HON. GARECH BROWNE
PRINCESS PURMA of MORVI
MAHARAJAH of MORVI
DINA GUINNESS
TEDDY GOLDSMITH
HON. ERNEST GUINNESS
1st EARL of IVEAGH
BENJAMIN GUINNESS
KENELM LEE GUINNESS
DIDO GOLDSMITH
CLIO GOLDSMITH
FRANCESCA THYSSEN
FIONA, BARONESS THYSSEN
DENISE SHORTO
ROBERTO SHORTO
BARONESS HENRIETTA BENTINCK
SPENNY, MARQUESS of NORTHAMPTON
NINA DYER
BARON HEINRICH THYSSEN
BARONESS BENTINCK
BARON STEVEN BENTINCK
PRINCE MAX von FURSTENBERG
PRINCE MAX EGON von FURSTENBERG
JOHN BENTLEY
PRINCESS TERESA of LIPPE
PRINCE FREDERICK von FURSTENBERG
SIR FRED WARNER
KITTY PERCY
JENNIFER PERCY
DOWAGER MARCHIONESS of BUTE
COUNTESS of GRANARD
OGDEN MILLS
SUSAN GORE
LORD JAMES CRICHTON-STUART
6th MARQUESS of BUTE
5th MARQUESS of BUTE
LORD ROBERT CRICHTON-STUART
LADY ROBERT CRICHTON-STUART
LADY BARBARA GORE

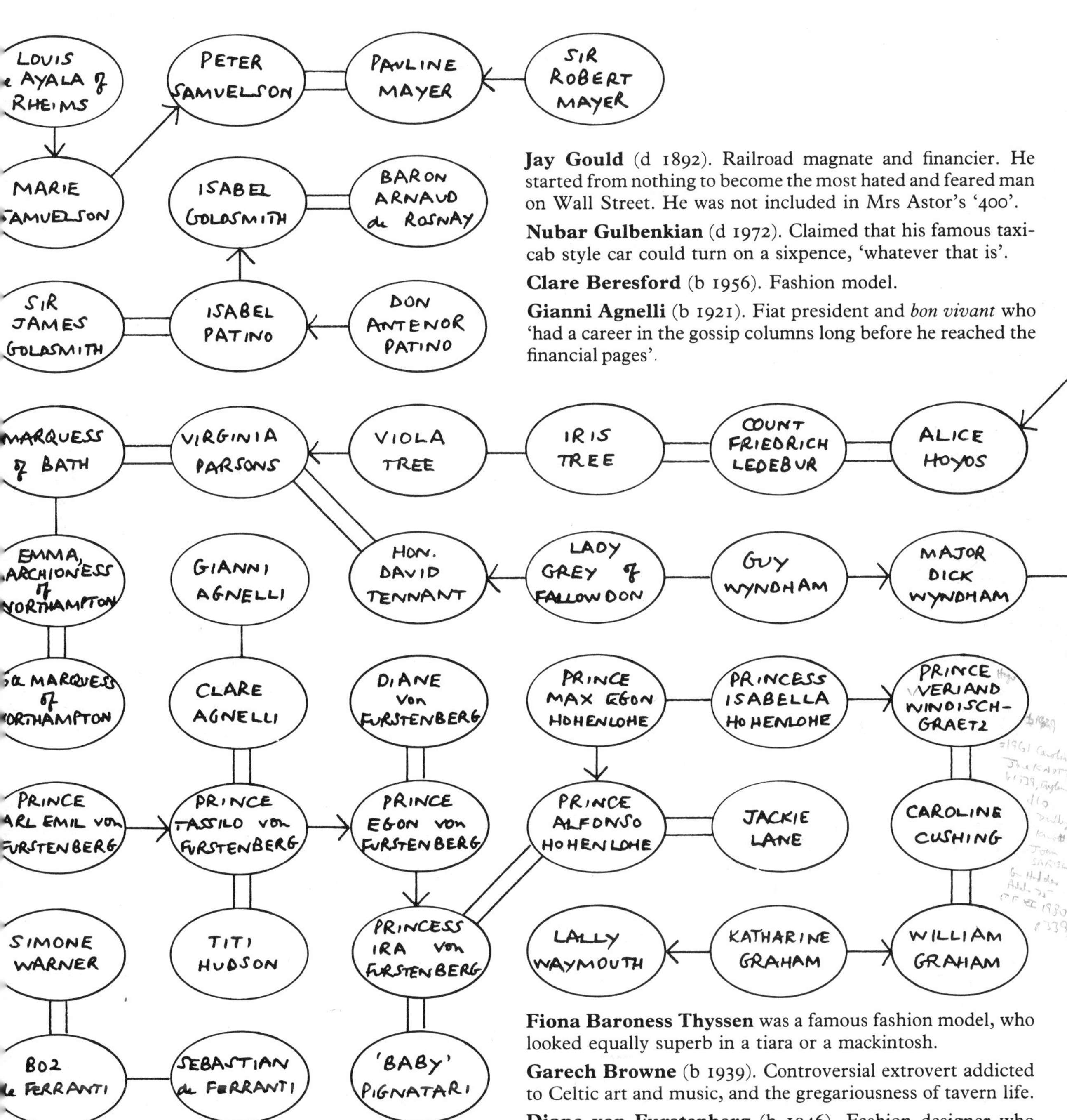
LOUIS
e AYALA of
RHEIMS
PETER
SAMUELSON
PAULINE
MAYER
SIR
ROBERT
MAYER
MARIE
SAMUELSON
ISABEL
GOLDSMITH
BARON
ARNAUD
de ROSNAY
SIR
JAMES
GOLDSMITH
ISABEL
PATINO
DON
ANTENOR
PATINO
MARQUESS
of BATH
VIRGINIA
PARSONS
VIOLA
TREE
IRIS
TREE
COUNT
FRIEDRICH
LEDEBUR
ALICE
HOYOS
EMMA,
ARCHIONESS
of
NORTHAMPTON
GIANNI
AGNELLI
HON.
DAVID
TENNANT
LADY
GREY of
FALLOWDON
GUY
WYNDHAM
MAJOR
DICK
WYNDHAM
MARQUESS
of
NORTHAMPTON
CLARE
AGNELLI
DIANE
Von
FURSTENBERG
PRINCE
MAX EGON
HOHENLOHE
PRINCESS
ISABELLA
HOHENLOHE
PRINCE
WERIAND
WINDISCH-
GRAETZ
PRINCE
ARL EMIL VON
FURSTENBERG
PRINCE
TASSILO VON
FURSTENBERG
PRINCE
EGON VON
FURSTENBERG
PRINCE
ALFONSO
HOHENLOHE
JACKIE
LANE
CAROLINE
CUSHING
SIMONE
WARNER
TITI
HUDSON
PRINCESS
IRA VON
FURSTENBERG
LALLY
WAYMOUTH
KATHARINE
GRAHAM
WILLIAM
GRAHAM
BOZ
de FERRANTI
SEBASTIAN
de FERRANTI
'BABY'
PIGNATARI

Jay Gould (d 1892). Railroad magnate and financier. He started from nothing to become the most hated and feared man on Wall Street. He was not included in Mrs Astor's '400'.

Nubar Gulbenkian (d 1972). Claimed that his famous taxi-cab style car could turn on a sixpence, 'whatever that is'.

Clare Beresford (b 1956). Fashion model.

Gianni Agnelli (b 1921). Fiat president and *bon vivant* who 'had a career in the gossip columns long before he reached the financial pages'.

Fiona Baroness Thyssen was a famous fashion model, who looked equally superb in a tiara or a mackintosh.

Garech Browne (b 1939). Controversial extrovert addicted to Celtic art and music, and the gregariousness of tavern life.

Diane von Furstenberg (b 1946). Fashion designer who heads a multi-million dollar business marketing clothes, furs, scarves, sun-glasses, handbags, cosmetics, shoes and over-the-counter fabrics.

Katharine Graham (b 1917). President of the *Washington Post*.

hn Bentley (b 1940). Old Harrovian tycoon.

aron Heinrich Thyssen (b 1921). Swiss industrialist and t collector.

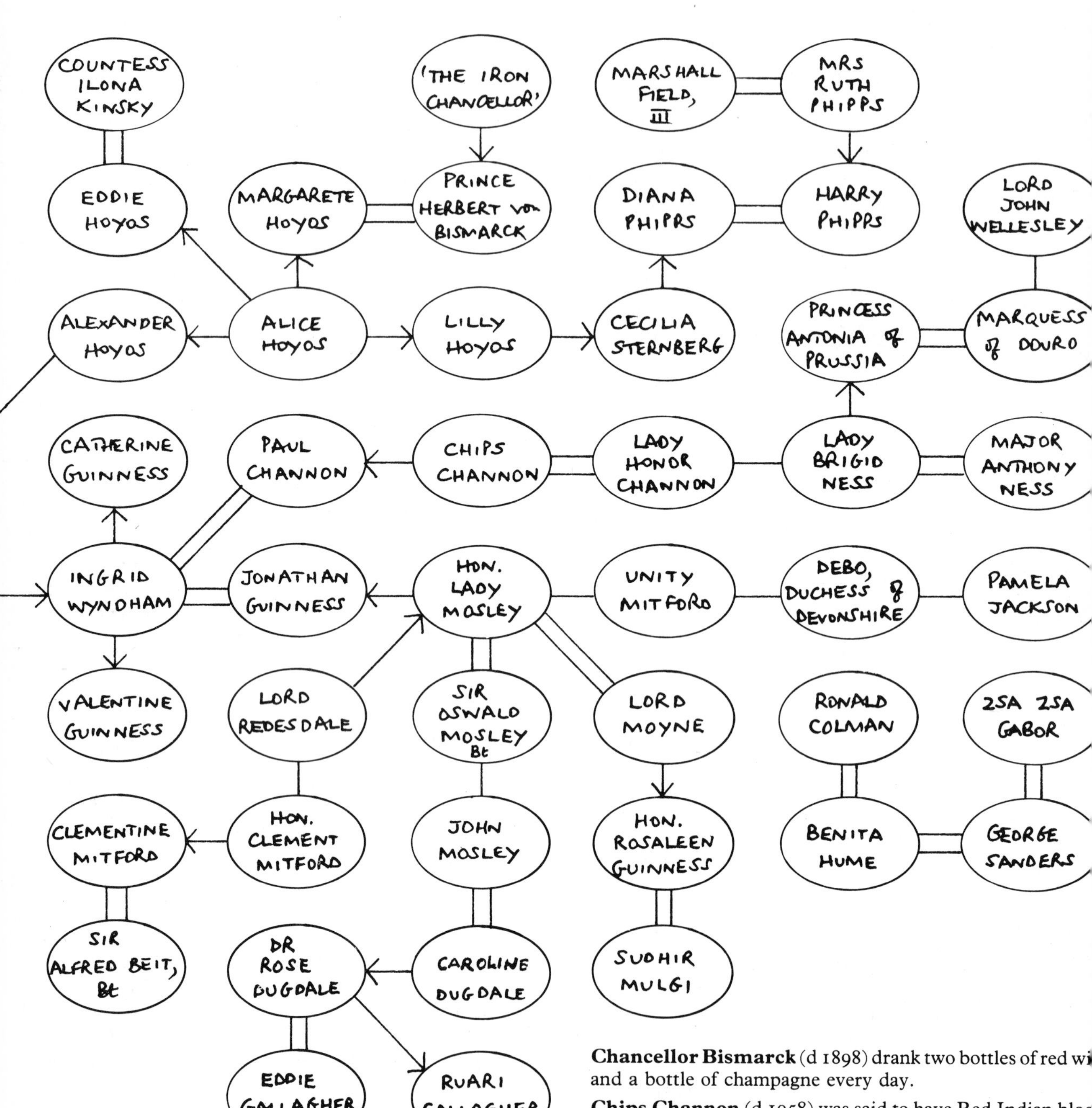
COUNTESS ILONA KINSKY
'THE IRON CHANCELLOR'
MARSHALL FIELD, III
MRS RUTH PHIPPS
EDDIE HOYOS
MARGARETE HOYOS
PRINCE HERBERT VON BISMARCK
DIANA PHIPPS
HARRY PHIPPS
LORD JOHN WELLESLEY
ALEXANDER HOYOS
ALICE HOYOS
LILLY HOYOS
CECILIA STERNBERG
PRINCESS ANTONIA OF PRUSSIA
MARQUESS OF DOURO
CATHERINE GUINNESS
PAUL CHANNON
CHIPS CHANNON
LADY HONOR CHANNON
LADY BRIGID NESS
MAJOR ANTHONY NESS
INGRID WYNDHAM
JONATHAN GUINNESS
HON. LADY MOSLEY
UNITY MITFORD
DEBO, DUCHESS OF DEVONSHIRE
PAMELA JACKSON
VALENTINE GUINNESS
LORD REDESDALE
SIR OSWALD MOSLEY Bt
LORD MOYNE
RONALD COLMAN
ZSA ZSA GABOR
CLEMENTINE MITFORD
HON. CLEMENT MITFORD
JOHN MOSLEY
HON. ROSALEEN GUINNESS
BENITA HUME
GEORGE SANDERS
SIR ALFRED BEIT, Bt
DR ROSE DUGDALE
CAROLINE DUGDALE
SUDHIR MULGI
EDDIE GALLAGHER
RUARI GALLAGHER

Unity Mitford (d 1948). A close friend of Adolf Hitler, she shot herself on the outbreak of the 2nd World War and never fully recovered from her injuries. On her tombstone is written 'Say not the struggle nought availeth'.

Chancellor Bismarck (d 1898) drank two bottles of red wi and a bottle of champagne every day.

Chips Channon (d 1958) was said to have Red Indian bloc

Valentine Guinness (b 1959). Lead singer with a pop gro called The Panic.

Dr Rose Dugdale (b 1941) described her coming out dan as 'one of those pornographic affairs which cost what six old age pensioners receive in six months'.

Sudhir Mulgi (b 1938). Indian businessman.

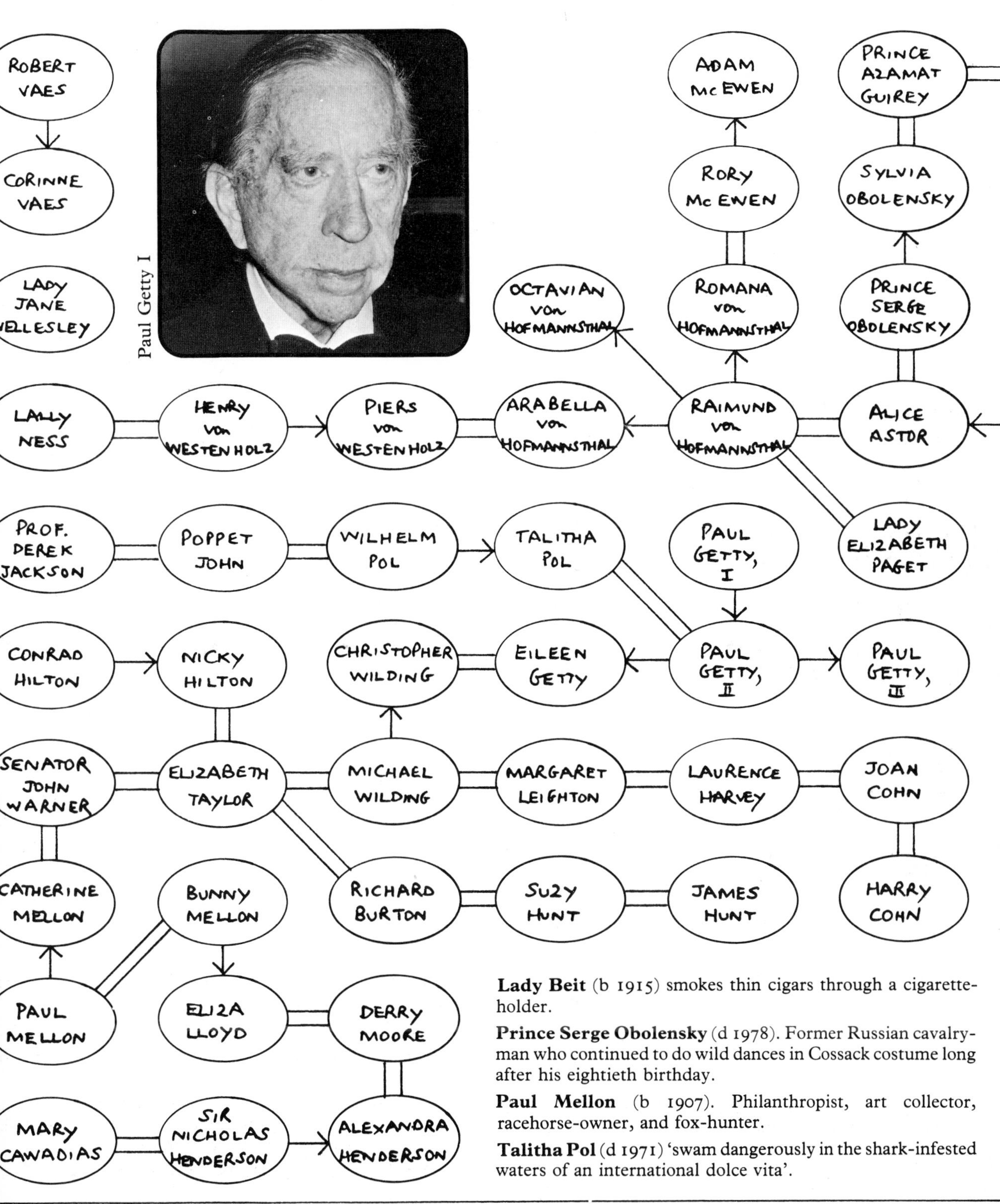
ROBERT VAES
CORINNE VAES
LADY JANE WELLESLEY
ADAM McEWEN
RORY McEWEN
PRINCE AZAMAT GUIREY
SYLVIA OBOLENSKY
OCTAVIAN von HOFMANNSTHAL
ROMANA von HOFMANNSTHAL
PRINCE SERGE OBOLENSKY
LALLY NESS
HENRY von WESTENHOLZ
PIERS von WESTENHOLZ
ARABELLA von HOFMANNSTHAL
RAIMUND von HOFMANNSTHAL
ALICE ASTOR
PROF. DEREK JACKSON
POPPET JOHN
WILHELM POL
TALITHA POL
PAUL GETTY, I
LADY ELIZABETH PAGET
CONRAD HILTON
NICKY HILTON
CHRISTOPHER WILDING
EILEEN GETTY
PAUL GETTY, II
PAUL GETTY, III
SENATOR JOHN WARNER
ELIZABETH TAYLOR
MICHAEL WILDING
MARGARET LEIGHTON
LAURENCE HARVEY
JOAN COHN
CATHERINE MELLON
BUNNY MELLON
RICHARD BURTON
SUZY HUNT
JAMES HUNT
HARRY COHN
PAUL MELLON
ELIZA LLOYD
DERRY MOORE
MARY CAWADIAS
SIR NICHOLAS HENDERSON
ALEXANDRA HENDERSON

Paul Getty I

Lady Beit (b 1915) smokes thin cigars through a cigarette-holder.

Prince Serge Obolensky (d 1978). Former Russian cavalryman who continued to do wild dances in Cossack costume long after his eightieth birthday.

Paul Mellon (b 1907). Philanthropist, art collector, racehorse-owner, and fox-hunter.

Talitha Pol (d 1971) 'swam dangerously in the shark-infested waters of an international dolce vita'.

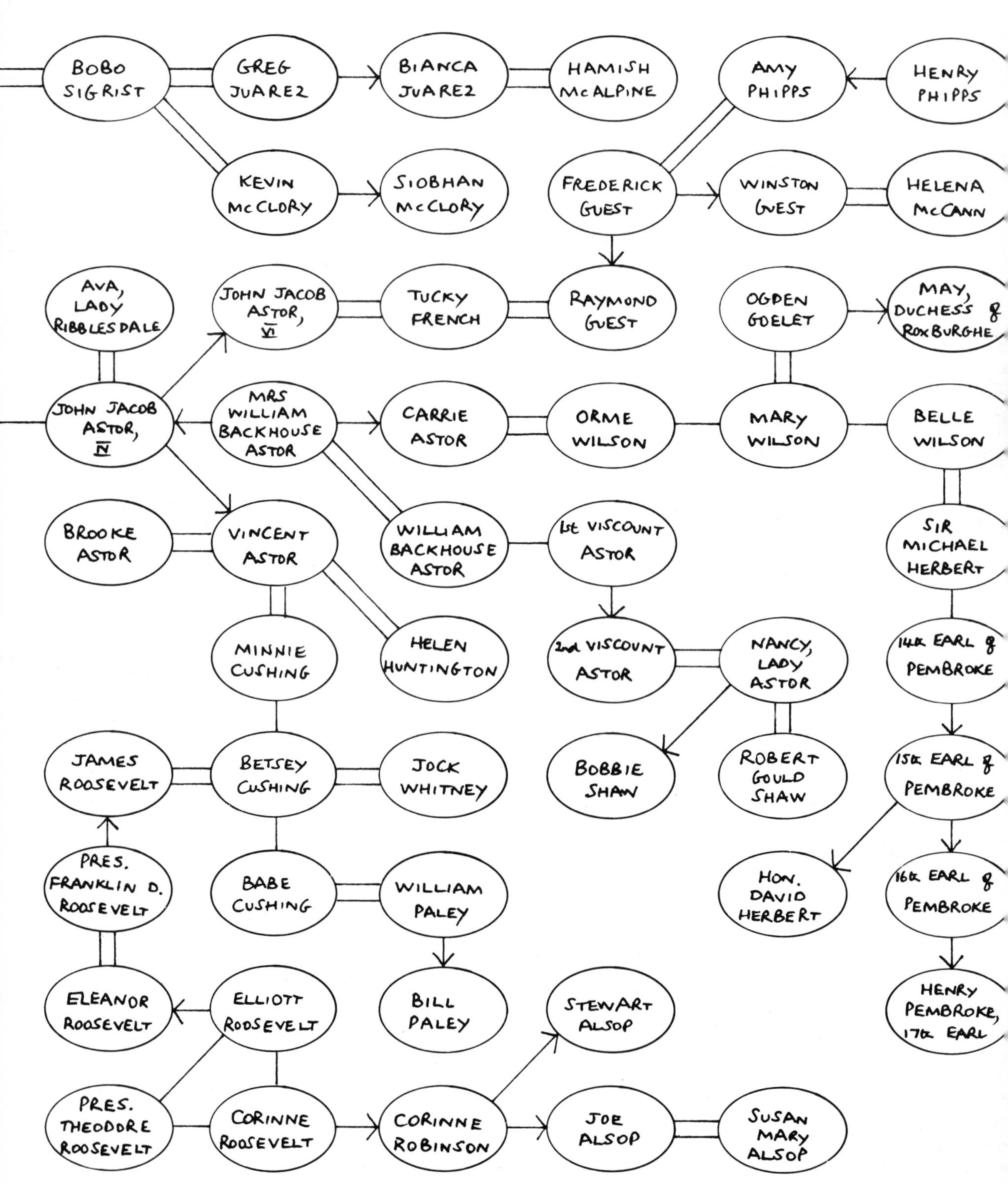
BOBO SIGRIST
GREG JUAREZ
BIANCA JUAREZ
HAMISH McALPINE
AMY PHIPPS
HENRY PHIPPS
KEVIN McCLORY
SIOBHAN McCLORY
FREDERICK GUEST
WINSTON GUEST
HELENA McCANN
AVA, LADY RIBBLESDALE
JOHN JACOB ASTOR, VI
TUCKY FRENCH
RAYMOND GUEST
OGDEN GOELET
MAY, DUCHESS OF ROXBURGHE
JOHN JACOB ASTOR, IV
MRS WILLIAM BACKHOUSE ASTOR
CARRIE ASTOR
ORME WILSON
MARY WILSON
BELLE WILSON
BROOKE ASTOR
VINCENT ASTOR
WILLIAM BACKHOUSE ASTOR
1st VISCOUNT ASTOR
SIR MICHAEL HERBERT
MINNIE CUSHING
HELEN HUNTINGTON
2nd VISCOUNT ASTOR
NANCY, LADY ASTOR
14th EARL OF PEMBROKE
JAMES ROOSEVELT
BETSEY CUSHING
JOCK WHITNEY
BOBBIE SHAW
ROBERT GOULD SHAW
15th EARL OF PEMBROKE
PRES. FRANKLIN D. ROOSEVELT
BABE CUSHING
WILLIAM PALEY
HON. DAVID HERBERT
16th EARL OF PEMBROKE
ELEANOR ROOSEVELT
ELLIOTT ROOSEVELT
BILL PALEY
STEWART ALSOP
HENRY PEMBROKE, 17th EARL
PRES. THEODORE ROOSEVELT
CORINNE ROOSEVELT
CORINNE ROBINSON
JOE ALSOP
SUSAN MARY ALSOP

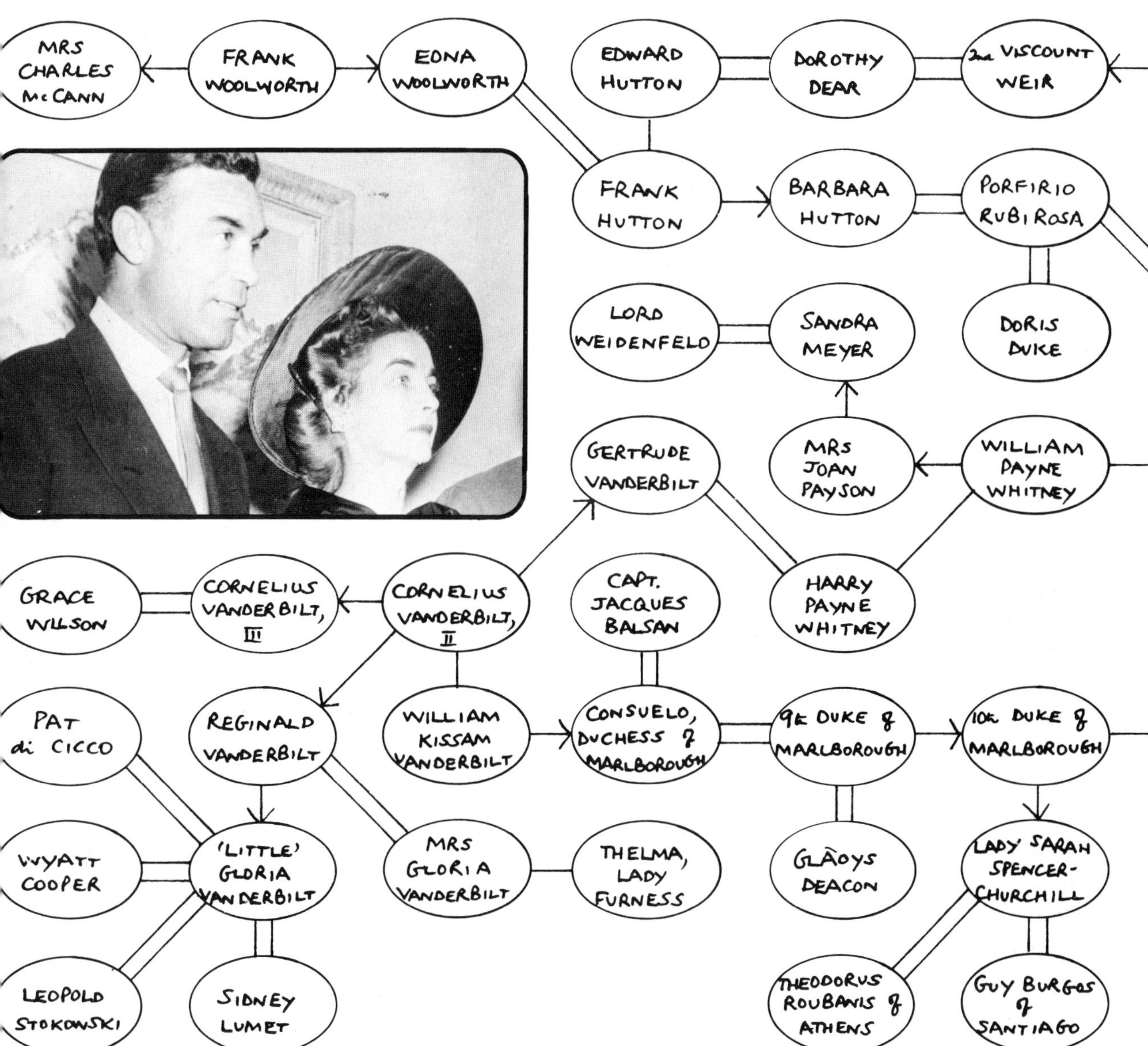

MRS CHARLES McCANN
FRANK WOOLWORTH
EDNA WOOLWORTH
EDWARD HUTTON
DOROTHY DEAR
2nd VISCOUNT WEIR
FRANK HUTTON
BARBARA HUTTON
PORFIRIO RUBIROSA
LORD WEIDENFELD
SANDRA MEYER
DORIS DUKE
GERTRUDE VANDERBILT
MRS JOAN PAYSON
WILLIAM PAYNE WHITNEY
GRACE WILSON
CORNELIUS VANDERBILT, III
CORNELIUS VANDERBILT, II
CAPT. JACQUES BALSAN
HARRY PAYNE WHITNEY
PAT di CICCO
REGINALD VANDERBILT
WILLIAM KISSAM VANDERBILT
CONSUELO, DUCHESS of MARLBOROUGH
9th DUKE of MARLBOROUGH
10th DUKE of MARLBOROUGH
WYATT COOPER
'LITTLE' GLORIA VANDERBILT
MRS GLORIA VANDERBILT
THELMA, LADY FURNESS
GLADYS DEACON
LADY SARAH SPENCER-CHURCHILL
LEOPOLD STOKOWSKI
SIDNEY LUMET
THEODORUS ROUBANIS of ATHENS
GUY BURGOS of SANTIAGO

John Jacob Astor IV died on the *Titanic* in 1912.

Mrs William Backhouse Astor (d 1907). Queen of New York society. She did not care that the ballroom of her 5th Avenue mansion could accommodate only 400 people. 'If you go outside that number you strike people who are either not at ease in a ballroom or else make other people not at ease.'

Vincent Astor (d 1969) left $129 million. His widow **Brooke**, former features editor of *House and Garden*, has made charitable gifts 'of breathtaking generosity'.

Leopold Stokowski (d 1977). Conductor and composer whose hands were the subject of much comment and some derision.

Gladys Duchess of Marlborough died in a mental hospital in 1977. Her jewellery and art collection were sold later at Christie's for £784,000.

Thelma Lady Furness (d 1970) first introduced the Prince of Wales to Mrs Wallis Simpson.

1st VISCOUNT WEIR
JAMES WEIR
JEAN WEIR
ROBERT DUCAS
JUNE DUCAS
HON. JAMES OGILVY
VICTOR MATURE
MARTHA STEPHENSON
PATRICIA PROVATOROFF
BOB DUCAS
FLOR de TRUJILLO
ANTHONY VEIGA
SUSAN STONE STEPHENSON
GEORGE SCHAFFT
PAULINE WHITNEY
DOROTHY WHITNEY
MAJOR WILLARD STRAIGHT
MILDRED 'BROWNIE' BROWN
JOCK MACLEAN
LORD QUEENBOROUGH
DOROTHY PAGET
MICHAEL STRAIGHT
WHITNEY STRAIGHT
LADY DAPHNE STRAIGHT
EVALYN WALSH MACLEAN
LORD CHARLES SPENCER-CHURCHILL
OLIVE, LADY BAILLIE
MICHAEL BOWATER
CAMILLA STRAIGHT
COUNTESS of WINCHILSEA
NED MACLEAN
GILLIAN SPRECKELS FULLER
JANE WYNDHAM
SIR IAN BOWATER
ANTHONY J. DREXEL of PHILADELPHIA
JAMES STEWART
LT.-COL. ROGER MOSTYN-OWEN
COL. HERBERT MOSTYN-OWEN
HON. MARK WYNDHAM
ANN WINN
REGGIE WINN
ALICE PERKINS
WILLIE MOSTYN-OWEN
ELSIE OPPENHEIMER
SIR MICHAEL OPPENHEIMER, Bt
SIR MICHAEL OPPENHEIMER, Bt
XANTHE OPPENHEIMER
IVO MOSLEY
GAIA SERVADIO
LADY OPPENHEIMER
SIR ERNEST OPPENHEIMER
HARRY OPPENHEIMER

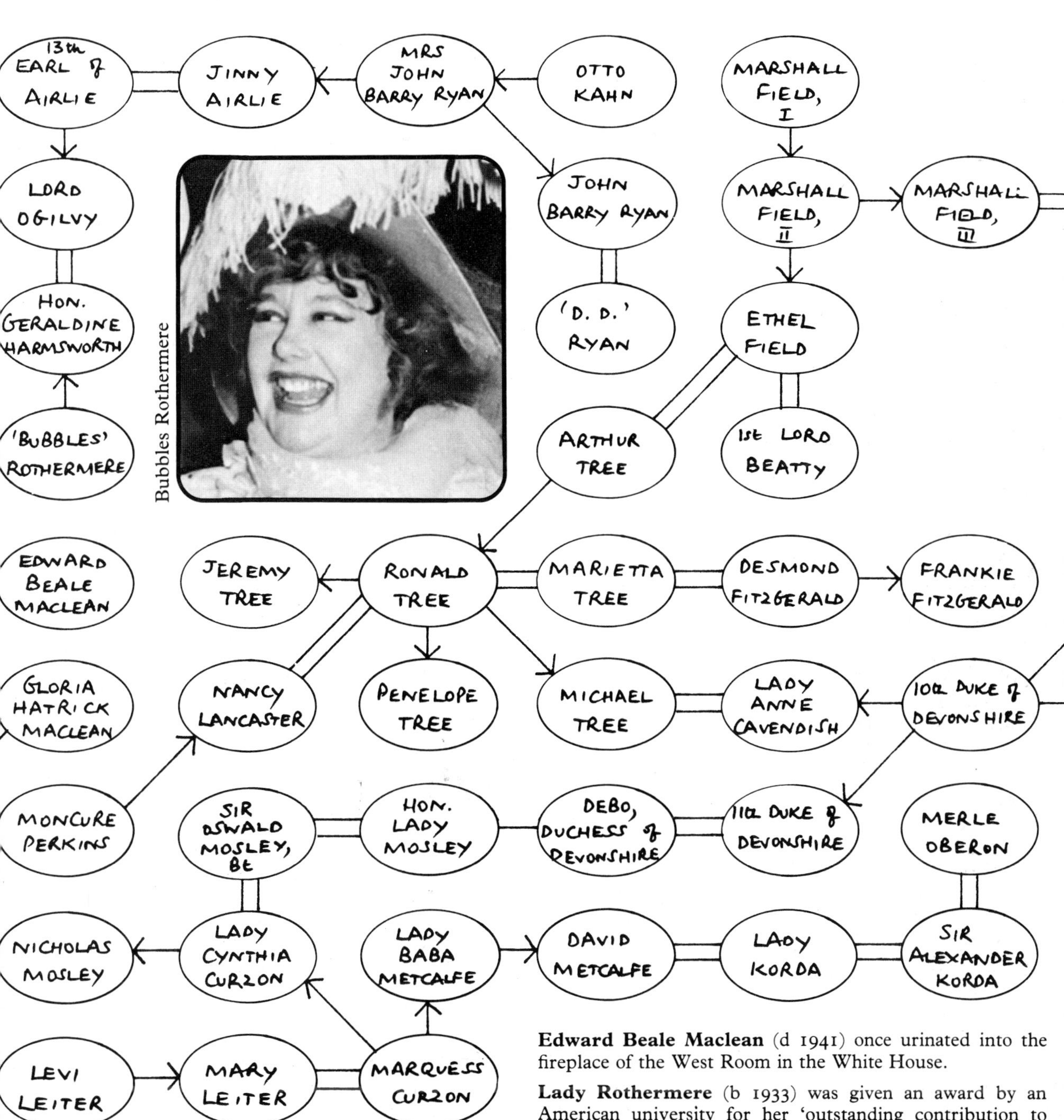
13th EARL of AIRLIE
JINNY AIRLIE
MRS JOHN BARRY RYAN
OTTO KAHN
MARSHALL FIELD, I
LORD OGILVY
JOHN BARRY RYAN
MARSHALL FIELD, II
MARSHALL FIELD, III
HON. GERALDINE HARMSWORTH
'D. D.' RYAN
ETHEL FIELD
'BUBBLES' ROTHERMERE
ARTHUR TREE
1st LORD BEATTY
EDWARD BEALE MACLEAN
JEREMY TREE
RONALD TREE
MARIETTA TREE
DESMOND FITZGERALD
FRANKIE FITZGERALD
GLORIA HATRICK MACLEAN
NANCY LANCASTER
PENELOPE TREE
MICHAEL TREE
LADY ANNE CAVENDISH
10th DUKE of DEVONSHIRE
MONCURE PERKINS
SIR OSWALD MOSLEY, Bt
HON. LADY MOSLEY
DEBO, DUCHESS of DEVONSHIRE
11th DUKE of DEVONSHIRE
MERLE OBERON
NICHOLAS MOSLEY
LADY CYNTHIA CURZON
LADY BABA METCALFE
DAVID METCALFE
LADY KORDA
SIR ALEXANDER KORDA
LEVI LEITER
MARY LEITER
MARQUESS CURZON
Bubbles Rothermere

Sir Ernest Oppenheimer (d 1957). Diamond and mining magnate who left a personal fortune of $183 million.

Evalyn Walsh Maclean (d 1947). Owner of the Hope Diamond. One of Washington's leading hostesses, she was usually too dazed from drugs or drink to recognise her guests.

Edward Beale Maclean (d 1941) once urinated into the fireplace of the West Room in the White House.

Lady Rothermere (b 1933) was given an award by an American university for her 'outstanding contribution to society through uncommon leadership and exemplary service'.

Otto Kahn (d 1934). Banker and art patron, who often remarked, 'I must atone for my wealth.'

Penelope Tree (b 1949). Fashion model who helped create the Swinging Sixties.

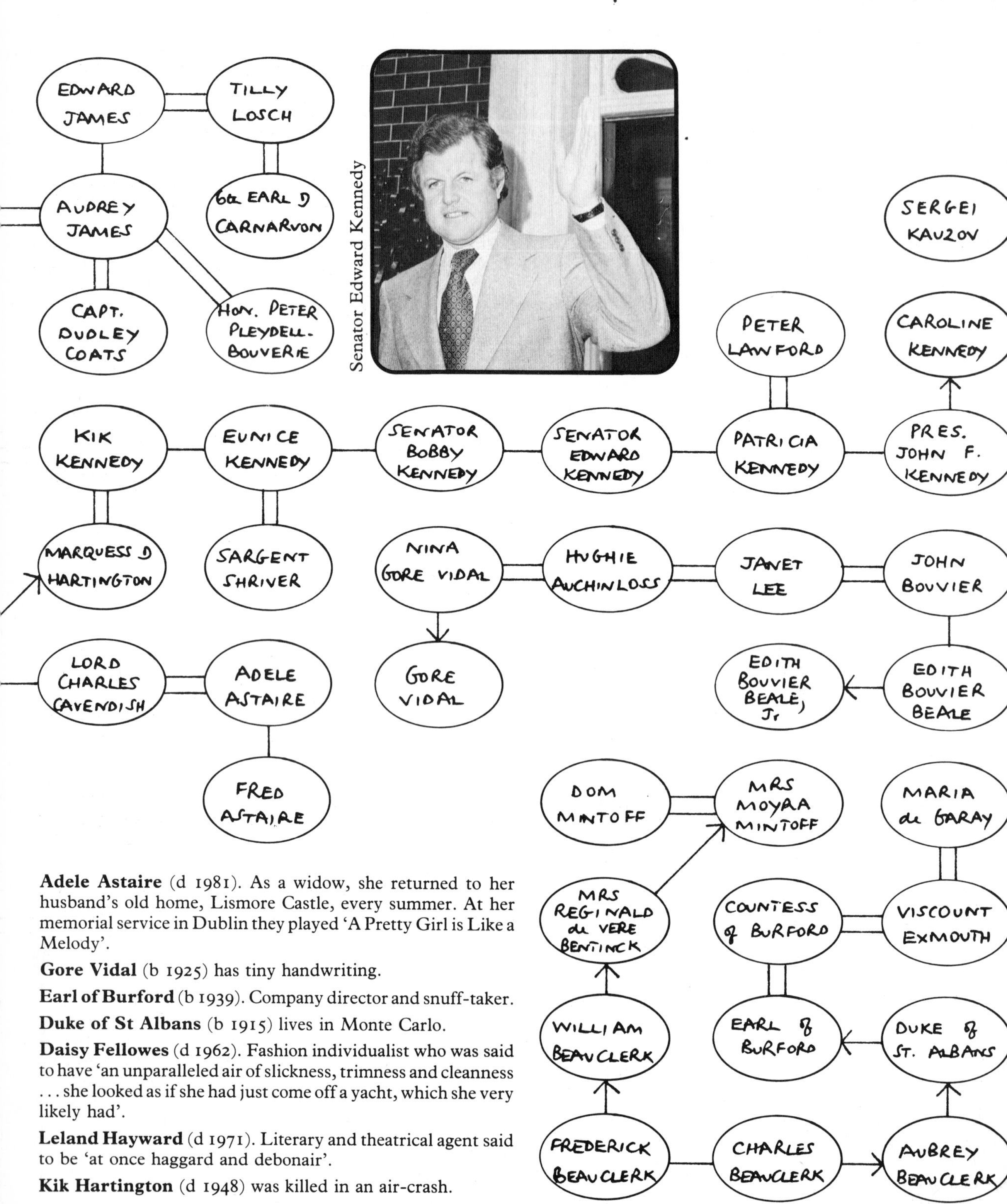
EDWARD JAMES
TILLY LOSCH
AUDREY JAMES
6th EARL of CARNARVON
CAPT. DUDLEY COATS
HON. PETER PLEYDELL-BOUVERIE
SERGEI KAUZOV
PETER LAWFORD
CAROLINE KENNEDY
KIK KENNEDY
EUNICE KENNEDY
SENATOR BOBBY KENNEDY
SENATOR EDWARD KENNEDY
PATRICIA KENNEDY
PRES. JOHN F. KENNEDY
MARQUESS of HARTINGTON
SARGENT SHRIVER
NINA GORE VIDAL
HUGHIE AUCHINLOSS
JANET LEE
JOHN BOUVIER
LORD CHARLES CAVENDISH
ADELE ASTAIRE
GORE VIDAL
EDITH BOUVIER BEALE, Jr
EDITH BOUVIER BEALE
FRED ASTAIRE
DOM MINTOFF
MRS MOYRA MINTOFF
MARIA de GARAY
MRS REGINALD de VERE BENTINCK
COUNTESS of BURFORD
VISCOUNT EXMOUTH
WILLIAM BEAUCLERK
EARL of BURFORD
DUKE of ST. ALBANS
FREDERICK BEAUCLERK
CHARLES BEAUCLERK
AUBREY BEAUCLERK

Senator Edward Kennedy

Adele Astaire (d 1981). As a widow, she returned to her husband's old home, Lismore Castle, every summer. At her memorial service in Dublin they played 'A Pretty Girl is Like a Melody'.

Gore Vidal (b 1925) has tiny handwriting.

Earl of Burford (b 1939). Company director and snuff-taker.

Duke of St Albans (b 1915) lives in Monte Carlo.

Daisy Fellowes (d 1962). Fashion individualist who was said to have 'an unparalleled air of slickness, trimness and cleanness . . . she looked as if she had just come off a yacht, which she very likely had'.

Leland Hayward (d 1971). Literary and theatrical agent said to be 'at once haggard and debonair'.

Kik Hartington (d 1948) was killed in an air-crash.

Henry Ford (b 1917). Sartorially impeccable and highly articulate industrialist.

Stavros Niarchos (b 1909). Pioneer of super-tankers who heads a group of companies controlling over 5.75 million tons of shipping (operational and building).

Isaac Singer (d 1875). Sewing machine manufacturer ostracised by New York society on account of his sixteen illegitimate children.

Bert Marlborough (d 1972). Owner of Blenheim Palace and one of the first dukes to enter the Stately Home league. 'I shut myself away behind the green railings in the east wing and on the whole life is liveable.'

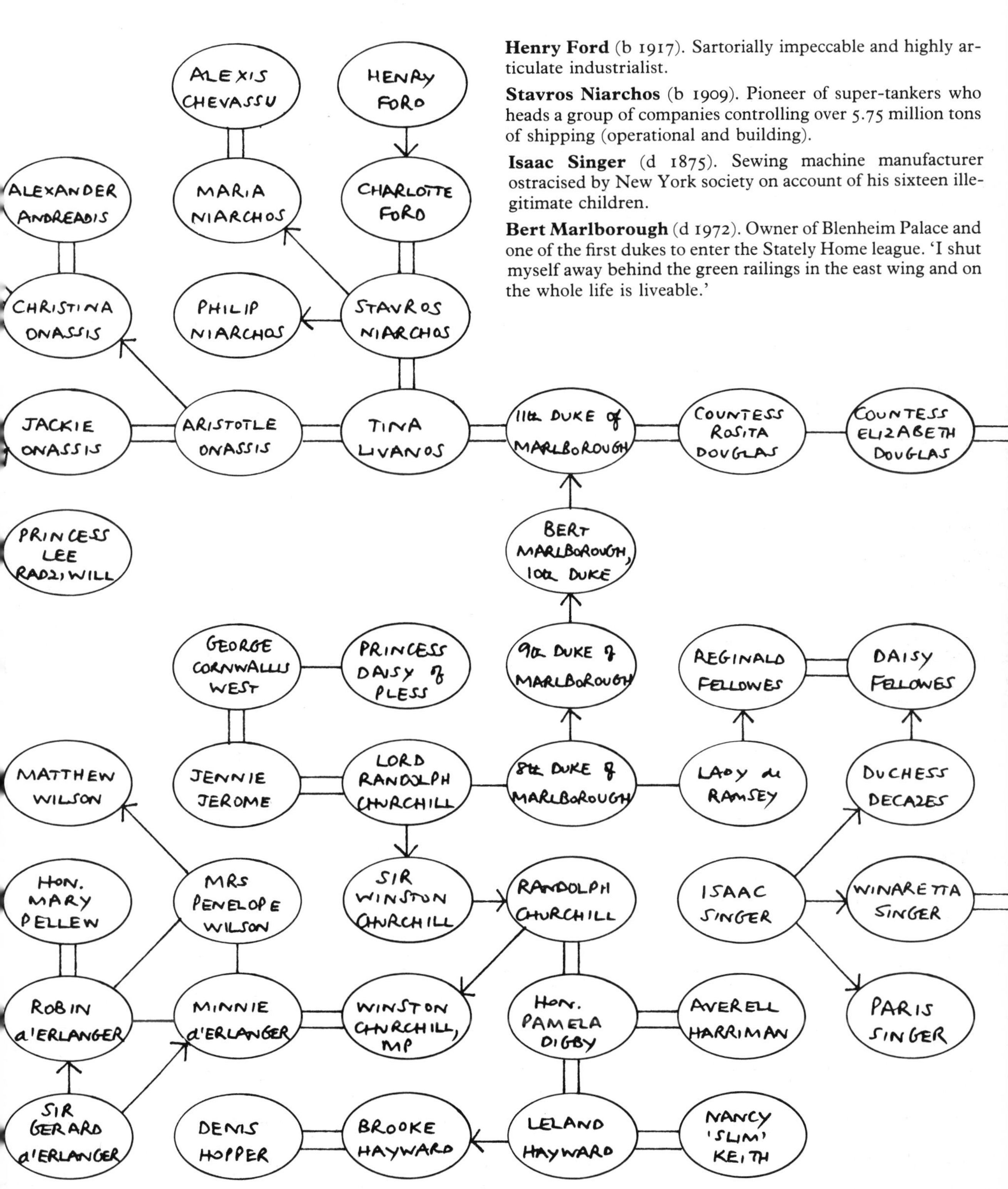

ALEXIS CHEVASSU
HENRY FORD
ALEXANDER ANDREADIS
MARIA NIARCHOS
CHARLOTTE FORD
CHRISTINA ONASSIS
PHILIP NIARCHOS
STAVROS NIARCHOS
JACKIE ONASSIS
ARISTOTLE ONASSIS
TINA LIVANOS
11th DUKE of MARLBOROUGH
COUNTESS ROSITA DOUGLAS
COUNTESS ELIZABETH DOUGLAS
PRINCESS LEE RADZIWILL
BERT MARLBOROUGH, 10th DUKE
GEORGE CORNWALLIS WEST
PRINCESS DAISY of PLESS
9th DUKE of MARLBOROUGH
REGINALD FELLOWES
DAISY FELLOWES
MATTHEW WILSON
JENNIE JEROME
LORD RANDOLPH CHURCHILL
8th DUKE of MARLBOROUGH
LADY de RAMSEY
DUCHESS DECAZES
HON. MARY PELLEW
MRS PENELOPE WILSON
SIR WINSTON CHURCHILL
RANDOLPH CHURCHILL
ISAAC SINGER
WINARETTA SINGER
ROBIN d'ERLANGER
MINNIE d'ERLANGER
WINSTON CHURCHILL, MP
HON. PAMELA DIGBY
AVERELL HARRIMAN
PARIS SINGER
SIR GERARD d'ERLANGER
DENIS HOPPER
BROOKE HAYWARD
LELAND HAYWARD
NANCY 'SLIM' KEITH

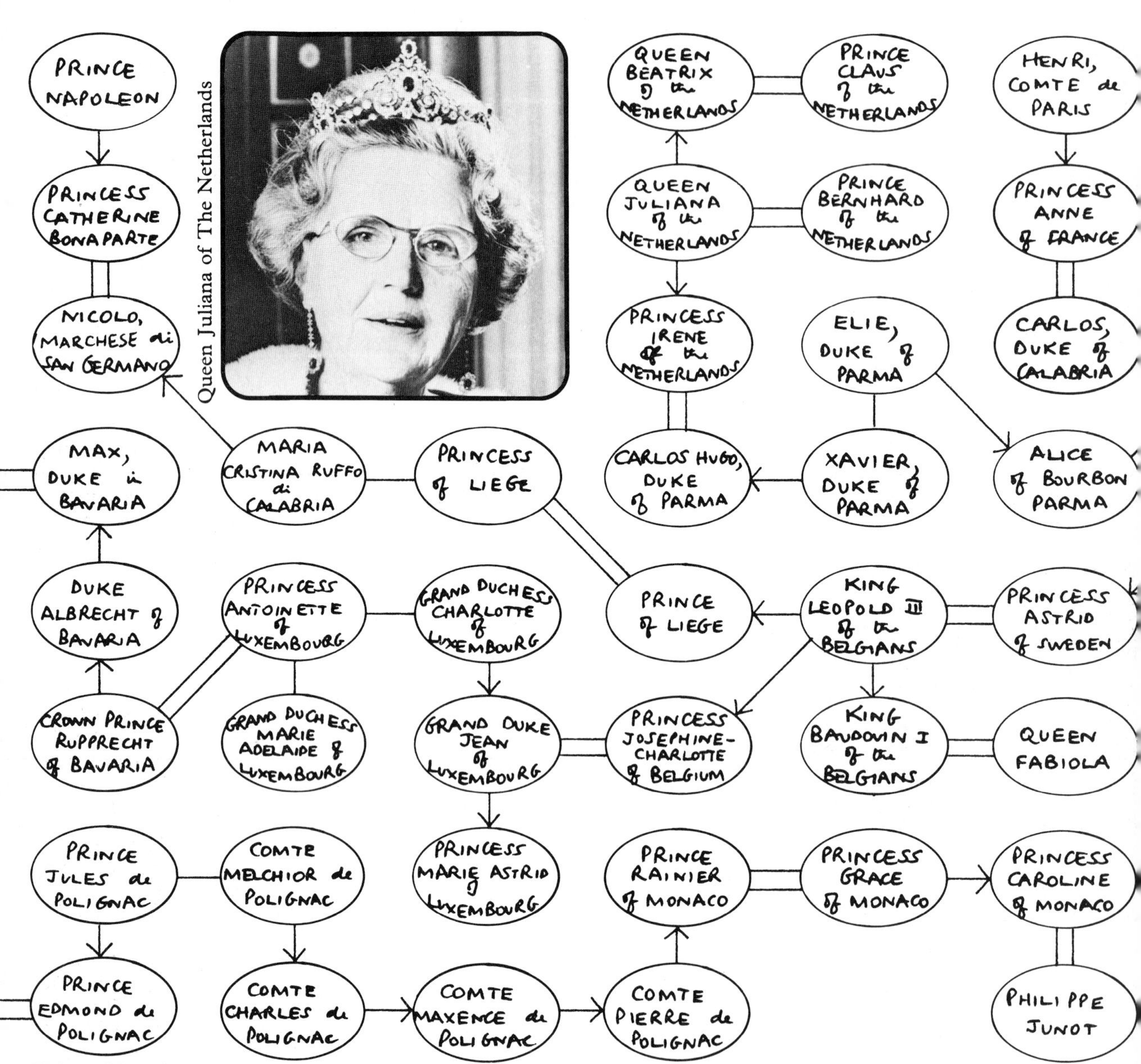
PRINCE NAPOLEON
PRINCESS CATHERINE BONAPARTE
NICOLO, MARCHESE di SAN GERMANO
MAX, DUKE in BAVARIA
MARIA CRISTINA RUFFO di CALABRIA
PRINCESS of LIEGE
DUKE ALBRECHT of BAVARIA
PRINCESS ANTOINETTE of LUXEMBOURG
GRAND DUCHESS CHARLOTTE of LUXEMBOURG
CROWN PRINCE RUPPRECHT of BAVARIA
GRAND DUCHESS MARIE ADELAIDE of LUXEMBOURG
GRAND DUKE JEAN of LUXEMBOURG
PRINCE JULES de POLIGNAC
COMTE MELCHIOR de POLIGNAC
PRINCESS MARIE ASTRID of LUXEMBOURG
PRINCE EDMOND de POLIGNAC
COMTE CHARLES de POLIGNAC
COMTE MAXENCE de POLIGNAC
COMTE PIERRE de POLIGNAC
QUEEN BEATRIX of the NETHERLANDS
PRINCE CLAUS of the NETHERLANDS
HENRI, COMTE de PARIS
QUEEN JULIANA of the NETHERLANDS
PRINCE BERNHARD of the NETHERLANDS
PRINCESS ANNE of FRANCE
PRINCESS IRENE of the NETHERLANDS
ELIE, DUKE of PARMA
CARLOS, DUKE of CALABRIA
CARLOS HUGO, DUKE of PARMA
XAVIER, DUKE of PARMA
ALICE of BOURBON PARMA
PRINCE of LIEGE
KING LEOPOLD III of the BELGIANS
PRINCESS ASTRID of SWEDEN
PRINCESS JOSEPHINE-CHARLOTTE of BELGIUM
KING BAUDOUIN I of the BELGIANS
QUEEN FABIOLA
PRINCE RAINIER of MONACO
PRINCESS GRACE of MONACO
PRINCESS CAROLINE of MONACO
PHILIPPE JUNOT

Queen Juliana of The Netherlands

Prince Napoleon (b 1914). Businessman and head of the Imperial House of Bonaparte.

Queen Astrid of the Belgians (d 1935) and **Princess Grace of Monaco** (d 1982) were both killed in motor accidents.

King Baudouin of the Belgians (b 1930) wears contact lenses.

Grand Duchess Marie Adelaide of Luxembourg (d 1924) drove herself to the frontier on the outbreak of the 1st World War and ordered the invading German army out of her country.

Henri Comte de Paris (b 1908). Heir to the French thron and former owner and editor of *Ici France* and *Le Courie Royal*. He still maintains a secrétariat at 102, rue de Mirc mesnil, Paris VII.

Queen Margrethe of Denmark (b 1940) never expresse controversial opinions, even among her closest friends.

Marquess of Carisbrooke (d 1960) reminded James Lees Milne of 'an old, spruce hen, cackling and scratching the dus in a chicken run – really, a typical old queen'.

Lady Iris Mountbatten (d 1982) once worked in a New Yor department store.

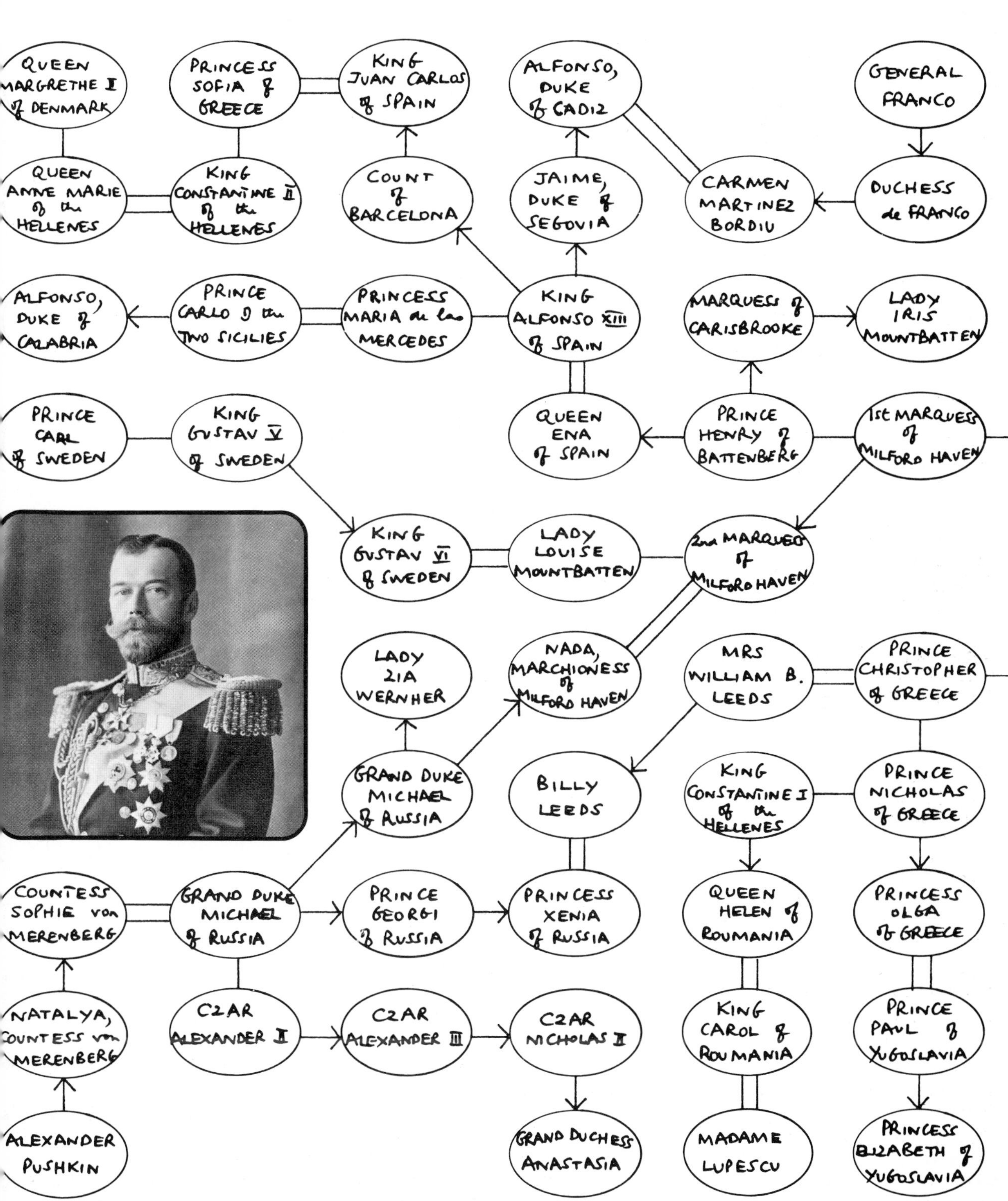
QUEEN MARGRETHE II of DENMARK
PRINCESS SOFIA of GREECE
KING JUAN CARLOS of SPAIN
ALFONSO, DUKE of CADIZ
GENERAL FRANCO
QUEEN ANNE MARIE of the HELLENES
KING CONSTANTINE II of the HELLENES
COUNT of BARCELONA
JAIME, DUKE of SEGOVIA
CARMEN MARTINEZ BORDIU
DUCHESS de FRANCO
ALFONSO, DUKE of CALABRIA
PRINCE CARLO of the TWO SICILIES
PRINCESS MARIA de las MERCEDES
KING ALFONSO XIII of SPAIN
MARQUESS of CARISBROOKE
LADY IRIS MOUNTBATTEN
PRINCE CARL of SWEDEN
KING GUSTAV V of SWEDEN
QUEEN ENA of SPAIN
PRINCE HENRY of BATTENBERG
1st MARQUESS of MILFORD HAVEN
KING GUSTAV VI of SWEDEN
LADY LOUISE MOUNTBATTEN
2nd MARQUESS of MILFORD HAVEN
LADY ZIA WERNHER
NADA, MARCHIONESS of MILFORD HAVEN
MRS WILLIAM B. LEEDS
PRINCE CHRISTOPHER of GREECE
GRAND DUKE MICHAEL of RUSSIA
BILLY LEEDS
KING CONSTANTINE I of the HELLENES
PRINCE NICHOLAS of GREECE
COUNTESS SOPHIE von MERENBERG
GRAND DUKE MICHAEL of RUSSIA
PRINCE GEORGI of RUSSIA
PRINCESS XENIA of RUSSIA
QUEEN HELEN of ROUMANIA
PRINCESS OLGA of GREECE
NATALYA, COUNTESS von MERENBERG
CZAR ALEXANDER II
CZAR ALEXANDER III
CZAR NICHOLAS II
KING CAROL of ROUMANIA
PRINCE PAUL of YUGOSLAVIA
ALEXANDER PUSHKIN
GRAND DUCHESS ANASTASIA
MADAME LUPESCU
PRINCESS ELIZABETH of YUGOSLAVIA

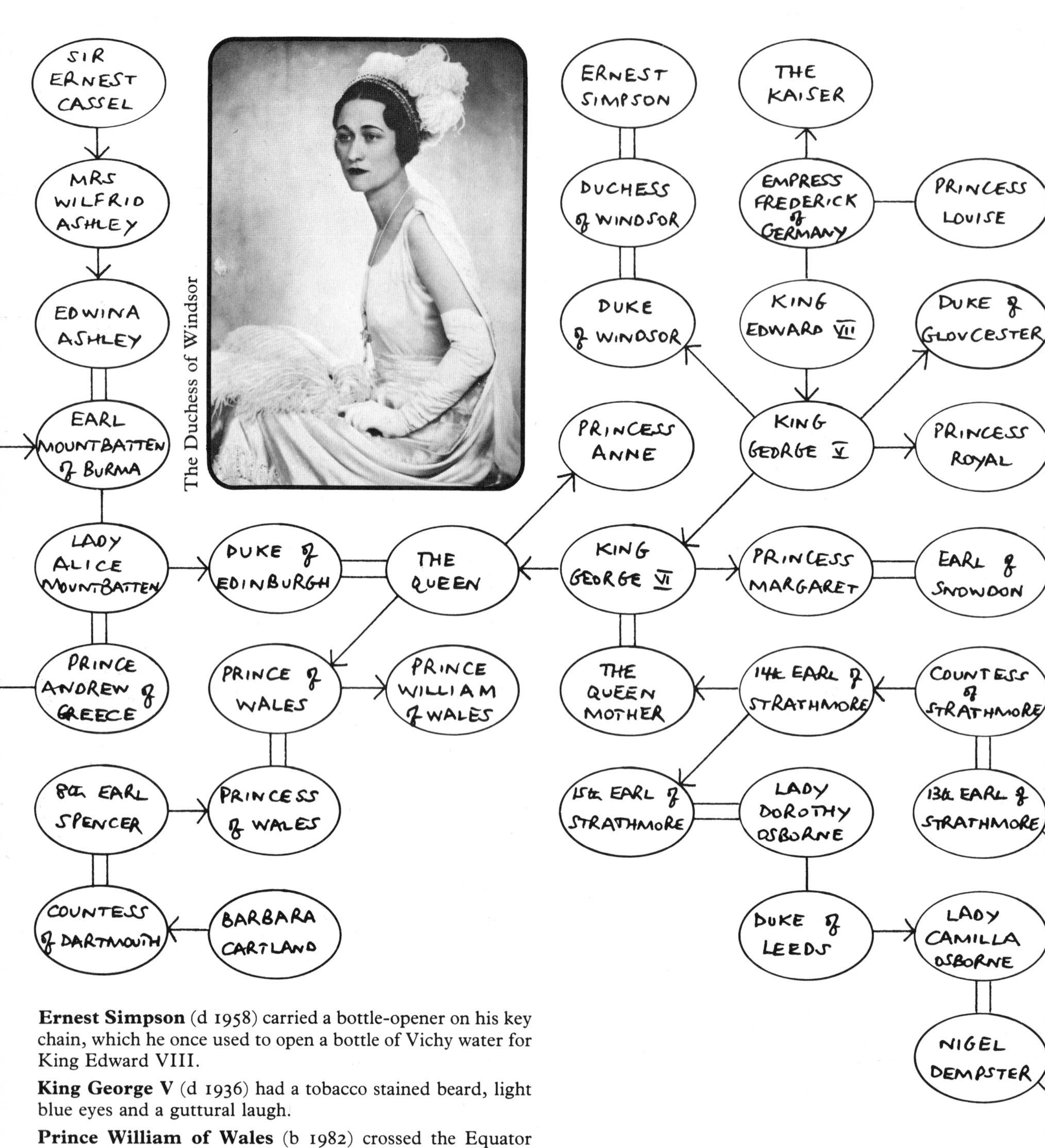
SIR ERNEST CASSEL
MRS WILFRID ASHLEY
EDWINA ASHLEY
EARL MOUNTBATTEN of BURMA
LADY ALICE MOUNTBATTEN
PRINCE ANDREW of GREECE
8th EARL SPENCER
COUNTESS of DARTMOUTH
BARBARA CARTLAND
DUKE of EDINBURGH
PRINCE of WALES
PRINCESS of WALES
THE QUEEN
PRINCE WILLIAM of WALES
PRINCESS ANNE
ERNEST SIMPSON
DUCHESS of WINDSOR
DUKE of WINDSOR
KING GEORGE VI
THE QUEEN MOTHER
15th EARL of STRATHMORE
THE KAISER
EMPRESS FREDERICK of GERMANY
KING EDWARD VII
KING GEORGE V
PRINCESS MARGARET
14th EARL of STRATHMORE
LADY DOROTHY OSBORNE
DUKE of LEEDS
PRINCESS LOUISE
DUKE of GLOUCESTER
PRINCESS ROYAL
EARL of SNOWDON
COUNTESS of STRATHMORE
13th EARL of STRATHMORE
LADY CAMILLA OSBORNE
NIGEL DEMPSTER

The Duchess of Windsor

Ernest Simpson (d 1958) carried a bottle-opener on his key chain, which he once used to open a bottle of Vichy water for King Edward VIII.

King George V (d 1936) had a tobacco stained beard, light blue eyes and a guttural laugh.

Prince William of Wales (b 1982) crossed the Equator before his first birthday.

Earl of Harewood (b 1923) has his hair cut at Ivan's in Jermyn Street.

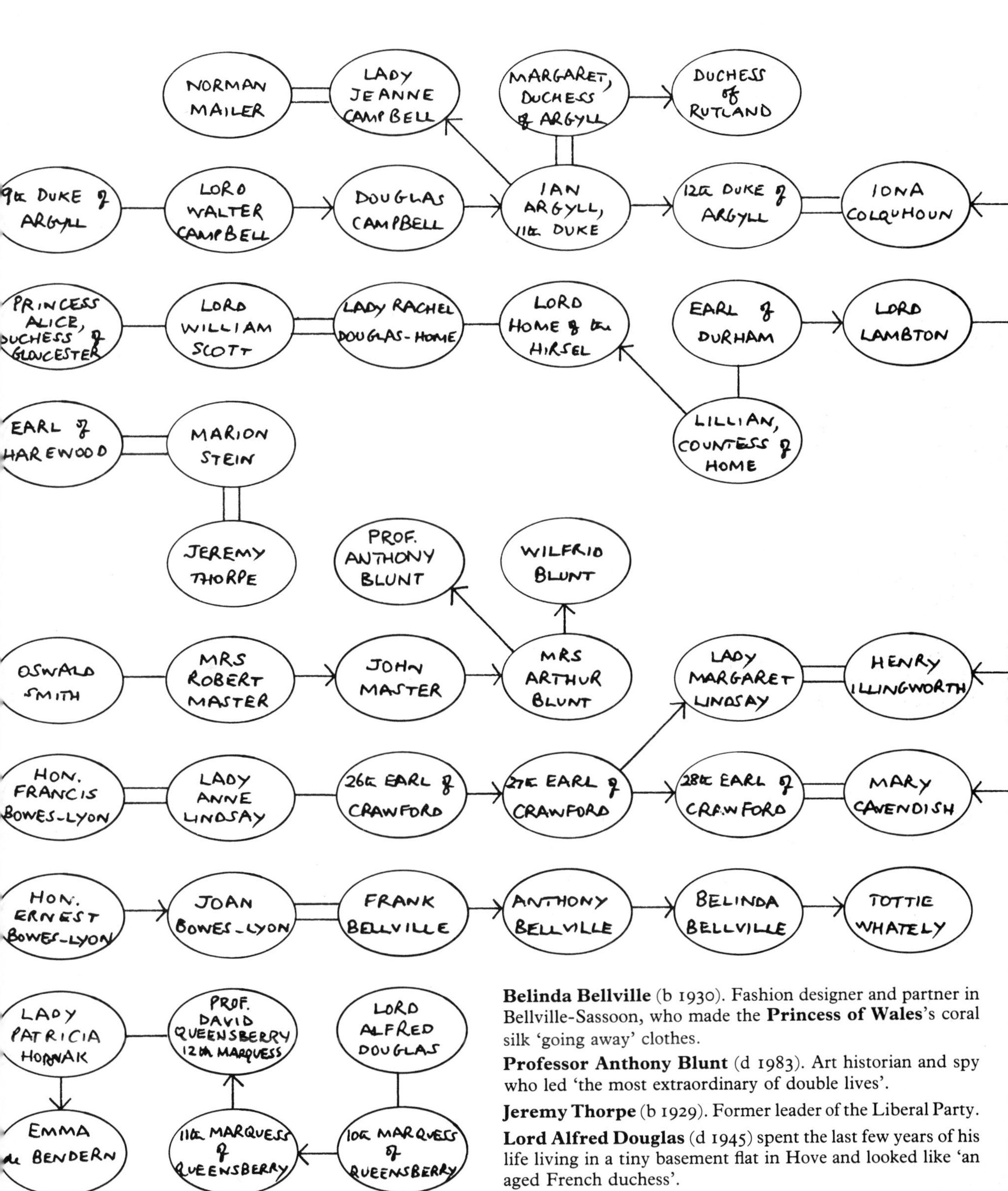
NORMAN MAILER
LADY JEANNE CAMPBELL
MARGARET, DUCHESS of ARGYLL
DUCHESS of RUTLAND
9th DUKE of ARGYLL
LORD WALTER CAMPBELL
DOUGLAS CAMPBELL
IAN ARGYLL, 11th DUKE
12th DUKE of ARGYLL
IONA COLQUHOUN
PRINCESS ALICE, UCHESS of GLOUCESTER
LORD WILLIAM SCOTT
LADY RACHEL DOUGLAS-HOME
LORD HOME of the HIRSEL
EARL of DURHAM
LORD LAMBTON
LILLIAN, COUNTESS of HOME
EARL of HAREWOOD
MARION STEIN
JEREMY THORPE
PROF. ANTHONY BLUNT
WILFRID BLUNT
OSWALD SMITH
MRS ROBERT MASTER
JOHN MASTER
MRS ARTHUR BLUNT
LADY MARGARET LINDSAY
HENRY ILLINGWORTH
HON. FRANCIS BOWES-LYON
LADY ANNE LINDSAY
26th EARL of CRAWFORD
27th EARL of CRAWFORD
28th EARL of CRAWFORD
MARY CAVENDISH
HON. ERNEST BOWES-LYON
JOAN BOWES-LYON
FRANK BELLVILLE
ANTHONY BELLVILLE
BELINDA BELLVILLE
TOTTIE WHATELY
LADY PATRICIA HORNAK
PROF. DAVID QUEENSBERRY 12th MARQUESS
LORD ALFRED DOUGLAS
EMMA
BENDERN
11th MARQUESS of QUEENSBERRY
10th MARQUESS of QUEENSBERRY

Belinda Bellville (b 1930). Fashion designer and partner in Bellville-Sassoon, who made the **Princess of Wales**'s coral silk 'going away' clothes.

Professor Anthony Blunt (d 1983). Art historian and spy who led 'the most extraordinary of double lives'.

Jeremy Thorpe (b 1929). Former leader of the Liberal Party.

Lord Alfred Douglas (d 1945) spent the last few years of his life living in a tiny basement flat in Hove and looked like 'an aged French duchess'.

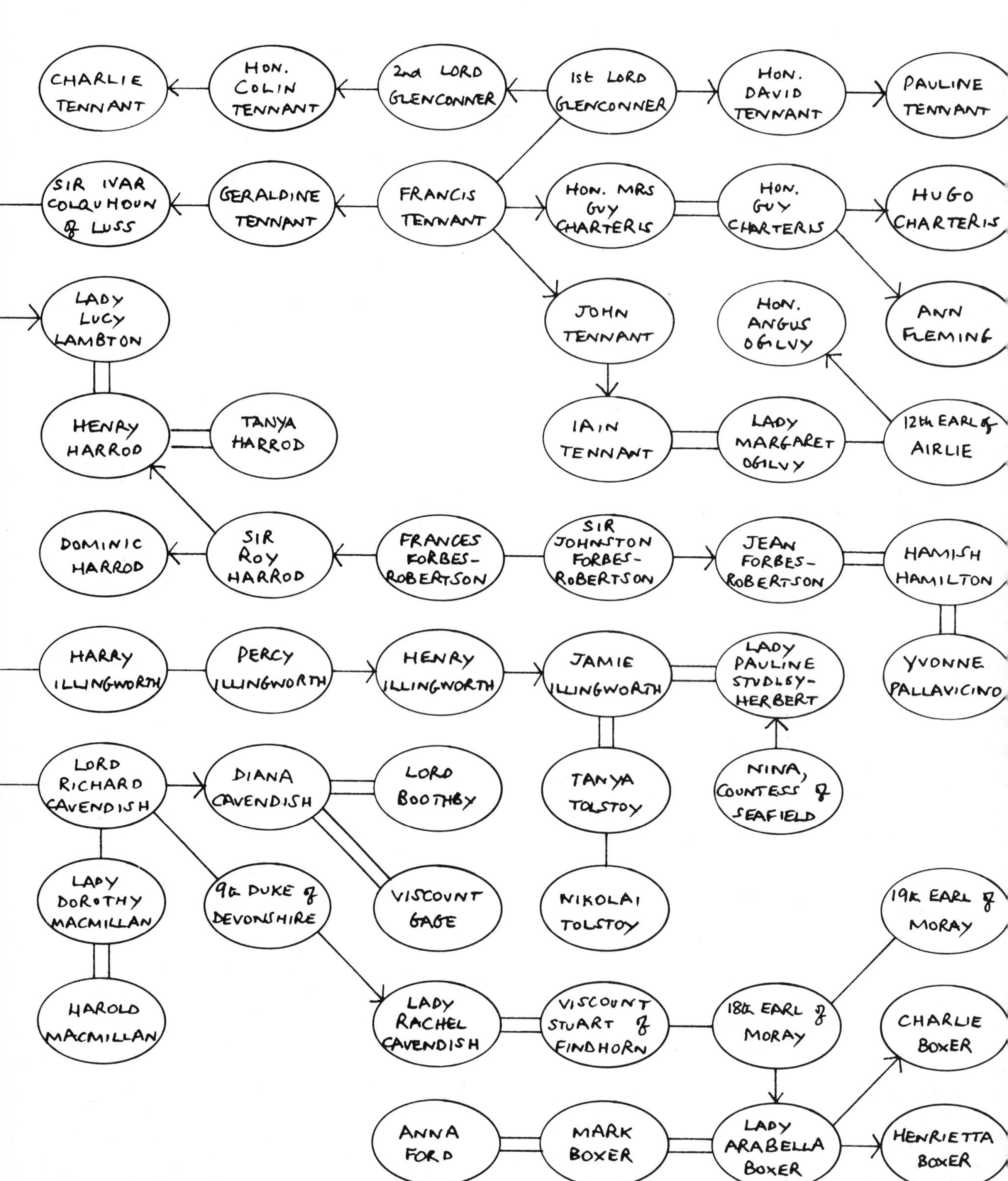
CHARLIE TENNANT
HON. COLIN TENNANT
2nd LORD GLENCONNER
1st LORD GLENCONNER
HON. DAVID TENNANT
PAULINE TENNANT
SIR IVAR COLQUHOUN of LUSS
GERALDINE TENNANT
FRANCIS TENNANT
HON. MRS GUY CHARTERIS
HON. GUY CHARTERIS
HUGO CHARTERIS
LADY LUCY LAMBTON
JOHN TENNANT
HON. ANGUS OGILVY
ANN FLEMING
HENRY HARROD
TANYA HARROD
IAIN TENNANT
LADY MARGARET OGILVY
12th EARL of AIRLIE
DOMINIC HARROD
SIR ROY HARROD
FRANCES FORBES-ROBERTSON
SIR JOHNSTON FORBES-ROBERTSON
JEAN FORBES-ROBERTSON
HAMISH HAMILTON
HARRY ILLINGWORTH
PERCY ILLINGWORTH
HENRY ILLINGWORTH
JAMIE ILLINGWORTH
LADY PAULINE STUDLEY-HERBERT
YVONNE PALLAVICINO
LORD RICHARD CAVENDISH
DIANA CAVENDISH
LORD BOOTHBY
TANYA TOLSTOY
NINA, COUNTESS of SEAFIELD
LADY DOROTHY MACMILLAN
9th DUKE of DEVONSHIRE
VISCOUNT GAGE
NIKOLAI TOLSTOY
19th EARL of MORAY
HAROLD MACMILLAN
LADY RACHEL CAVENDISH
VISCOUNT STUART of FINDHORN
18th EARL of MORAY
CHARLIE BOXER
ANNA FORD
MARK BOXER
LADY ARABELLA BOXER
HENRIETTA BOXER

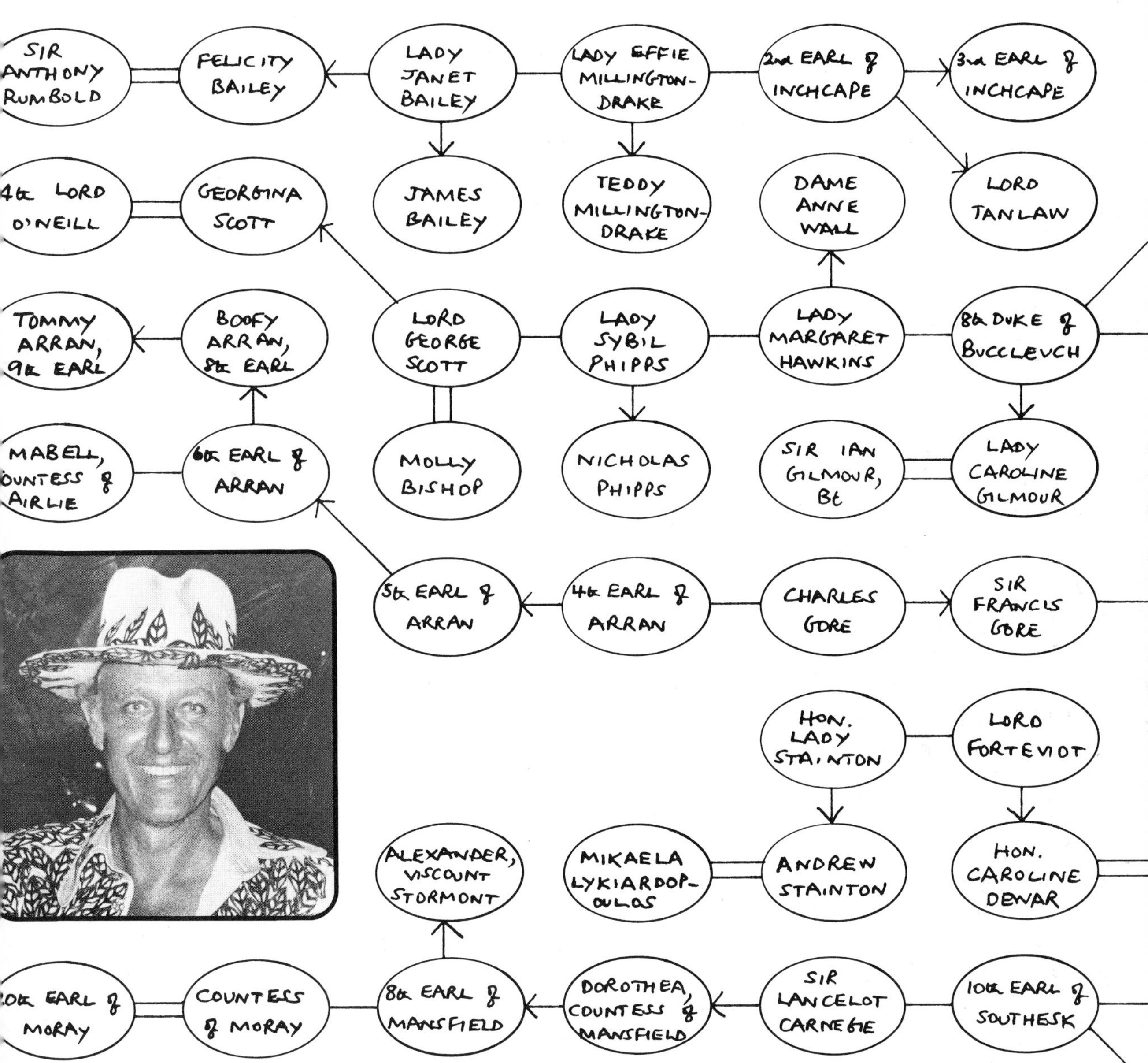
SIR ANTHONY RUMBOLD
FELICITY BAILEY
LADY JANET BAILEY
LADY EFFIE MILLINGTON-DRAKE
2nd EARL of INCHCAPE
3rd EARL of INCHCAPE
4th LORD O'NEILL
GEORGINA SCOTT
JAMES BAILEY
TEDDY MILLINGTON-DRAKE
DAME ANNE WALL
LORD TANLAW
TOMMY ARRAN, 9th EARL
BOOFY ARRAN, 8th EARL
LORD GEORGE SCOTT
LADY SYBIL PHIPPS
LADY MARGARET HAWKINS
8th DUKE of BUCCLEUCH
MABELL, OUNTESS of AIRLIE
6th EARL of ARRAN
MOLLY BISHOP
NICHOLAS PHIPPS
SIR IAN GILMOUR, Bt
LADY CAROLINE GILMOUR
5th EARL of ARRAN
4th EARL of ARRAN
CHARLES GORE
SIR FRANCIS GORE
HON. LADY STAINTON
LORD FORTEVIOT
ALEXANDER, VISCOUNT STORMONT
MIKAELA LYKIARDOPOULOS
ANDREW STAINTON
HON. CAROLINE DEWAR
0th EARL of MORAY
COUNTESS of MORAY
8th EARL of MANSFIELD
DOROTHEA, COUNTESS of MANSFIELD
SIR LANCELOT CARNEGIE
10th EARL of SOUTHESK

Ion. Colin Tennant (b 1926). Former owner of the island of Iustique which he bought in 1959 for £50,000.

'auline Tennant (b 1929). Brilliant raconteur with sparkling ıminous eyes.

Iamish Hamilton (b 1900). Founder of the famous publishing house that bears his name.

th Earl of Arran (d 1983). Newspaper columnist who iloted the Sex Offences and Badgers Protection Bills through ıe House of Lords.

Nina Countess of Seafield (d 1969). Owned 70,000 acres and lived at Cullen House in Banffshire, which has forty bedrooms and seven miles of corridors.

Teddy Millington-Drake (b 1932). Landscape painter.

8th Duke of Buccleuch (d 1973). Owner of nearly half a million acres, he placed his vast estate into the hands of trustees and kept only a nominal shareholding for himself.

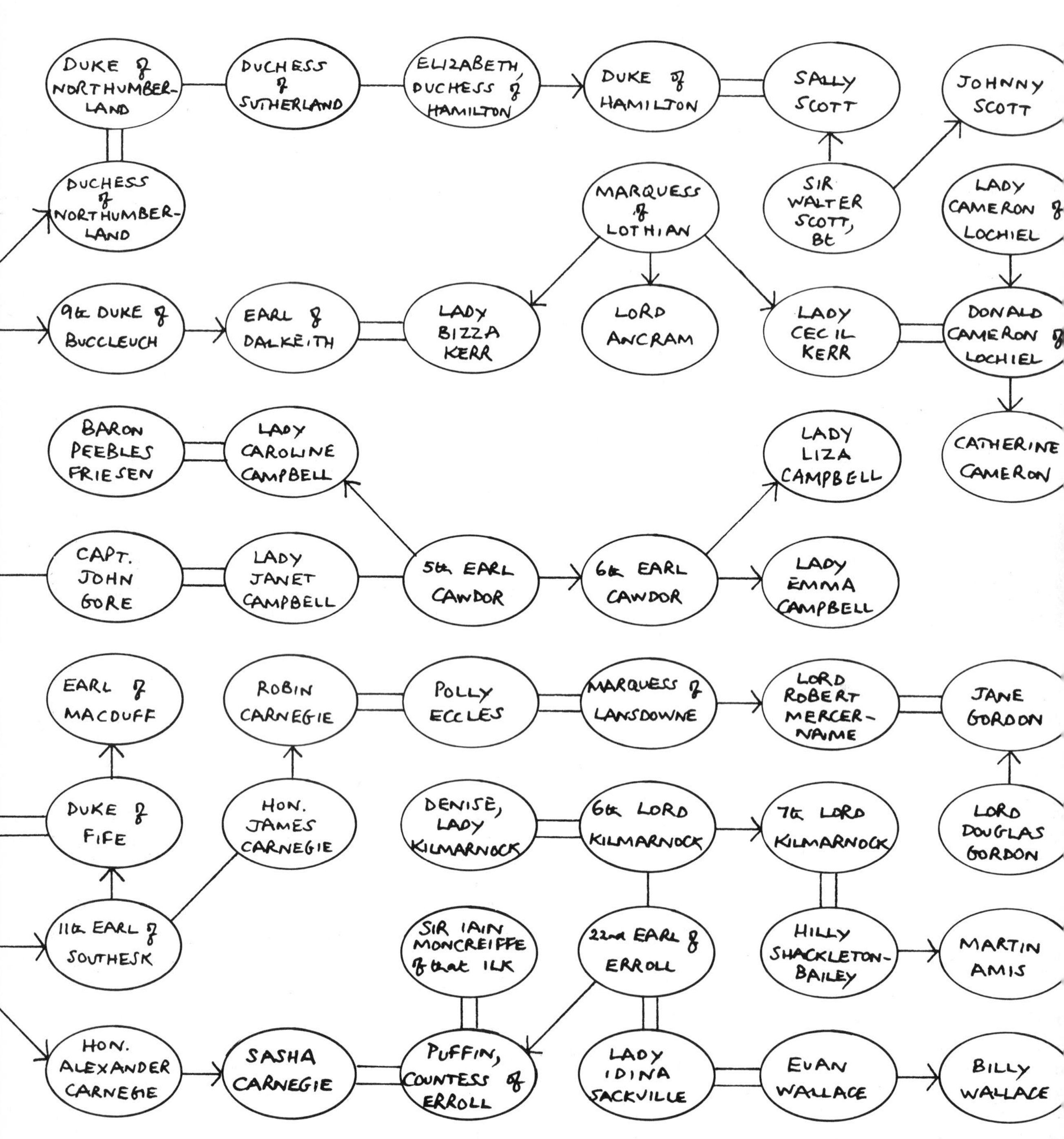
DUKE of NORTHUMBERLAND
DUCHESS of SUTHERLAND
ELIZABETH, DUCHESS of HAMILTON
DUKE of HAMILTON
SALLY SCOTT
JOHNNY SCOTT
DUCHESS of NORTHUMBERLAND
MARQUESS of LOTHIAN
SIR WALTER SCOTT, Bt
LADY CAMERON of LOCHIEL
9th DUKE of BUCCLEUCH
EARL of DALKEITH
LADY BIZZA KERR
LORD ANCRAM
LADY CECIL KERR
DONALD CAMERON of LOCHIEL
BARON PEEBLES FRIESEN
LADY CAROLINE CAMPBELL
LADY LIZA CAMPBELL
CATHERINE CAMERON
CAPT. JOHN GORE
LADY JANET CAMPBELL
5th EARL CAWDOR
6th EARL CAWDOR
LADY EMMA CAMPBELL
EARL of MACDUFF
ROBIN CARNEGIE
POLLY ECCLES
MARQUESS of LANSDOWNE
LORD ROBERT MERCER-NAIME
JANE GORDON
DUKE of FIFE
HON. JAMES CARNEGIE
DENISE, LADY KILMARNOCK
6th LORD KILMARNOCK
7th LORD KILMARNOCK
LORD DOUGLAS GORDON
11th EARL of SOUTHESK
SIR IAIN MONCREIFFE of that ILK
22nd EARL of ERROLL
HILLY SHACKLETON-BAILEY
MARTIN AMIS
HON. ALEXANDER CARNEGIE
SASHA CARNEGIE
PUFFIN, COUNTESS of ERROLL
LADY IDINA SACKVILLE
EVAN WALLACE
BILLY WALLACE

Duke of Hamilton (b 1938). Former test pilot, skin-diver and racing motorist.

Duke of Fife (b 1929). Former chairman of the Amateur Boxing Association.

Denise Lady Kilmarnock travelled on the first run of the re-launched Orient Express.

22nd Earl of Erroll (d 1941). Hereditary High Constable of Scotland who was murdered in Kenya.

atherine Cameron (b 1975). Bridesmaid at the wedding of e Prince and Princess of Wales.

uke of Atholl (b 1931). Owner of 120,000 acres and the only an in the country who is permitted to keep a private army.

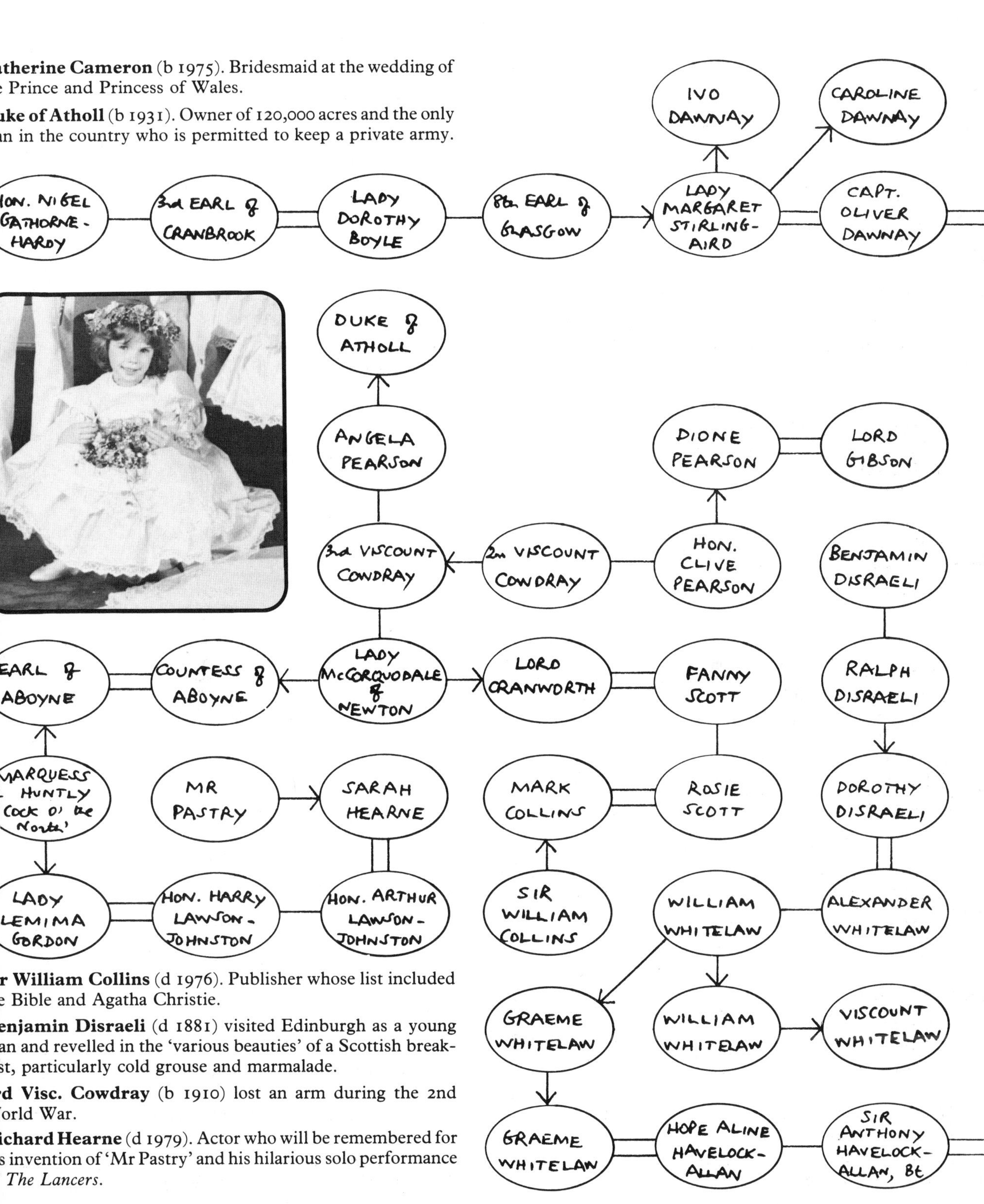

IVO DAWNAY
CAROLINE DAWNAY
HON. NIGEL GATHORNE-HARDY
3rd EARL OF CRANBROOK
LADY DOROTHY BOYLE
8th EARL OF GLASGOW
LADY MARGARET STIRLING-AIRD
CAPT. OLIVER DAWNAY
DUKE OF ATHOLL
ANGELA PEARSON
DIONE PEARSON
LORD GIBSON
3rd VISCOUNT COWDRAY
2nd VISCOUNT COWDRAY
HON. CLIVE PEARSON
BENJAMIN DISRAELI
EARL OF ABOYNE
COUNTESS OF ABOYNE
LADY McCORQUODALE OF NEWTON
LORD CRANWORTH
FANNY SCOTT
RALPH DISRAELI
MARQUESS OF HUNTLY 'COCK O' THE NORTH'
MR PASTRY
SARAH HEARNE
MARK COLLINS
ROSIE SCOTT
DOROTHY DISRAELI
LADY LEMIMA GORDON
HON. HARRY LAWSON-JOHNSTON
HON. ARTHUR LAWSON-JOHNSTON
SIR WILLIAM COLLINS
WILLIAM WHITELAW
ALEXANDER WHITELAW
GRAEME WHITELAW
WILLIAM WHITELAW
VISCOUNT WHITELAW
GRAEME WHITELAW
HOPE ALINE HAVELOCK-ALLAN
SIR ANTHONY HAVELOCK-ALLAN, Bt

r William Collins (d 1976). Publisher whose list included e Bible and Agatha Christie.

enjamin Disraeli (d 1881) visited Edinburgh as a young an and revelled in the 'various beauties' of a Scottish breakst, particularly cold grouse and marmalade.

rd Visc. Cowdray (b 1910) lost an arm during the 2nd orld War.

ichard Hearne (d 1979). Actor who will be remembered for s invention of 'Mr Pastry' and his hilarious solo performance *The Lancers.*

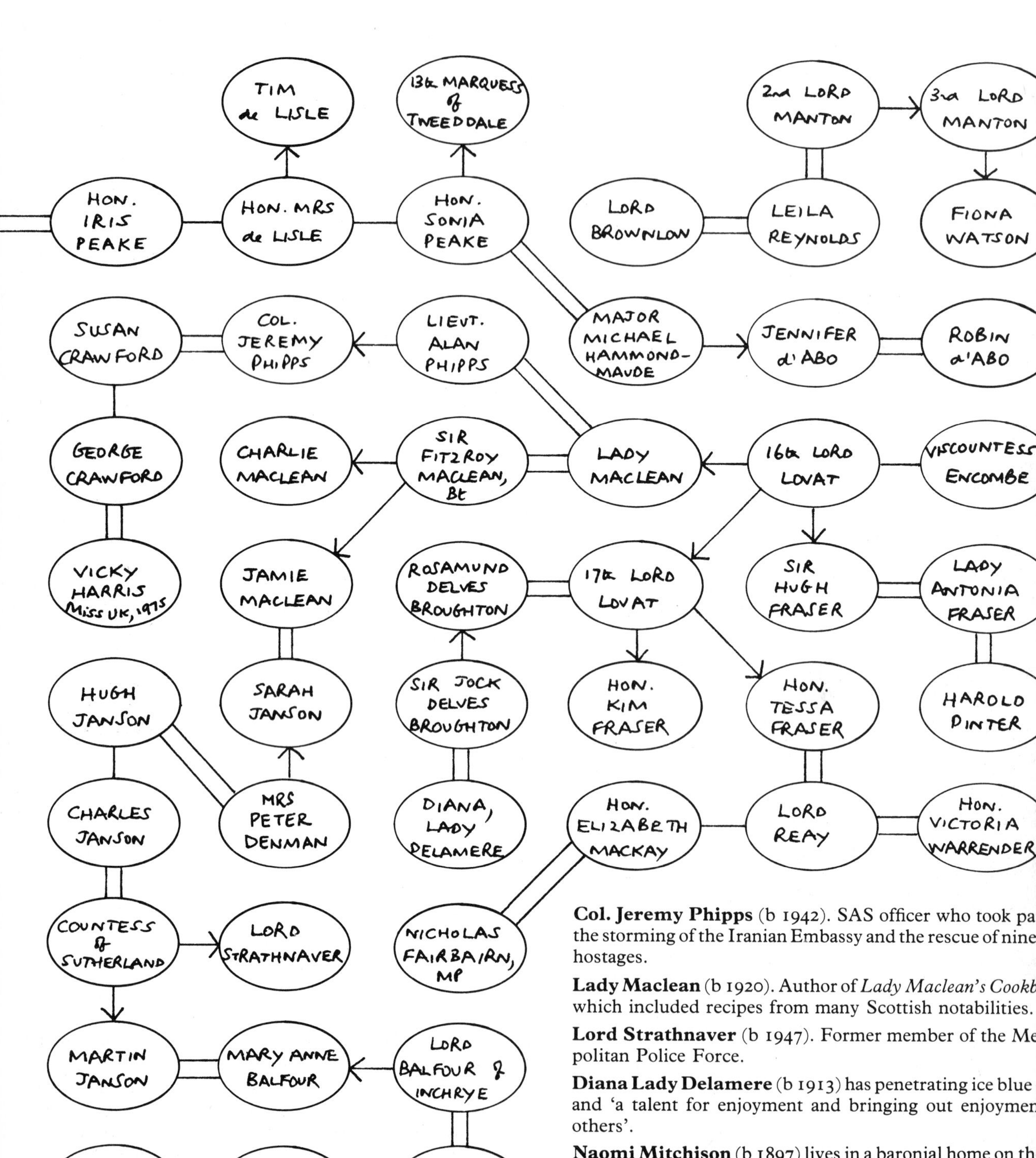
TIM de LISLE
13th MARQUESS of TWEEDDALE
2nd LORD MANTON
3rd LORD MANTON
HON. IRIS PEAKE
HON. MRS de LISLE
HON. SONIA PEAKE
LORD BROWNLOW
LEILA REYNOLDS
FIONA WATSON
SUSAN CRAWFORD
COL. JEREMY PHIPPS
LIEUT. ALAN PHIPPS
MAJOR MICHAEL HAMMOND-MAUDE
JENNIFER d'ABO
ROBIN d'ABO
GEORGE CRAWFORD
CHARLIE MACLEAN
SIR FITZROY MACLEAN, Bt
LADY MACLEAN
16th LORD LOVAT
VISCOUNTESS ENCOMBE
VICKY HARRIS Miss UK, 1975
JAMIE MACLEAN
ROSAMUND DELVES BROUGHTON
17th LORD LOVAT
SIR HUGH FRASER
LADY ANTONIA FRASER
HUGH JANSON
SARAH JANSON
SIR JOCK DELVES BROUGHTON
HON. KIM FRASER
HON. TESSA FRASER
HAROLD PINTER
CHARLES JANSON
MRS PETER DENMAN
DIANA, LADY DELAMERE
HON. ELIZABETH MACKAY
LORD REAY
HON. VICTORIA WARRENDER
COUNTESS of SUTHERLAND
LORD STRATHNAVER
NICHOLAS FAIRBAIRN, MP
MARTIN JANSON
MARY ANNE BALFOUR
LORD BALFOUR of INCHRYE
VALERIE HOBSON
JACK PROFUMO, CBE
MARY PROFUMO

Col. Jeremy Phipps (b 1942). SAS officer who took pa[rt in] the storming of the Iranian Embassy and the rescue of nine[teen] hostages.

Lady Maclean (b 1920). Author of *Lady Maclean's Cookb[ook]* which included recipes from many Scottish notabilities.

Lord Strathnaver (b 1947). Former member of the Me[tro]politan Police Force.

Diana Lady Delamere (b 1913) has penetrating ice blue [eyes] and 'a talent for enjoyment and bringing out enjoymen[t in] others'.

Naomi Mitchison (b 1897) lives in a baronial home on th[e far-]flung peninsula the Mull of Kintyre.

John Mitchison (b 1922). Professor of zoology at Edinbu[rgh] University and author of *The Biology of the Cell Cycle*.

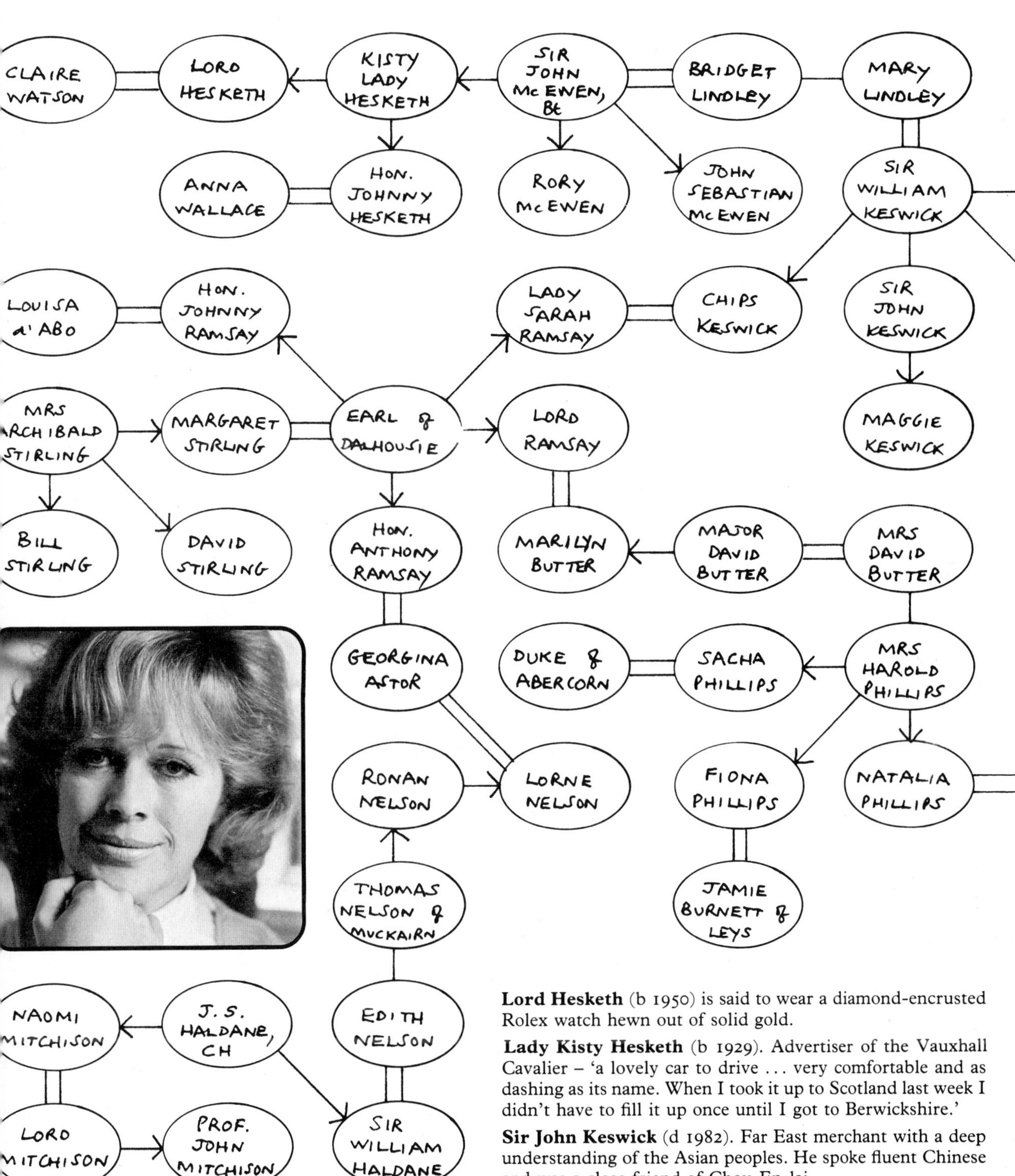
CLAIRE WATSON
LORD HESKETH
KISTY LADY HESKETH
SIR JOHN McEWEN, Bt
BRIDGET LINDLEY
MARY LINDLEY
ANNA WALLACE
HON. JOHNNY HESKETH
RORY McEWEN
JOHN SEBASTIAN McEWEN
SIR WILLIAM KESWICK
LOUISA d'ABO
HON. JOHNNY RAMSAY
LADY SARAH RAMSAY
CHIPS KESWICK
SIR JOHN KESWICK
MRS ARCHIBALD STIRLING
MARGARET STIRLING
EARL of DALHOUSIE
LORD RAMSAY
MAGGIE KESWICK
BILL STIRLING
DAVID STIRLING
HON. ANTHONY RAMSAY
MARILYN BUTTER
MAJOR DAVID BUTTER
MRS DAVID BUTTER
GEORGINA ASTOR
DUKE of ABERCORN
SACHA PHILLIPS
MRS HAROLD PHILLIPS
RONAN NELSON
LORNE NELSON
FIONA PHILLIPS
NATALIA PHILLIPS
THOMAS NELSON of MUCKAIRN
JAMIE BURNETT of LEYS
NAOMI MITCHISON
J. S. HALDANE, CH
EDITH NELSON
LORD MITCHISON
PROF. JOHN MITCHISON
SIR WILLIAM HALDANE

Lord Hesketh (b 1950) is said to wear a diamond-encrusted Rolex watch hewn out of solid gold.

Lady Kisty Hesketh (b 1929). Advertiser of the Vauxhall Cavalier – 'a lovely car to drive ... very comfortable and as dashing as its name. When I took it up to Scotland last week I didn't have to fill it up once until I got to Berwickshire.'

Sir John Keswick (d 1982). Far East merchant with a deep understanding of the Asian peoples. He spoke fluent Chinese and was a close friend of Chou-En-lai.

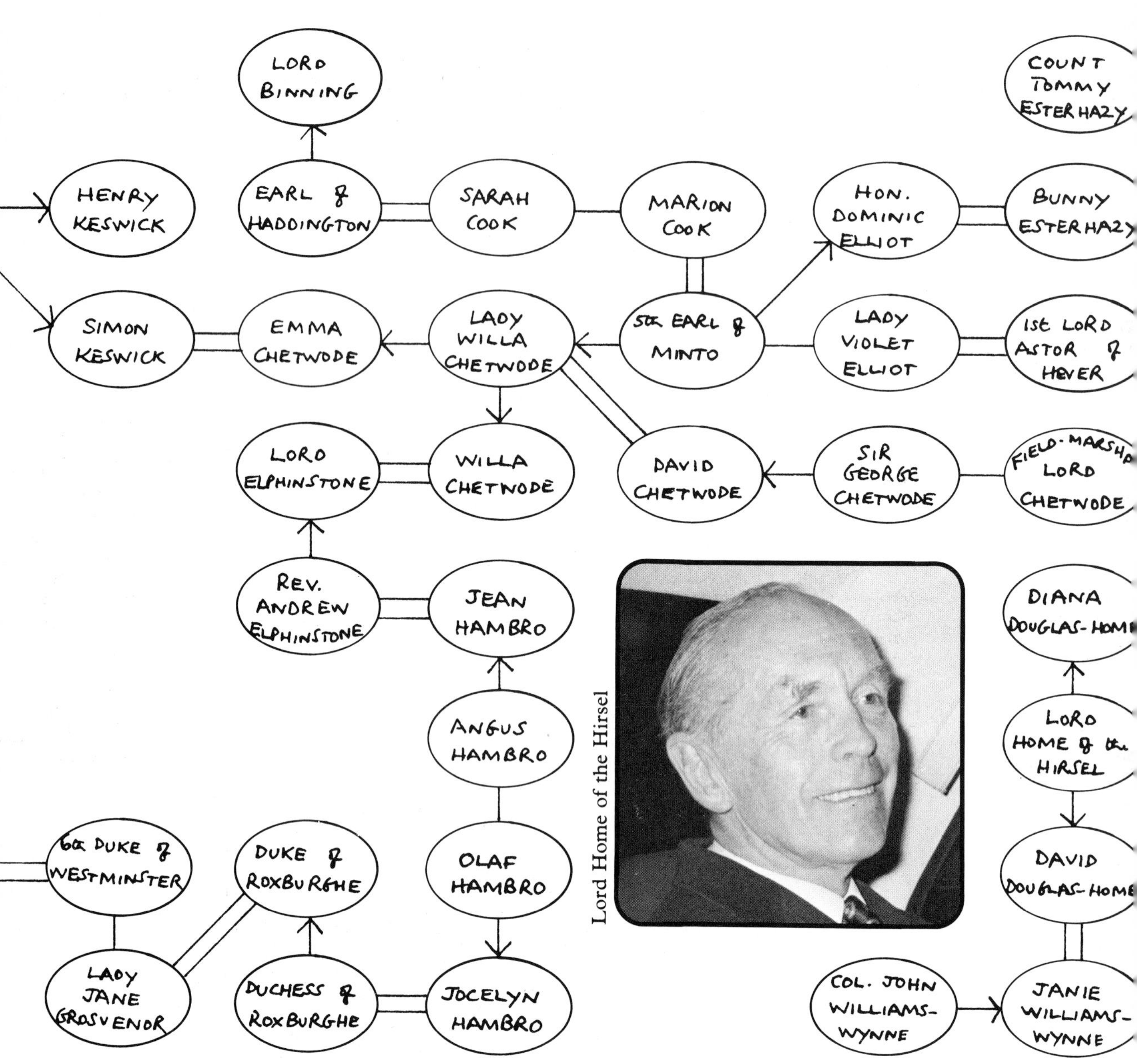
LORD BINNING
COUNT TOMMY ESTERHAZY
HENRY KESWICK
EARL OF HADDINGTON
SARAH COOK
MARION COOK
HON. DOMINIC ELLIOT
BUNNY ESTERHAZ
SIMON KESWICK
EMMA CHETWODE
LADY WILLA CHETWODE
5th EARL OF MINTO
LADY VIOLET ELLIOT
1st LORD ASTOR OF HEVER
LORD ELPHINSTONE
WILLA CHETWODE
DAVID CHETWODE
SIR GEORGE CHETWODE
FIELD-MARSH LORD CHETWODE
REV. ANDREW ELPHINSTONE
JEAN HAMBRO
DIANA DOUGLAS-HOM
ANGUS HAMBRO
LORD HOME OF THE HIRSEL
6th DUKE OF WESTMINSTER
DUKE OF ROXBURGHE
OLAF HAMBRO
DAVID DOUGLAS-HOME
LADY JANE GROSVENOR
DUCHESS OF ROXBURGHE
JOCELYN HAMBRO
COL. JOHN WILLIAMS-WYNNE
JANIE WILLIAMS-WYNNE

Lord Home of the Hirsel

Henry Keswick (b 1938). Chairman Matheson & Co. and former proprietor of the *Spectator*.

Earl of Haddington (b 1894). Poet, former steeplechase rider and embroiderer (petit point).

Duke of Roxburghe (b 1954). Crack shot, ace tennis player and owner of the rambling and picturesque Floors Castle.

Field Marshal Earl Haig (d 1928) was Commander-i Chief of the armed forces 1915–19. His bedside readi during the 1st World War included *The Bible, Scottish Met Psalms, Pilgrim's Progress* and a life of Cromwell.

2nd Earl Haig (b 1918). Painter and member of the Quee Body Guard for Scotland.

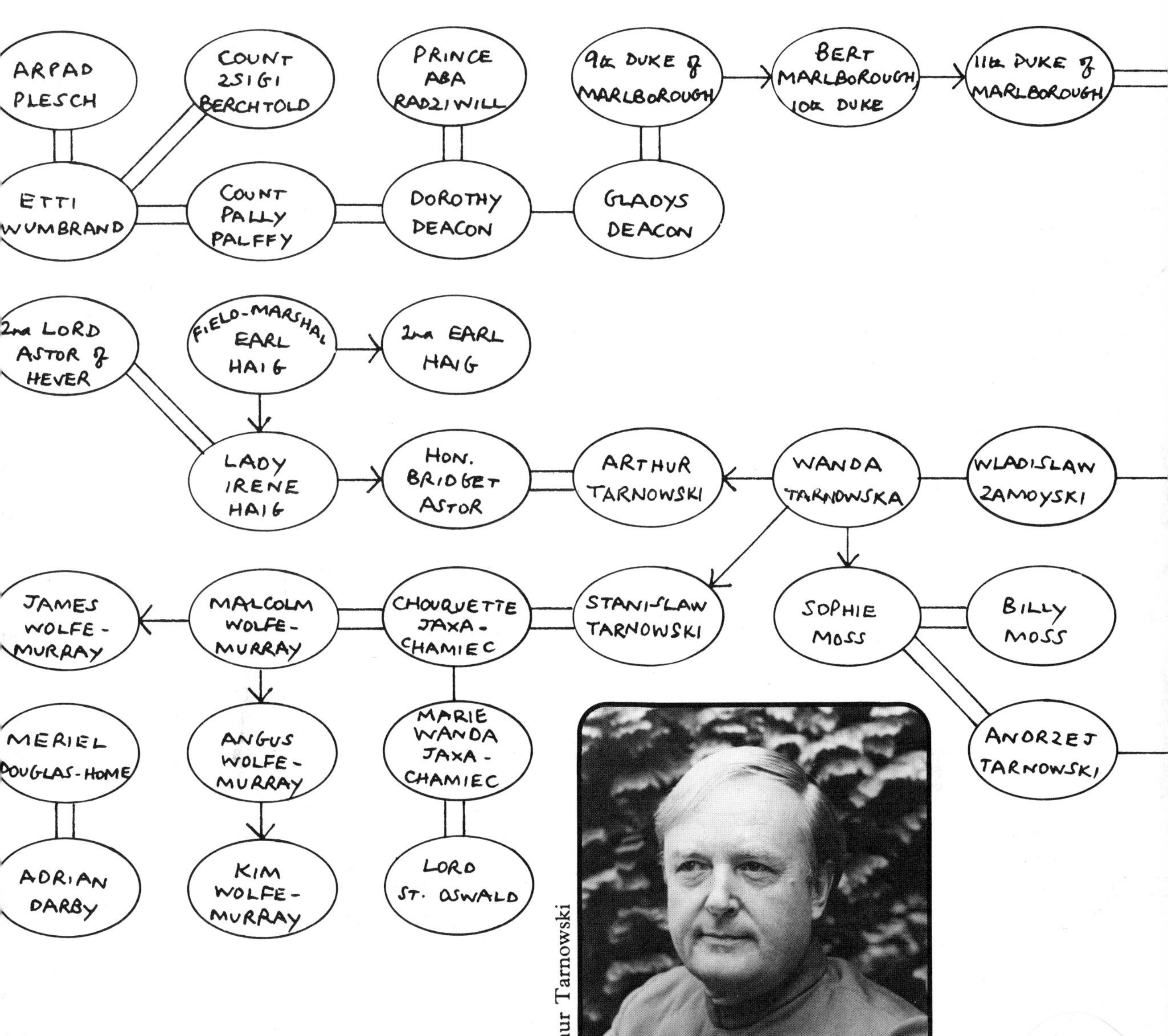
ARPAD PLESCH
COUNT ZSIGI BERCHTOLD
PRINCE ABA RADZIWILL
9th DUKE of MARLBOROUGH
BERT MARLBOROUGH, 10th DUKE
11th DUKE of MARLBOROUGH
ETTI WUMBRAND
COUNT PALLY PALFFY
DOROTHY DEACON
GLADYS DEACON
2nd LORD ASTOR of HEVER
FIELD-MARSHAL EARL HAIG
2nd EARL HAIG
LADY IRENE HAIG
HON. BRIDGET ASTOR
ARTHUR TARNOWSKI
WANDA TARNOWSKA
WLADISLAW ZAMOYSKI
JAMES WOLFE-MURRAY
MALCOLM WOLFE-MURRAY
CHOUQUETTE JAXA-CHAMIEC
STANISLAW TARNOWSKI
SOPHIE MOSS
BILLY MOSS
MERIEL DOUGLAS-HOME
ANGUS WOLFE-MURRAY
MARIE WANDA JAXA-CHAMIEC
ANDRZEJ TARNOWSKI
ADRIAN DARBY
KIM WOLFE-MURRAY
LORD ST. OSWALD

Arthur Tarnowski

Hon. Bridget Astor (b 1948). Professional photographer, specialising in children's portraiture.

Arthur Tarnowski (b 1930). Writer and explorer who refuses to be restricted by his wheelchair.

Angus Wolfe-Murray (b 1937). Novelist who now runs a removal service between London and Edinburgh.

Arpad Plesch (d 1974). Hungarian-born lawyer, financier, racehorse owner and collector of botanical books. His fortune was said to have come from Cuban sugar.

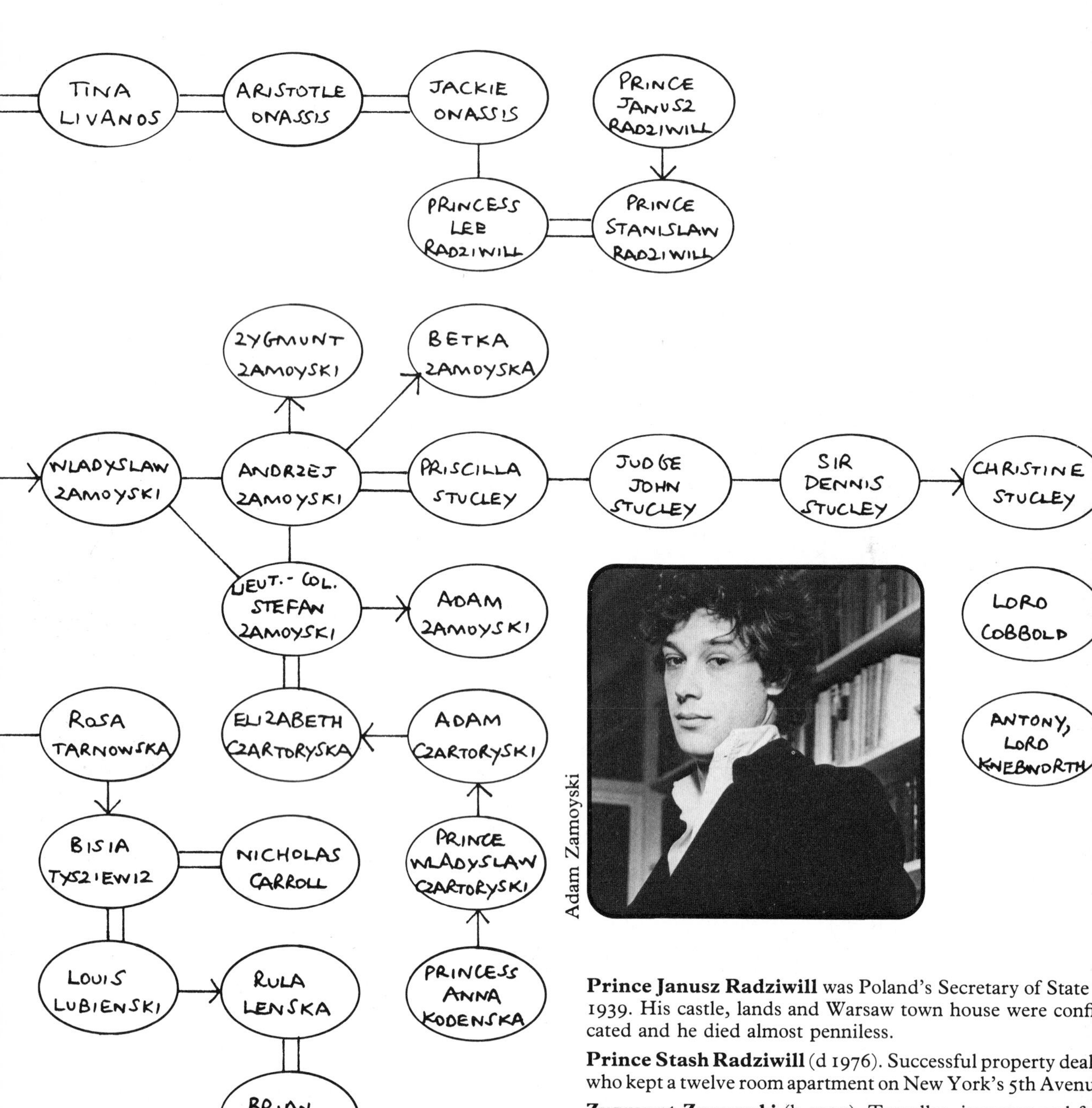
TINA LIVANOS
ARISTOTLE ONASSIS
JACKIE ONASSIS
PRINCE JANUSZ RADZIWILL
PRINCESS LEE RADZIWILL
PRINCE STANISLAW RADZIWILL
ZYGMUNT ZAMOYSKI
BETKA ZAMOYSKA
WLADYSLAW ZAMOYSKI
ANDRZEJ ZAMOYSKI
PRISCILLA STUCLEY
JUDGE JOHN STUCLEY
SIR DENNIS STUCLEY
CHRISTINE STUCLEY
LIEUT.-COL. STEFAN ZAMOYSKI
ADAM ZAMOYSKI
LORD COBBOLD
ROSA TARNOWSKA
ELIZABETH CZARTORYSKA
ADAM CZARTORYSKI
ANTONY, LORD KNEBWORTH
BISIA TYSZIEWIZ
NICHOLAS CARROLL
PRINCE WLADYSLAW CZARTORYSKI
LOUIS LUBIENSKI
RULA LENSKA
PRINCESS ANNA KODENSKA
BRIAN DEACON

Adam Zamoyski

Rula Lenska (b 1947). Actress and star of *Rock Follies*, said to project 'upmarket glamour'.

Princess Lee Radziwill (b 1933). International socialite, interior decorator and former actress who once rented Andy Warhol's house on Long Island.

Prince Janusz Radziwill was Poland's Secretary of State 1939. His castle, lands and Warsaw town house were confi cated and he died almost penniless.

Prince Stash Radziwill (d 1976). Successful property deal who kept a twelve room apartment on New York's 5th Avenu

Zygmunt Zamoyski (b 1937). Traveller, inventor and fo mer prison officer.

Betka Zamoyska (b 1948). Freelance journalist and T critic.

Priscilla Zamoyska (b 1911). Novelist and school-teach who was on the staff at Cranborne Chase.

Adam Zamoyski (b 1949). Biographer of Chopin ar Paderewski.

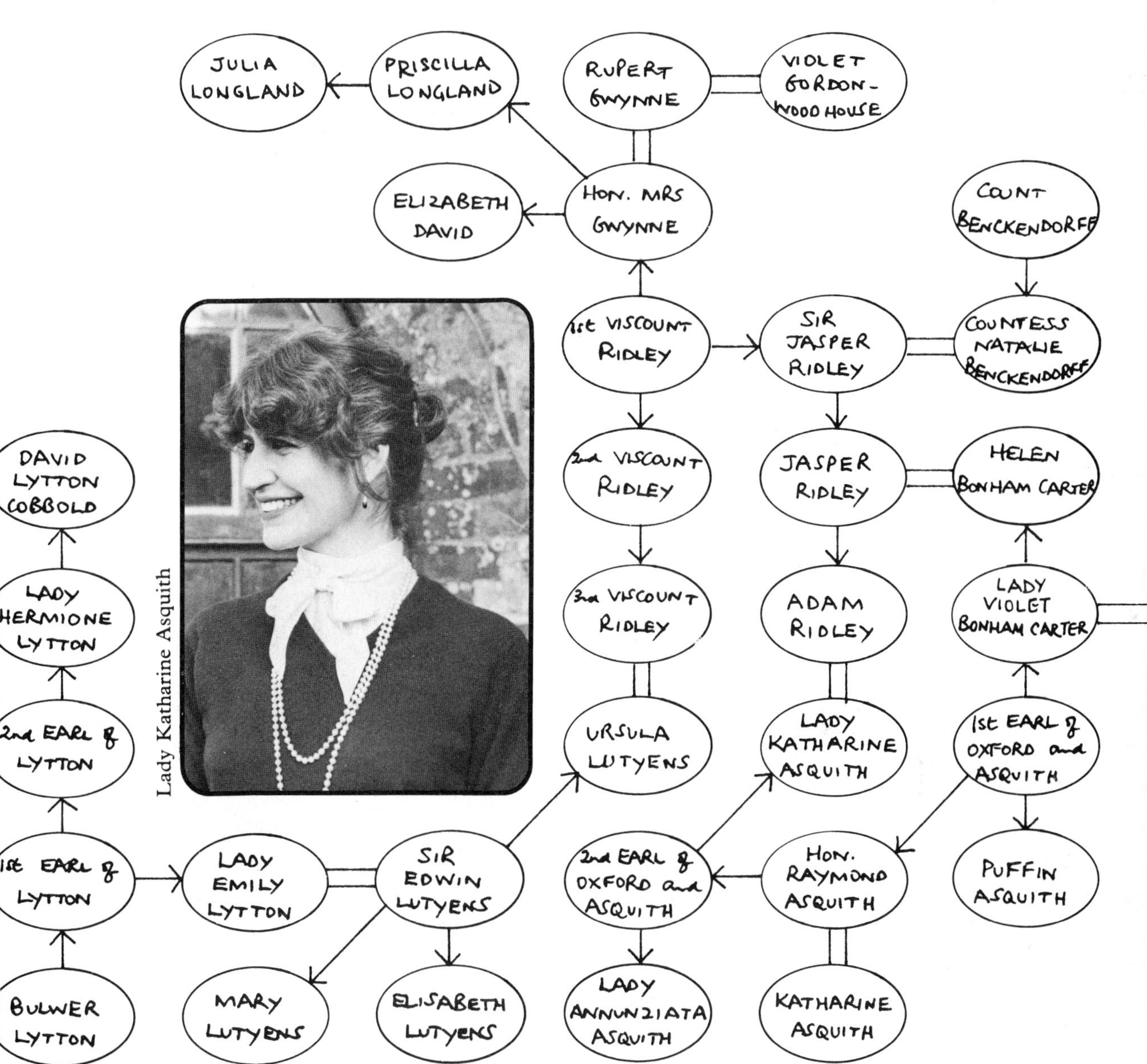
JULIA LONGLAND
PRISCILLA LONGLAND
RUPERT GWYNNE
VIOLET GORDON-WOODHOUSE
ELIZABETH DAVID
HON. MRS GWYNNE
COUNT BENCKENDORFF
1st VISCOUNT RIDLEY
SIR JASPER RIDLEY
COUNTESS NATALIE BENCKENDORFF
DAVID LYTTON COBBOLD
2nd VISCOUNT RIDLEY
JASPER RIDLEY
HELEN BONHAM CARTER
LADY HERMIONE LYTTON
3rd VISCOUNT RIDLEY
ADAM RIDLEY
LADY VIOLET BONHAM CARTER
2nd EARL of LYTTON
URSULA LUTYENS
LADY KATHARINE ASQUITH
1st EARL of OXFORD and ASQUITH
1st EARL of LYTTON
LADY EMILY LYTTON
SIR EDWIN LUTYENS
2nd EARL of OXFORD and ASQUITH
HON. RAYMOND ASQUITH
PUFFIN ASQUITH
BULWER LYTTON
MARY LUTYENS
ELISABETH LUTYENS
LADY ANNUNZIATA ASQUITH
KATHARINE ASQUITH
Lady Katharine Asquith

Violet Gordon-Woodhouse collected early musical instruments and lived at Nether Lypiatt Manor, now the home of Prince and Princess Michael of Kent.

Elizabeth David (b 1913). Cookery writer. Her first book *Mediterranean Food* struck a cheerful note in the austere post-war years.

Sir Edwin Lutyens (d 1944). Architect who designed ideal houses for pre-war weekend parties, with lots of courtyards, loggias, terraces and pergolas.

Lord Oxford and Asquith (d 1928). The first Prime Minister to go to the cinema. 'He laughed heartily and made continuous witty comments.'

Lady Annunziata Asquith (b 1948). Model, journalist and author.

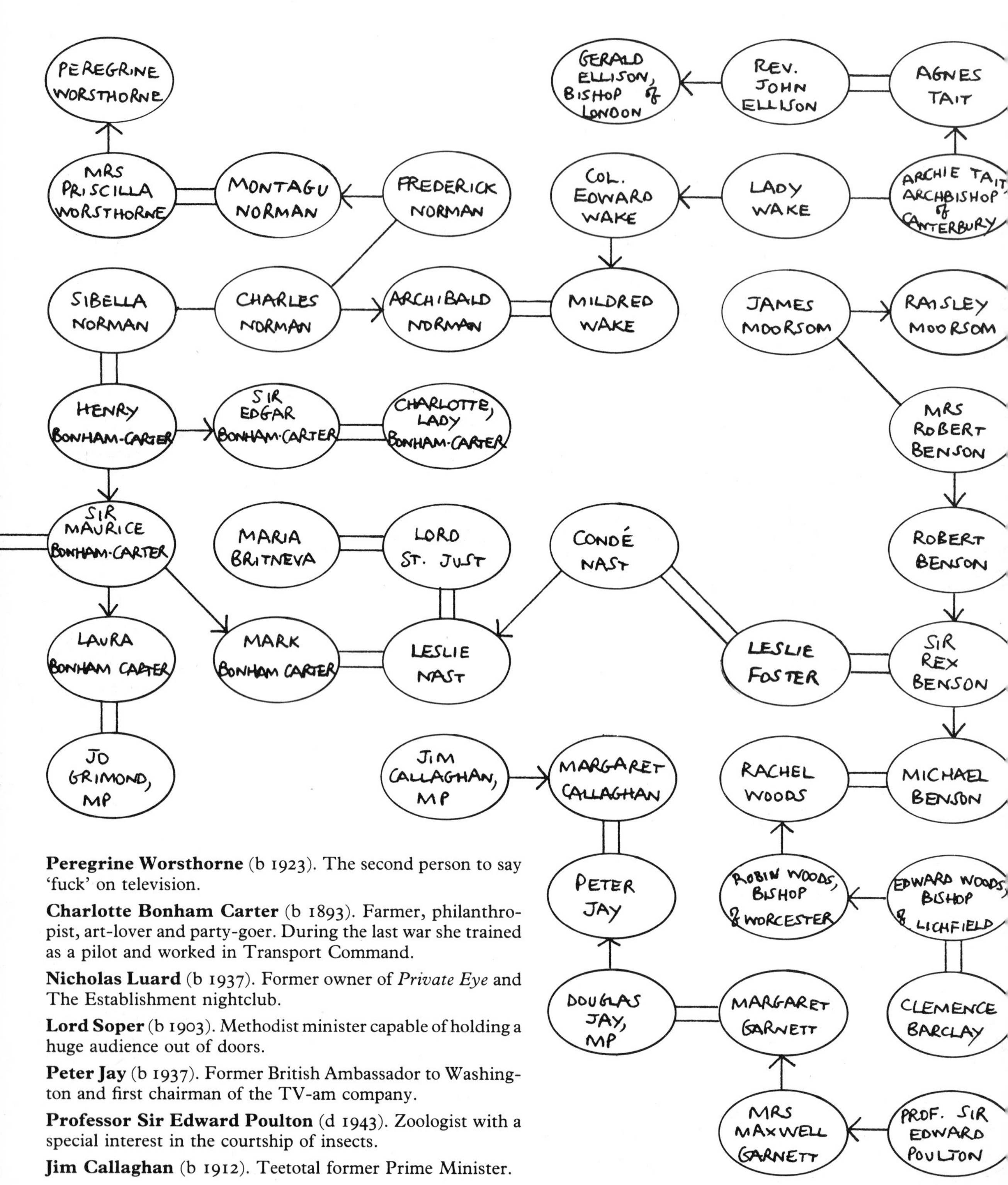
PEREGRINE WORSTHORNE
MRS PRISCILLA WORSTHORNE
MONTAGU NORMAN
FREDERICK NORMAN
GERALD ELLISON, BISHOP OF LONDON
REV. JOHN ELLISON
AGNES TAIT
COL. EDWARD WAKE
LADY WAKE
ARCHIE TAIT ARCHBISHOP OF CANTERBURY
SIBELLA NORMAN
CHARLES NORMAN
ARCHIBALD NORMAN
MILDRED WAKE
JAMES MOORSOM
RAISLEY MOORSOM
HENRY BONHAM-CARTER
SIR EDGAR BONHAM-CARTER
CHARLOTTE, LADY BONHAM-CARTER
MRS ROBERT BENSON
SIR MAURICE BONHAM-CARTER
MARIA BRITNEVA
LORD ST. JUST
CONDÉ NAST
ROBERT BENSON
LAURA BONHAM CARTER
MARK BONHAM CARTER
LESLIE NAST
LESLIE FOSTER
SIR REX BENSON
JO GRIMOND, MP
JIM CALLAGHAN, MP
MARGARET CALLAGHAN
RACHEL WOODS
MICHAEL BENSON
PETER JAY
ROBIN WOODS, BISHOP OF WORCESTER
EDWARD WOODS, BISHOP OF LICHFIELD
DOUGLAS JAY, MP
MARGARET GARNETT
CLEMENCE BARCLAY
MRS MAXWELL GARNETT
PROF. SIR EDWARD POULTON

Peregrine Worsthorne (b 1923). The second person to say 'fuck' on television.

Charlotte Bonham Carter (b 1893). Farmer, philanthropist, art-lover and party-goer. During the last war she trained as a pilot and worked in Transport Command.

Nicholas Luard (b 1937). Former owner of *Private Eye* and The Establishment nightclub.

Lord Soper (b 1903). Methodist minister capable of holding a huge audience out of doors.

Peter Jay (b 1937). Former British Ambassador to Washington and first chairman of the TV-am company.

Professor Sir Edward Poulton (d 1943). Zoologist with a special interest in the courtship of insects.

Jim Callaghan (b 1912). Teetotal former Prime Minister.

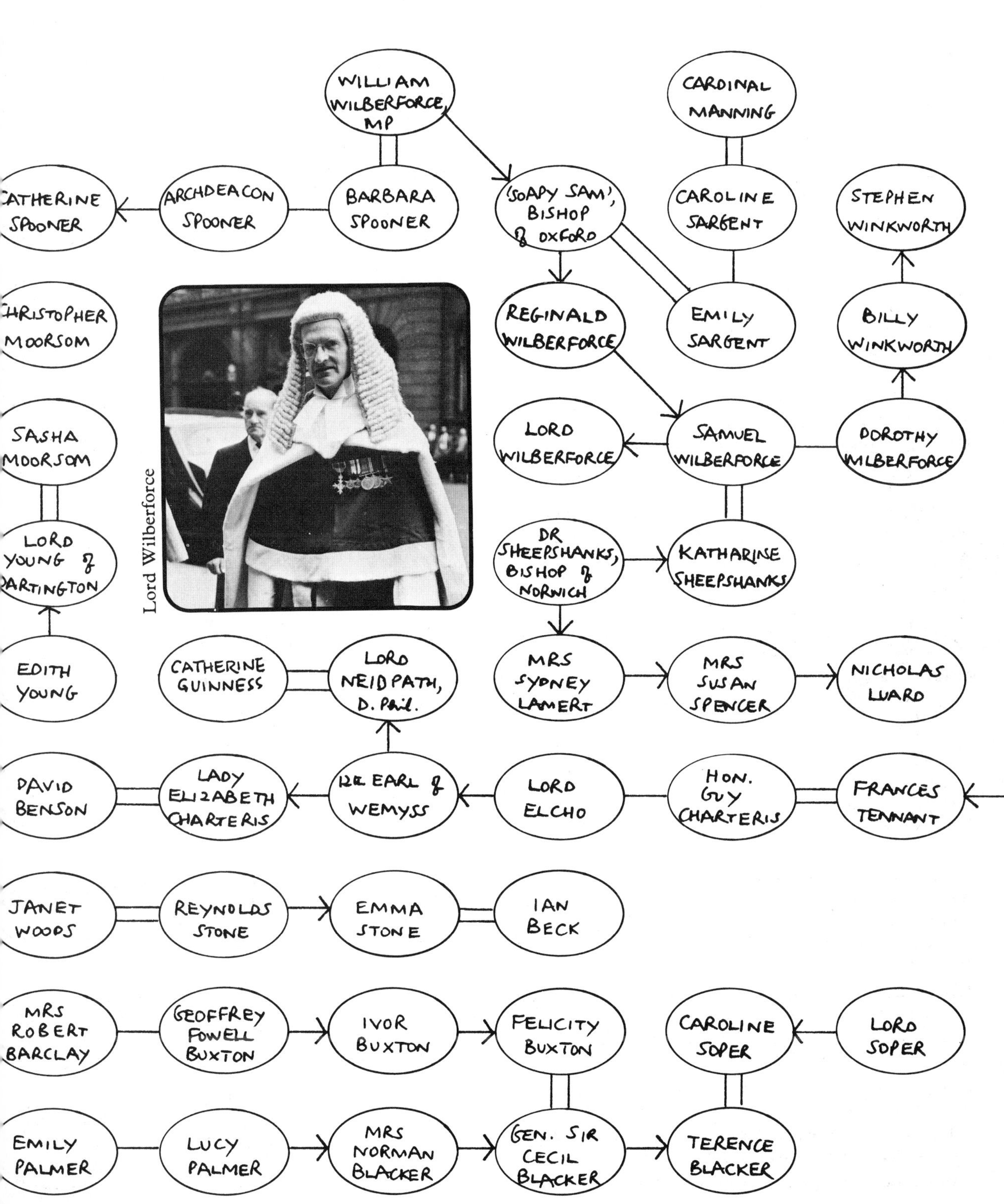
WILLIAM WILBERFORCE, MP
CARDINAL MANNING
CATHERINE SPOONER
ARCHDEACON SPOONER
BARBARA SPOONER
'SOAPY SAM', BISHOP OF OXFORD
CAROLINE SARGENT
STEPHEN WINKWORTH
CHRISTOPHER MOORSOM
REGINALD WILBERFORCE
EMILY SARGENT
BILLY WINKWORTH
SASHA MOORSOM
LORD WILBERFORCE
SAMUEL WILBERFORCE
DOROTHY WILBERFORCE
LORD YOUNG OF DARTINGTON
DR SHEEPSHANKS, BISHOP OF NORWICH
KATHARINE SHEEPSHANKS
EDITH YOUNG
CATHERINE GUINNESS
LORD NEIDPATH, D. Phil.
MRS SYDNEY LAMERT
MRS SUSAN SPENCER
NICHOLAS LUARD
DAVID BENSON
LADY ELIZABETH CHARTERIS
12th EARL OF WEMYSS
LORD ELCHO
HON. GUY CHARTERIS
FRANCES TENNANT
JANET WOODS
REYNOLDS STONE
EMMA STONE
IAN BECK
MRS ROBERT BARCLAY
GEOFFREY FOWELL BUXTON
IVOR BUXTON
FELICITY BUXTON
CAROLINE SOPER
LORD SOPER
EMILY PALMER
LUCY PALMER
MRS NORMAN BLACKER
GEN. SIR CECIL BLACKER
TERENCE BLACKER

Lord Wilberforce

Prince Rupert Lowenstein (b 1933). Financial adviser to the Rolling Stones.

Sir Victor Gollancz (d 1967). Left wing publisher who was fond of the phrase 'un-put-downable'.

Sheila Kitzinger (b 1929). Author of *The Good Birth Guide*, *The Place of Birth*, *The Experience of Breastfeeding* and other books on natural childbirth.

HON. MRS LOWRY-CORR

POLLY TOYNBEE
PHILIP TOYNBEE
CLAUD COCKBURN
HENRY GREEN
DIG YORKE

JOHN WELLS
PROF. RICHARD WOLLHEIM
ANN WOLLHEIM
ALEXANDER COCKBURN
SEBASTIAN YORKE

TERESA GATACRE
ALEXANDER CHANCELLOR
ELIZABETH POWELL
EMMA TENNANT
CHRISTOPHER BOOKER
GEORGIA TENNANT

SUSANNA JOHNSTON
LADY CHANCELLOR
PAMELA, LADY GLENCONNER
2nd LORD GLENCONNER
HON. DAVID TENNANT
VIRGINIA PARSONS

FRANCIS TENNANT
NANCY, LADY CRATHORNE
MARGOT, LADY OXFORD
1st LORD GLENCONNER
HAROLD TENNANT
DAME MARGARET WAKEHURST

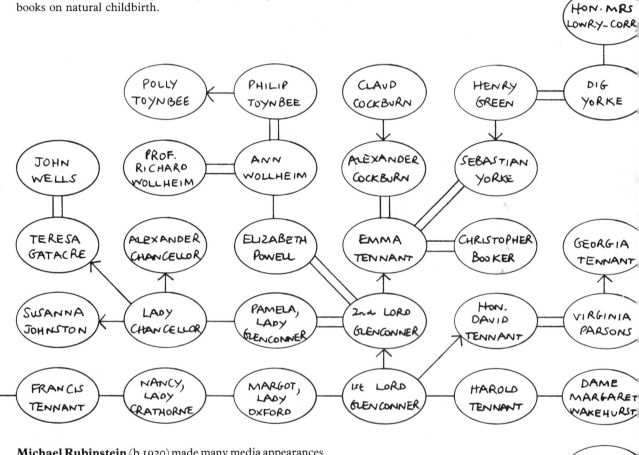

Michael Rubinstein (b 1920) made many media appearances as the legal adviser of Sir Anthony Blunt at the time of the publication of *Climate of Treason*.

Sir Stephen Spender (b 1909) is 6 ft 3 ins tall, has blue eyes and an unruly shock of white hair.

Prokoviev (d 1953). Soviet composer with highly individual style.

Henry Green was the pen-name of Henry Yorke (d 1973). His family firm, Pontifex, made lavatories.

Jeremy Sandford (b 1934) and **Nell Dunn** (b 1936) caused a sensation in 1959 when they exchanged their spacious home in Cheyne Walk for a humble terraced house in Battersea.

Jonathan Gathorne-Hardy (b 1933). Author of *The Rise and Fall of the British Nanny*.

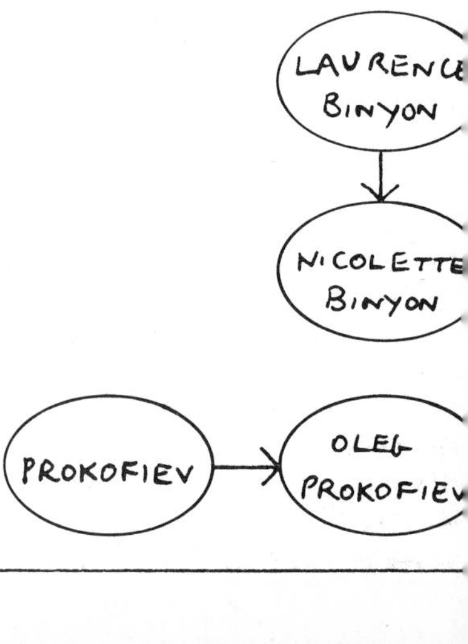
LAURENCE BINYON
NICOLETTE BINYON
PROKOFIEV
OLEG PROKOFIEV

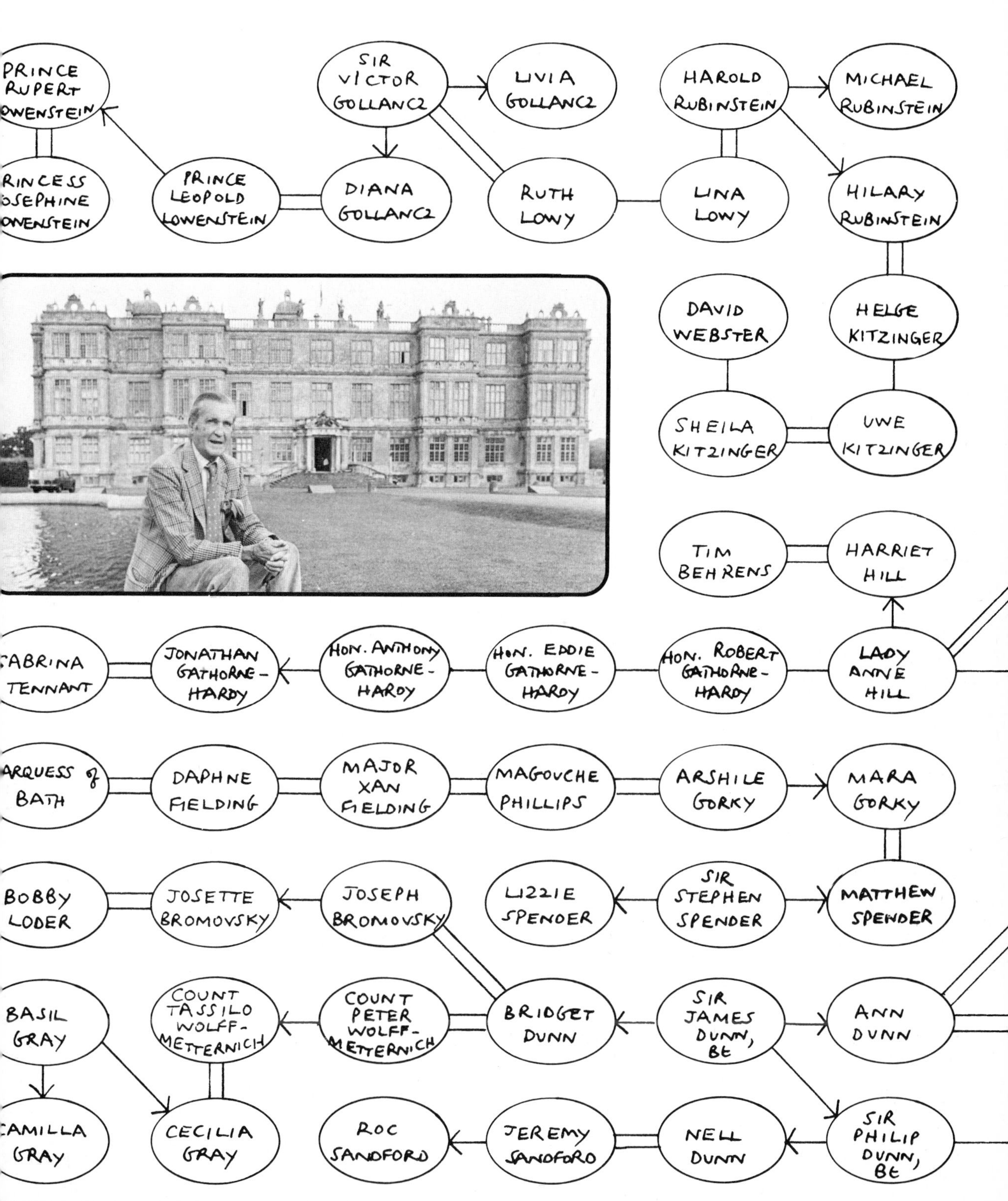
PRINCE RUPERT OWENSTEIN
RINCESS OSEPHINE OWENSTEIN
PRINCE LEOPOLD LOWENSTEIN
SIR VICTOR GOLLANCZ
DIANA GOLLANCZ
LIVIA GOLLANCZ
RUTH LOWY
HAROLD RUBINSTEIN
LINA LOWY
MICHAEL RUBINSTEIN
HILARY RUBINSTEIN
DAVID WEBSTER
HELGE KITZINGER
SHEILA KITZINGER
UWE KITZINGER
TIM BEHRENS
HARRIET HILL
ABRINA TENNANT
JONATHAN GATHORNE-HARDY
HON. ANTHONY GATHORNE-HARDY
HON. EDDIE GATHORNE-HARDY
HON. ROBERT GATHORNE-HARDY
LADY ANNE HILL
ARQUESS of BATH
DAPHNE FIELDING
MAJOR XAN FIELDING
MAGOUCHE PHILLIPS
ARSHILE GORKY
MARA GORKY
BOBBY LODER
JOSETTE BROMOVSKY
JOSEPH BROMOVSKY
LIZZIE SPENDER
SIR STEPHEN SPENDER
MATTHEW SPENDER
BASIL GRAY
COUNT TASSILO WOLFF-METTERNICH
COUNT PETER WOLFF-METTERNICH
BRIDGET DUNN
SIR JAMES DUNN, BT
ANN DUNN
AMILLA GRAY
CECILIA GRAY
ROC SANDFORD
JEREMY SANDFORD
NELL DUNN
SIR PHILIP DUNN, BT

Ann Barr is co-author of *The Official Sloane Ranger Handbook.*

Lucian Freud (b 1922). Painter noted for his bright woollen scarves and the 'decidedly *zazou* cut' of his trousers.

Mary St John Hutchinson (d 1977). Leading Bloomsb personality who never published her memoirs and avoi researchers who wished to pump her about her emi friends. 'Delightfully feminine, she lent chic to a ribbon glove by the way she wore it.'

Donald Maclean (d 1983). Spy.

Min Hogg is Editor of *The World of Interiors.*

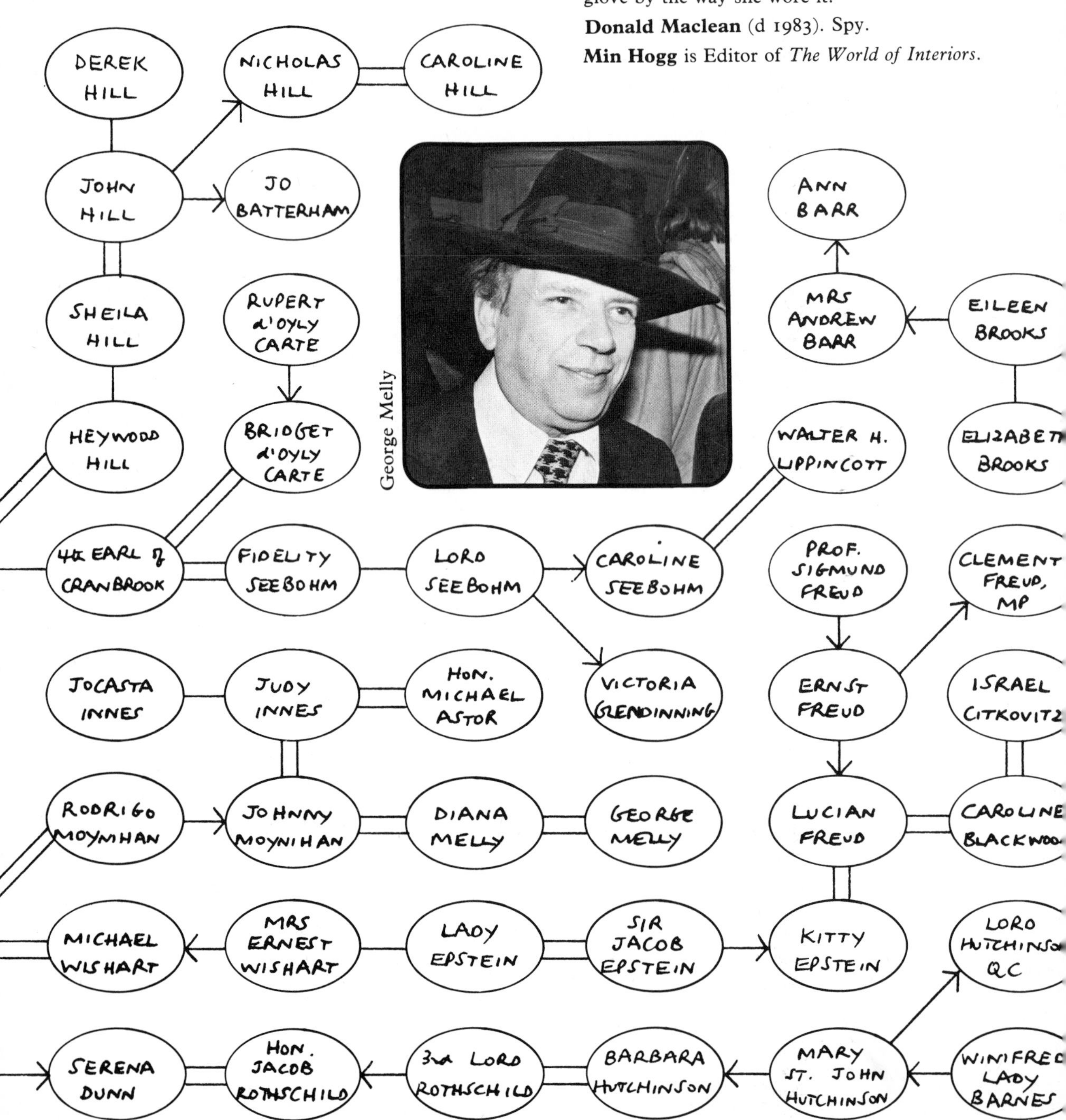
DEREK HILL
NICHOLAS HILL
CAROLINE HILL
JOHN HILL
JO BATTERHAM
ANN BARR
SHEILA HILL
RUPERT d'OYLY CARTE
MRS ANDREW BARR
EILEEN BROOKS
HEYWOOD HILL
BRIDGET d'OYLY CARTE
WALTER H. LIPPINCOTT
ELIZABET BROOKS
4th EARL of CRANBROOK
FIDELITY SEEBOHM
LORD SEEBOHM
CAROLINE SEEBOHM
PROF. SIGMUND FREUD
CLEMENT FREUD, MP
JOCASTA INNES
JUDY INNES
HON. MICHAEL ASTOR
VICTORIA GLENDINNING
ERNST FREUD
ISRAEL CITKOVITZ
RODRIGO MOYNIHAN
JOHNNY MOYNIHAN
DIANA MELLY
GEORGE MELLY
LUCIAN FREUD
CAROLINE BLACKWOO
MICHAEL WISHART
MRS ERNEST WISHART
LADY EPSTEIN
SIR JACOB EPSTEIN
KITTY EPSTEIN
LORD HUTCHINSO QC
SERENA DUNN
HON. JACOB ROTHSCHILD
3rd LORD ROTHSCHILD
BARBARA HUTCHINSON
MARY ST. JOHN HUTCHINSON
WINIFRED LADY BARNES
George Melly

Anthony Powell (b 1905) first met his wife at a party given by Lady Pansy Lamb. 'No more words were exchanged than were needed for the offering and accepting of a glass of gin and tonic.'

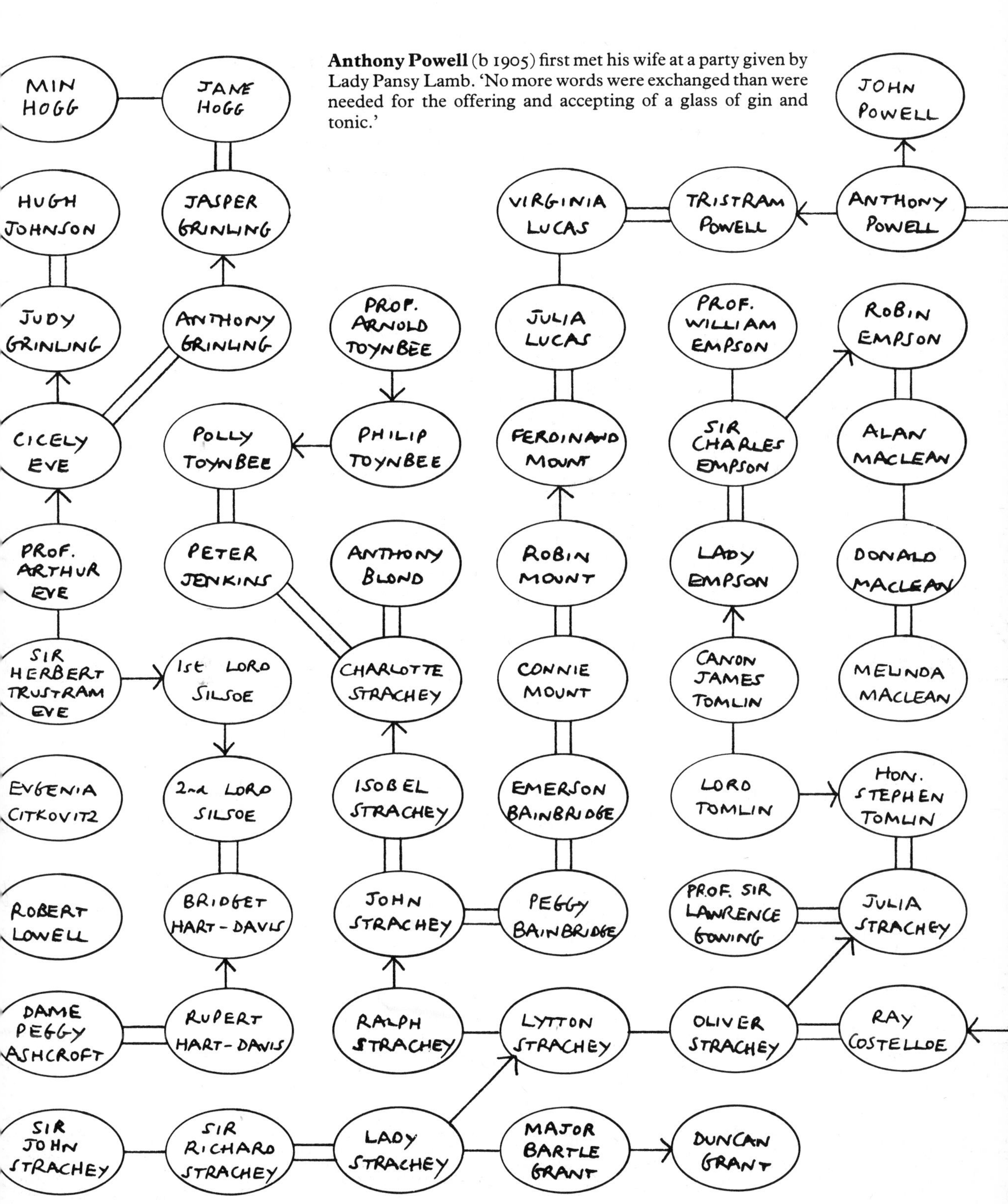
MIN HOGG
JANE HOGG
JOHN POWELL
HUGH JOHNSON
JASPER GRINLING
VIRGINIA LUCAS
TRISTRAM POWELL
ANTHONY POWELL
JUDY GRINLING
ANTHONY GRINLING
PROF. ARNOLD TOYNBEE
JULIA LUCAS
PROF. WILLIAM EMPSON
ROBIN EMPSON
CICELY EVE
POLLY TOYNBEE
PHILIP TOYNBEE
FERDINAND MOUNT
SIR CHARLES EMPSON
ALAN MACLEAN
PROF. ARTHUR EVE
PETER JENKINS
ANTHONY BLOND
ROBIN MOUNT
LADY EMPSON
DONALD MACLEAN
SIR HERBERT TRUSTRAM EVE
1st LORD SILSOE
CHARLOTTE STRACHEY
CONNIE MOUNT
CANON JAMES TOMLIN
MELINDA MACLEAN
EVGENIA CITKOVITZ
2nd LORD SILSOE
ISOBEL STRACHEY
EMERSON BAINBRIDGE
LORD TOMLIN
HON. STEPHEN TOMLIN
ROBERT LOWELL
BRIDGET HART-DAVIS
JOHN STRACHEY
PEGGY BAINBRIDGE
PROF. SIR LAWRENCE GOWING
JULIA STRACHEY
DAME PEGGY ASHCROFT
RUPERT HART-DAVIS
RALPH STRACHEY
LYTTON STRACHEY
OLIVER STRACHEY
RAY COSTELLOE
SIR JOHN STRACHEY
SIR RICHARD STRACHEY
LADY STRACHEY
MAJOR BARTLE GRANT
DUNCAN GRANT

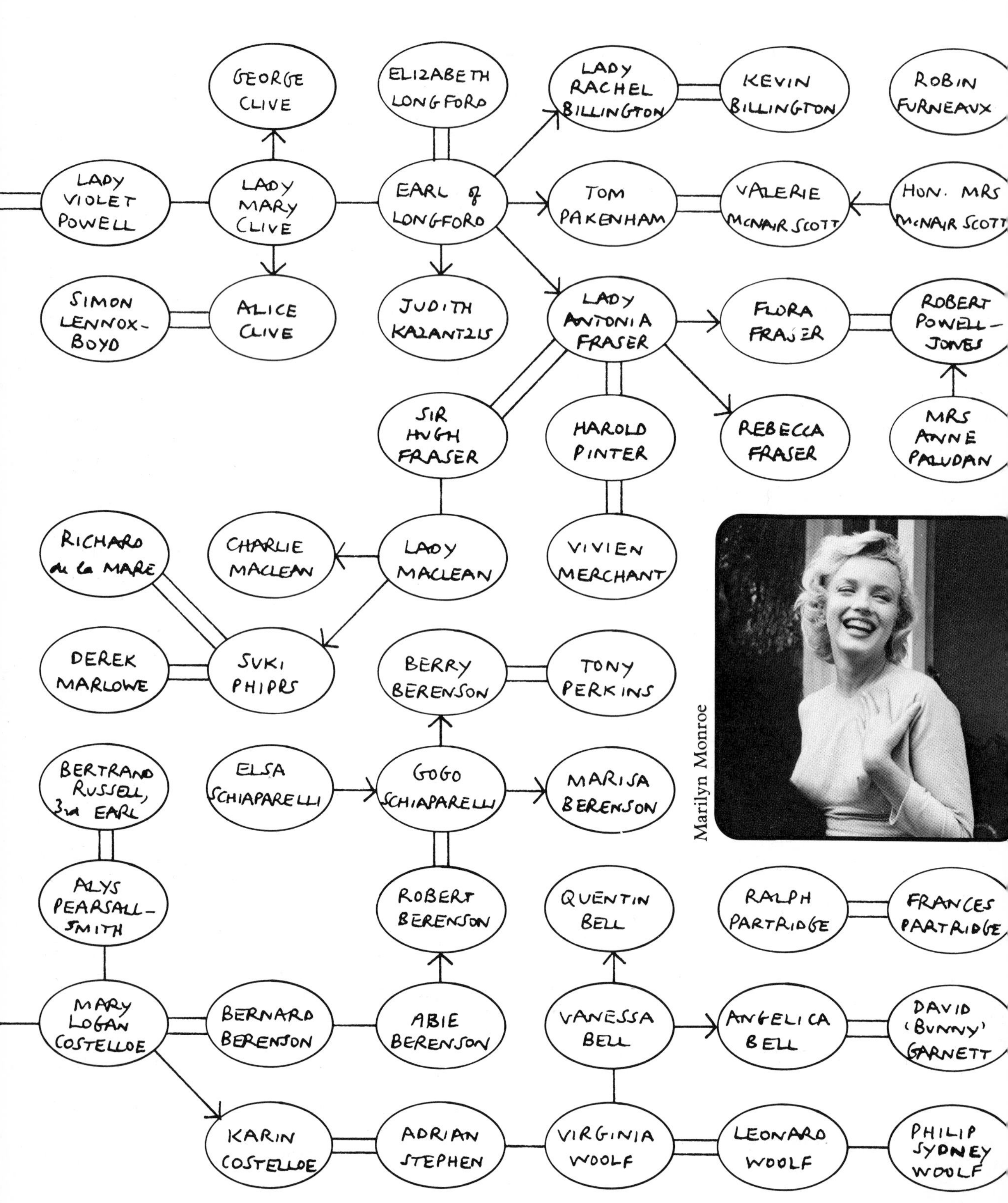
GEORGE CLIVE
ELIZABETH LONGFORD
LADY RACHEL BILLINGTON
KEVIN BILLINGTON
ROBIN FURNEAUX
LADY VIOLET POWELL
LADY MARY CLIVE
EARL of LONGFORD
TOM PAKENHAM
VALERIE McNAIR SCOTT
HON. MRS McNAIR SCOTT
SIMON LENNOX-BOYD
ALICE CLIVE
JUDITH KAZANTZIS
LADY ANTONIA FRASER
FLORA FRASER
ROBERT POWELL-JONES
SIR HUGH FRASER
HAROLD PINTER
REBECCA FRASER
MRS ANNE PALUDAN
RICHARD de la MARE
CHARLIE MACLEAN
LADY MACLEAN
VIVIEN MERCHANT
DEREK MARLOWE
SUKI PHIPPS
BERRY BERENSON
TONY PERKINS
BERTRAND RUSSELL, 3rd EARL
ELSA SCHIAPARELLI
GOGO SCHIAPARELLI
MARISA BERENSON
ALYS PEARSALL-SMITH
ROBERT BERENSON
QUENTIN BELL
RALPH PARTRIDGE
FRANCES PARTRIDGE
MARY LOGAN COSTELLOE
BERNARD BERENSON
ABIE BERENSON
VANESSA BELL
ANGELICA BELL
DAVID 'BUNNY' GARNETT
KARIN COSTELLOE
ADRIAN STEPHEN
VIRGINIA WOOLF
LEONARD WOOLF
PHILIP SYDNEY WOOLF

Marilyn Monroe

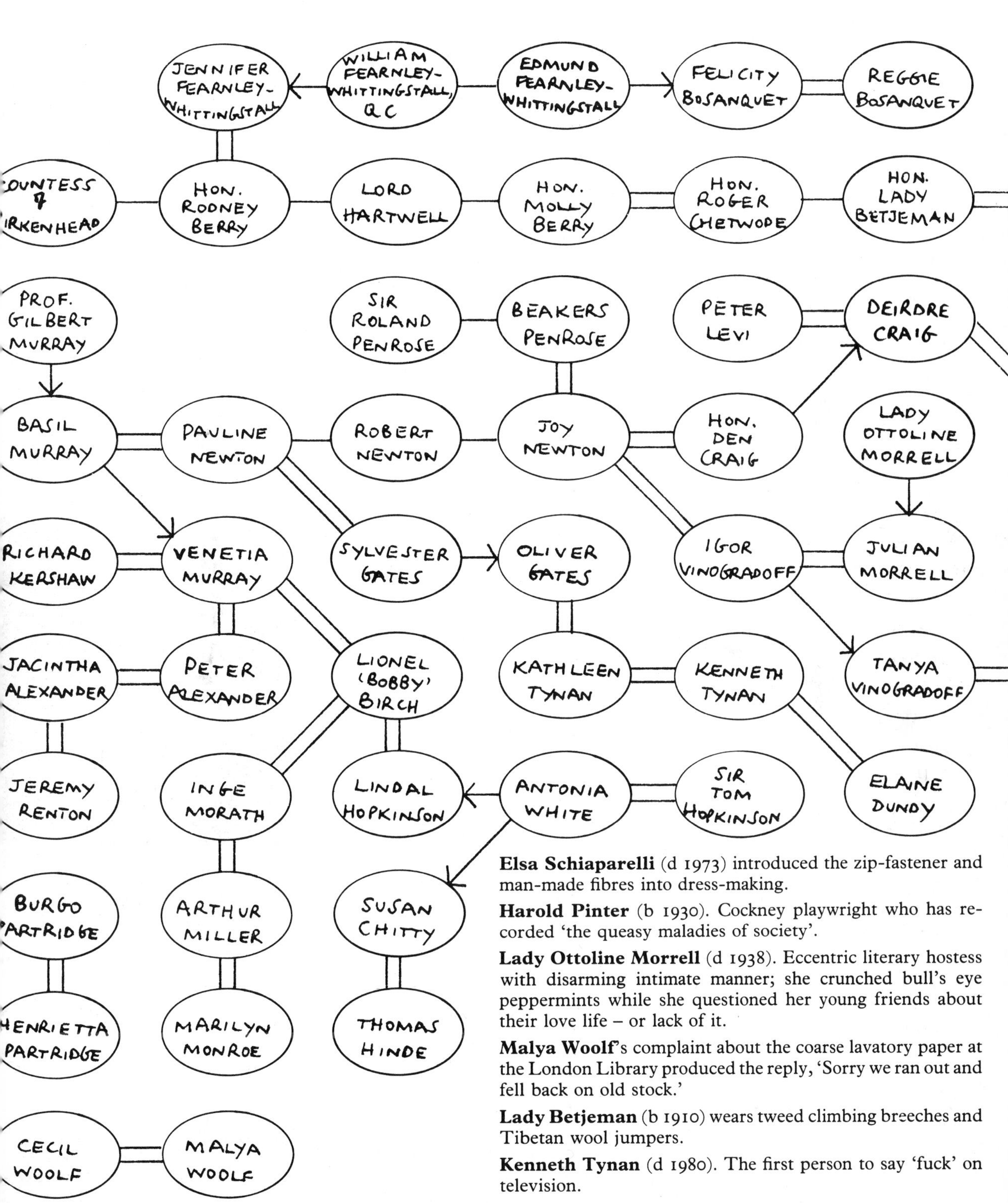
JENNIFER FEARNLEY-WHITTINGSTALL
WILLIAM FEARNLEY-WHITTINGSTALL, QC
EDMUND FEARNLEY-WHITTINGSTALL
FELICITY BOSANQUET
REGGIE BOSANQUET
COUNTESS OF BIRKENHEAD
HON. RODNEY BERRY
LORD HARTWELL
HON. MOLLY BERRY
HON. ROGER CHETWODE
HON. LADY BETJEMAN
PROF. GILBERT MURRAY
SIR ROLAND PENROSE
BEAKERS PENROSE
PETER LEVI
DEIRDRE CRAIG
BASIL MURRAY
PAULINE NEWTON
ROBERT NEWTON
JOY NEWTON
HON. DEN CRAIG
LADY OTTOLINE MORRELL
RICHARD KERSHAW
VENETIA MURRAY
SYLVESTER GATES
OLIVER GATES
IGOR VINOGRADOFF
JULIAN MORRELL
JACINTHA ALEXANDER
PETER ALEXANDER
LIONEL ('BOBBY') BIRCH
KATHLEEN TYNAN
KENNETH TYNAN
TANYA VINOGRADOFF
JEREMY RENTON
INGE MORATH
LINDAL HOPKINSON
ANTONIA WHITE
SIR TOM HOPKINSON
ELAINE DUNDY
BURGO PARTRIDGE
ARTHUR MILLER
SUSAN CHITTY
HENRIETTA PARTRIDGE
MARILYN MONROE
THOMAS HINDE
CECIL WOOLF
MALYA WOOLF

Elsa Schiaparelli (d 1973) introduced the zip-fastener and man-made fibres into dress-making.

Harold Pinter (b 1930). Cockney playwright who has recorded 'the queasy maladies of society'.

Lady Ottoline Morrell (d 1938). Eccentric literary hostess with disarming intimate manner; she crunched bull's eye peppermints while she questioned her young friends about their love life – or lack of it.

Malya Woolf's complaint about the coarse lavatory paper at the London Library produced the reply, 'Sorry we ran out and fell back on old stock.'

Lady Betjeman (b 1910) wears tweed climbing breeches and Tibetan wool jumpers.

Kenneth Tynan (d 1980). The first person to say 'fuck' on television.

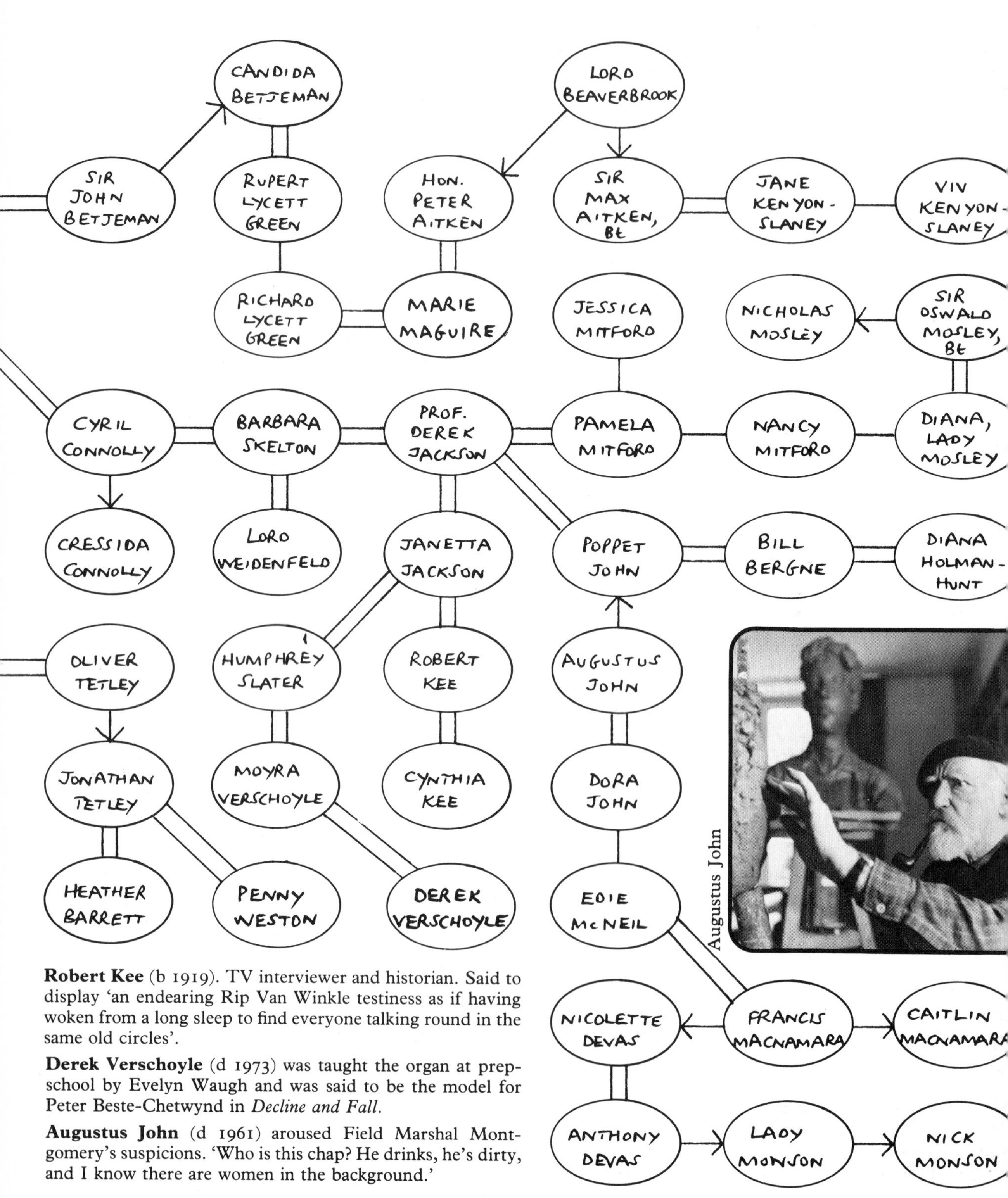
CANDIDA BETJEMAN
LORD BEAVERBROOK
SIR JOHN BETJEMAN
RUPERT LYCETT GREEN
HON. PETER AITKEN
SIR MAX AITKEN, Bt
JANE KENYON-SLANEY
VIV KENYON-SLANEY
RICHARD LYCETT GREEN
MARIE MAGUIRE
JESSICA MITFORD
NICHOLAS MOSLEY
SIR OSWALD MOSLEY, Bt
CYRIL CONNOLLY
BARBARA SKELTON
PROF. DEREK JACKSON
PAMELA MITFORD
NANCY MITFORD
DIANA, LADY MOSLEY
CRESSIDA CONNOLLY
LORD WEIDENFELD
JANETTA JACKSON
POPPET JOHN
BILL BERGNE
DIANA HOLMAN-HUNT
OLIVER TETLEY
HUMPHREY SLATER
ROBERT KEE
AUGUSTUS JOHN
JONATHAN TETLEY
MOYRA VERSCHOYLE
CYNTHIA KEE
DORA JOHN
HEATHER BARRETT
PENNY WESTON
DEREK VERSCHOYLE
EDIE McNEIL
NICOLETTE DEVAS
FRANCIS MACNAMARA
CAITLIN MACNAMARA
ANTHONY DEVAS
LADY MONSON
NICK MONSON

Augustus John

Robert Kee (b 1919). TV interviewer and historian. Said to display 'an endearing Rip Van Winkle testiness as if having woken from a long sleep to find everyone talking round in the same old circles'.

Derek Verschoyle (d 1973) was taught the organ at prep-school by Evelyn Waugh and was said to be the model for Peter Beste-Chetwynd in *Decline and Fall*.

Augustus John (d 1961) aroused Field Marshal Montgomery's suspicions. 'Who is this chap? He drinks, he's dirty, and I know there are women in the background.'

merset Maugham (d 1965) appeared at the wedding of ince Rainier and Grace Kelly wearing a tail coat and trousers ade in 1906.

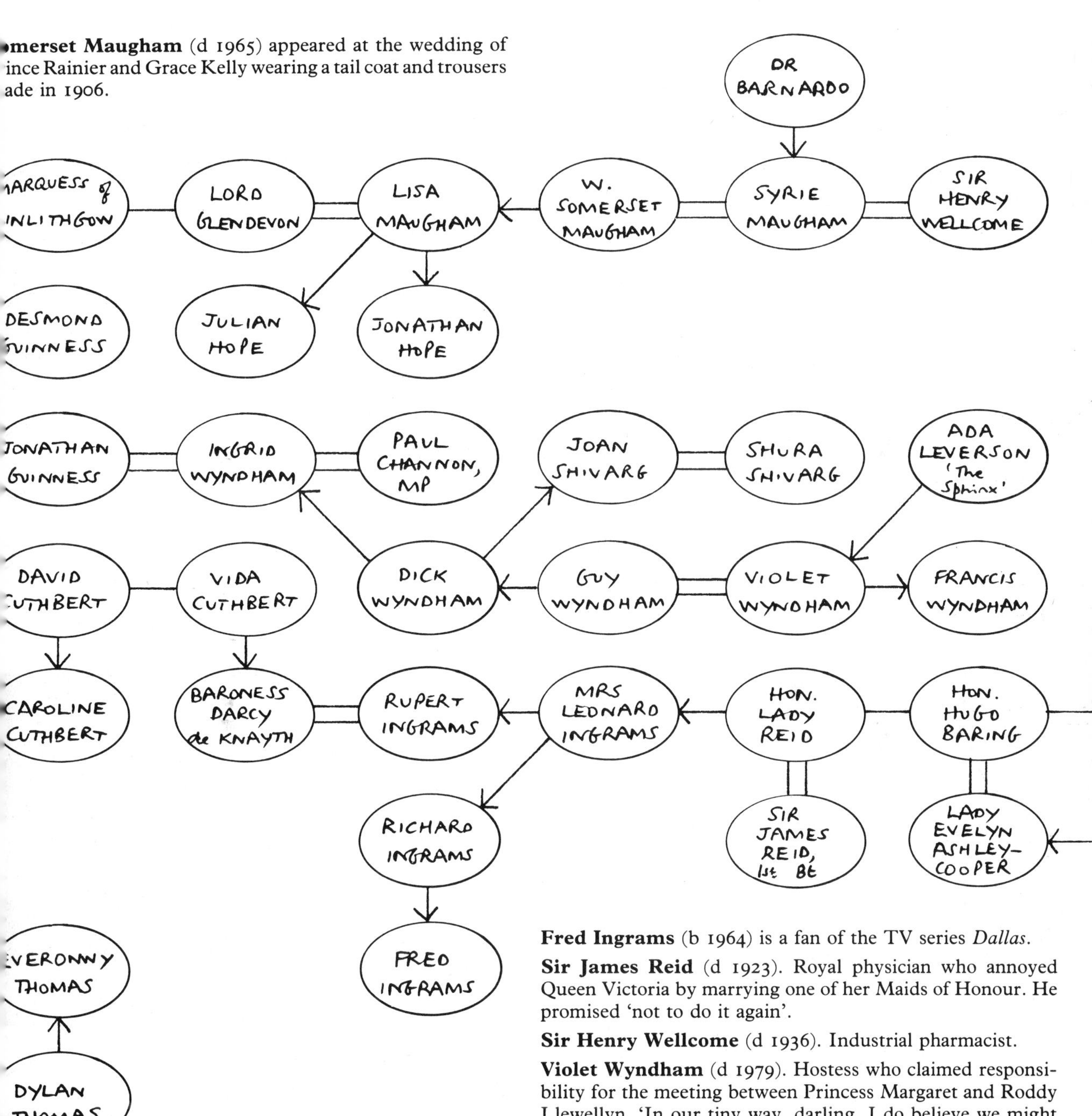
DR BARNARDO
MARQUESS of LINLITHGOW
LORD GLENDEVON
LISA MAUGHAM
W. SOMERSET MAUGHAM
SYRIE MAUGHAM
SIR HENRY WELLCOME
DESMOND GUINNESS
JULIAN HOPE
JONATHAN HOPE
JONATHAN GUINNESS
INGRID WYNDHAM
PAUL CHANNON, MP
JOAN SHIVARG
SHURA SHIVARG
ADA LEVERSON 'The Sphinx'
DAVID CUTHBERT
VIDA CUTHBERT
DICK WYNDHAM
GUY WYNDHAM
VIOLET WYNDHAM
FRANCIS WYNDHAM
CAROLINE CUTHBERT
BARONESS DARCY de KNAYTH
RUPERT INGRAMS
MRS LEONARD INGRAMS
HON. LADY REID
HON. HUGO BARING
RICHARD INGRAMS
SIR JAMES REID, 1st Bt
LADY EVELYN ASHLEY-COOPER
FRED INGRAMS
EVERONNY THOMAS
DYLAN THOMAS

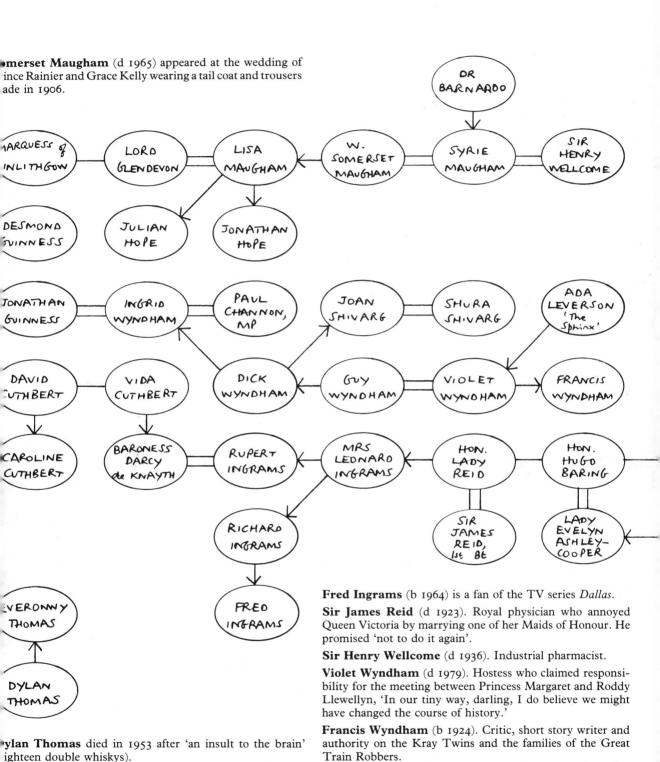

Fred Ingrams (b 1964) is a fan of the TV series *Dallas*.

Sir James Reid (d 1923). Royal physician who annoyed Queen Victoria by marrying one of her Maids of Honour. He promised 'not to do it again'.

Sir Henry Wellcome (d 1936). Industrial pharmacist.

Violet Wyndham (d 1979). Hostess who claimed responsibility for the meeting between Princess Margaret and Roddy Llewellyn, 'In our tiny way, darling, I do believe we might have changed the course of history.'

Francis Wyndham (b 1924). Critic, short story writer and authority on the Kray Twins and the families of the Great Train Robbers.

Dick Wyndham (d 1948) left his wine cellar to Cyril Connolly.

ylan Thomas died in 1953 after 'an insult to the brain' ighteen double whiskys).

ichard Ingrams (b 1937) served in Korea and Malaya as an cting Sergeant in the Royal Army Educational Corps.

Mark Girouard (b 1931). Writer and architectural historian.

Charles Addams (b 1912). *New Yorker* cartoonist who 'invites us to enter a world which has nothing to do with the one in which we live'.

Marika Hanbury-Tenison (d 1982). One of the first cook writers to tackle deep-freeze cooking. Her most popular b was on how to use up left-overs.

Richard Foster (b 1945). Portrait painter and wat colourist.

Dicky Muir is the owner of La Popote restaurant Knightsbridge.

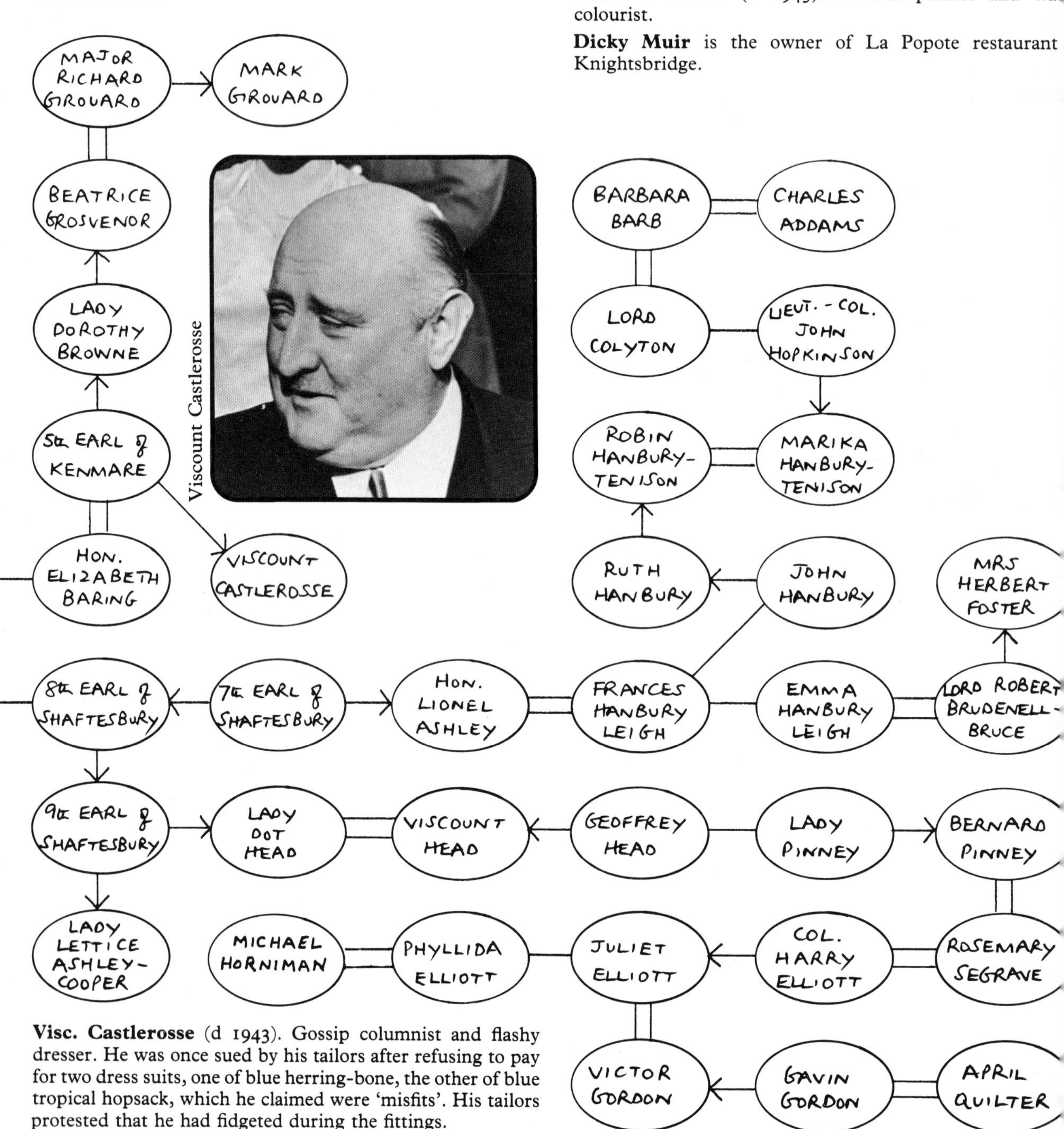

MAJOR RICHARD GIROUARD
MARK GIROUARD
BEATRICE GROSVENOR
LADY DOROTHY BROWNE
5th EARL of KENMARE
HON. ELIZABETH BARING
VISCOUNT CASTLEROSSE
Viscount Castlerosse
BARBARA BARB
CHARLES ADDAMS
LORD COLYTON
LIEUT.-COL. JOHN HOPKINSON
ROBIN HANBURY-TENISON
MARIKA HANBURY-TENISON
RUTH HANBURY
JOHN HANBURY
MRS HERBERT FOSTER
8th EARL of SHAFTESBURY
7th EARL of SHAFTESBURY
HON. LIONEL ASHLEY
FRANCES HANBURY LEIGH
EMMA HANBURY LEIGH
LORD ROBERT BRUDENELL-BRUCE
9th EARL of SHAFTESBURY
LADY DOT HEAD
VISCOUNT HEAD
GEOFFREY HEAD
LADY PINNEY
BERNARD PINNEY
LADY LETTICE ASHLEY-COOPER
MICHAEL HORNIMAN
PHYLLIDA ELLIOTT
JULIET ELLIOTT
COL. HARRY ELLIOTT
ROSEMARY SEGRAVE
VICTOR GORDON
GAVIN GORDON
APRIL QUILTER

Visc. Castlerosse (d 1943). Gossip columnist and flashy dresser. He was once sued by his tailors after refusing to pay for two dress suits, one of blue herring-bone, the other of blue tropical hopsack, which he claimed were 'misfits'. His tailors protested that he had fidgeted during the fittings.

nrietta Rous (b 1947). Wessex Regionalist candidate who od against Jeremy Thorpe at the 1979 General Election. e won fifty votes.

ordon Richardson (b 1915). Former governor of the Bank England.

ger Whittaker (b 1936). Singer, song-writer and inter- tional cabaret performer.

hn Pudney author of *The Smallest Room*, a history of the atory.

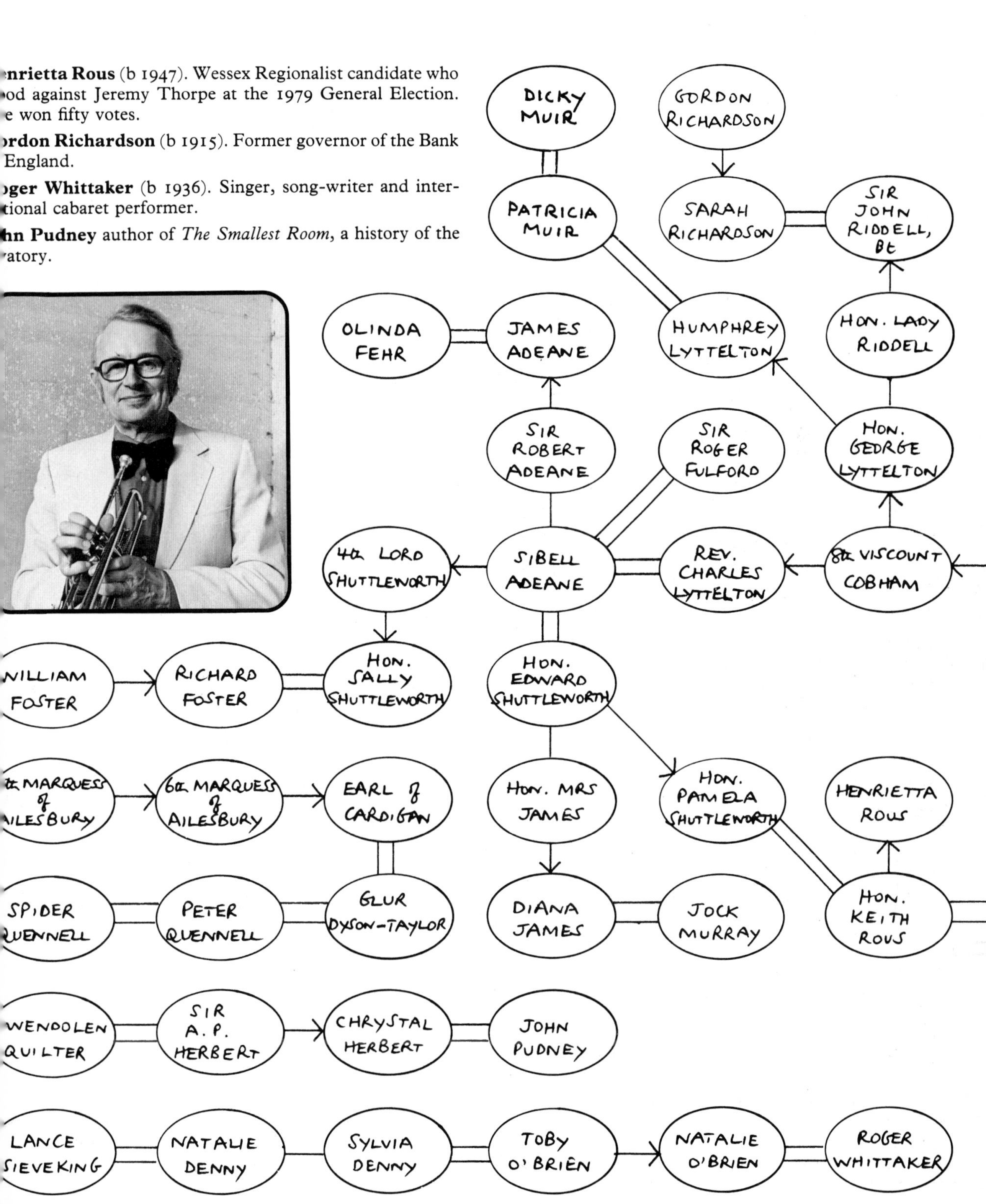

DICKY MUIR
GORDON RICHARDSON
PATRICIA MUIR
SARAH RICHARDSON
SIR JOHN RIDDELL, Bt
OLINDA FEHR
JAMES ADEANE
HUMPHREY LYTTELTON
HON. LADY RIDDELL
SIR ROBERT ADEANE
SIR ROGER FULFORD
HON. GEORGE LYTTELTON
4th LORD SHUTTLEWORTH
SIBELL ADEANE
REV. CHARLES LYTTELTON
8th VISCOUNT COBHAM
WILLIAM FOSTER
RICHARD FOSTER
HON. SALLY SHUTTLEWORTH
HON. EDWARD SHUTTLEWORTH
th MARQUESS of AILESBURY
6th MARQUESS of AILESBURY
EARL of CARDIGAN
HON. MRS JAMES
HON. PAMELA SHUTTLEWORTH
HENRIETTA ROUS
SPIDER QUENNELL
PETER QUENNELL
GLUR DYSON-TAYLOR
DIANA JAMES
JOCK MURRAY
HON. KEITH ROUS
WENDOLEN QUILTER
SIR A. P. HERBERT
CHRYSTAL HERBERT
JOHN PUDNEY
LANCE SIEVEKING
NATALIE DENNY
SYLVIA DENNY
TOBY O'BRIEN
NATALIE O'BRIEN
ROGER WHITTAKER

Piers Paul Read (b 1941). Roman Catholic writer who once shared a flat with Derek Marlowe and Tom Stoppard.

Mark Bonham Carter (b 1922). Former chairman of the Race Relations Board, whose Sussex manor house was once scrawled with the words 'Nigger lover'.

Nigel Dempster (b 1941). Gossip columnist who told television viewers, 'I am paid a certain sum of money to spy for my readers, to seek out the curious lives, the mistakes and the unhappiness of those who have got a privileged position.'

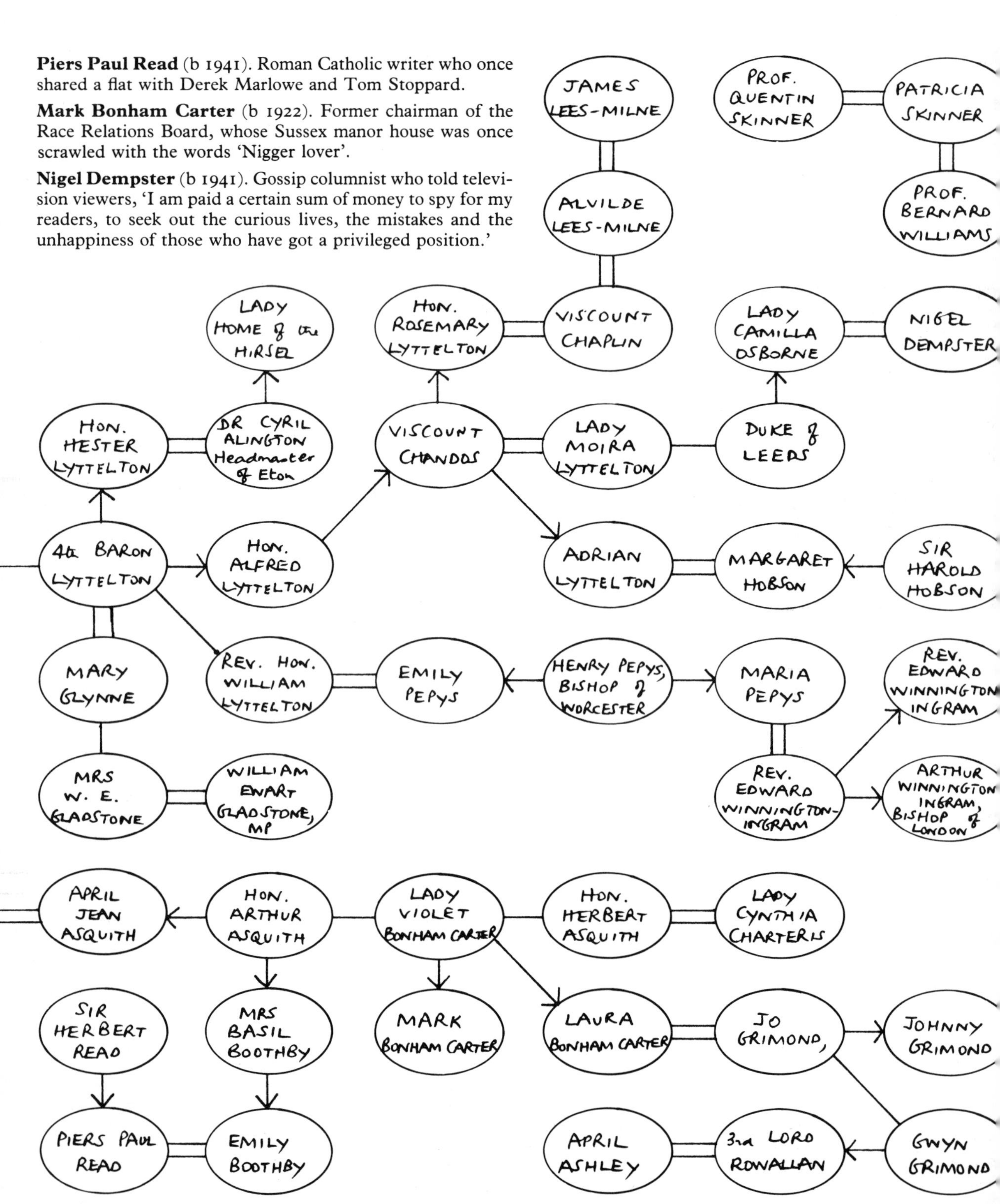
JAMES LEES-MILNE
PROF. QUENTIN SKINNER
PATRICIA SKINNER
ALVILDE LEES-MILNE
PROF. BERNARD WILLIAMS
LADY HOME of the HIRSEL
HON. ROSEMARY LYTTELTON
VISCOUNT CHAPLIN
LADY CAMILLA OSBORNE
NIGEL DEMPSTER
HON. HESTER LYTTELTON
DR CYRIL ALINGTON Headmaster of Eton
VISCOUNT CHANDOS
LADY MOIRA LYTTELTON
DUKE of LEEDS
4th BARON LYTTELTON
HON. ALFRED LYTTELTON
ADRIAN LYTTELTON
MARGARET HOBSON
SIR HAROLD HOBSON
MARY GLYNNE
REV. HON. WILLIAM LYTTELTON
EMILY PEPYS
HENRY PEPYS, BISHOP of WORCESTER
MARIA PEPYS
REV. EDWARD WINNINGTON INGRAM
MRS W. E. GLADSTONE
WILLIAM EWART GLADSTONE, MP
REV. EDWARD WINNINGTON-INGRAM
ARTHUR WINNINGTON INGRAM, BISHOP of LONDON
APRIL JEAN ASQUITH
HON. ARTHUR ASQUITH
LADY VIOLET BONHAM CARTER
HON. HERBERT ASQUITH
LADY CYNTHIA CHARTERIS
SIR HERBERT READ
MRS BASIL BOOTHBY
MARK BONHAM CARTER
LAURA BONHAM CARTER
JO GRIMOND,
JOHNNY GRIMOND
PIERS PAUL READ
EMILY BOOTHBY
APRIL ASHLEY
3rd LORD ROWALLAN
GWYN GRIMOND

hirley Williams (b 1930) has her hair cut at the Army & avy Stores.

isc. Montgomery of Alamein (d 1976) toured the City of ondon after the 2nd World War with one of his shoe laces ndone.

Sir Gerald du Maurier (d 1934) told the Earl of Carnarvon, 'The secret of acting is to be yourself.'

Hon. George Bruce (b 1930). Landscape, portrait and flower painter, who is rarely seen in a suit.

Lord Northcliffe (d 1922) ended up living in a hut on the roof of the Duke of Devonshire's house in Carlton Gardens.

1st Lord Rothermere (d 1940) gave his mistresses mink coats and diamond brooches. One of his typists received a ring containing a diamond the size of a pigeon's egg.

SHIRLEY WILLIAMS
SIR GEORGE CATLIN
VERA BRITTAIN
JOHN BRITTAIN-CATLIN
JENNIFER MANNASEH
LORD BALFOUR of BURLEIGH
HON. GEORGE BRUCE
FIELD-MARSHAL VISCOUNT MONTGOMERY of ALAMEIN
2nd VISCOUNT MONTGOMERY
TESSA BROWNING
EARL ATTLEE
VIOLET MILLAR
DAPHNE du MAURIER
HENRY MILLAR
SIR GERALD du MAURIER
HARRIET BERNARD
ARTHUR BERNARD
MRS CHARLES BLAND
HON. KATHERINE BRUCE
CHARLES MILLAR
BEATRIX du MAURIER
GEORGE CHRISTIE of GLYNDEBOURNE
PATRICIA NICHOLSON
BRIAN NICHOLSON
THOMAS RIVIERE BLAND
GERALD MILLAR
SIR OLIVER MILLAR
CELIA JOHNSON
MRS RALPH DENNIS
HENRIETTA NICHOLSON
MARY MILLAR
VISCOUNT NORTHCLIFFE
GERALDINE HARMSWORTH
KATE FLEMING
PETER FLEMING
IAN FLEMING
ANN FLEMING
2nd LORD ROTHERMERE
1st LORD ROTHERMERE
2nd LORD ROWALLAN
HON. JOSEPH CORBETT
HON. CATHERINE ACTON
HON. RICHARD ACTON
JUDITH TODD
GARFIELD TODD

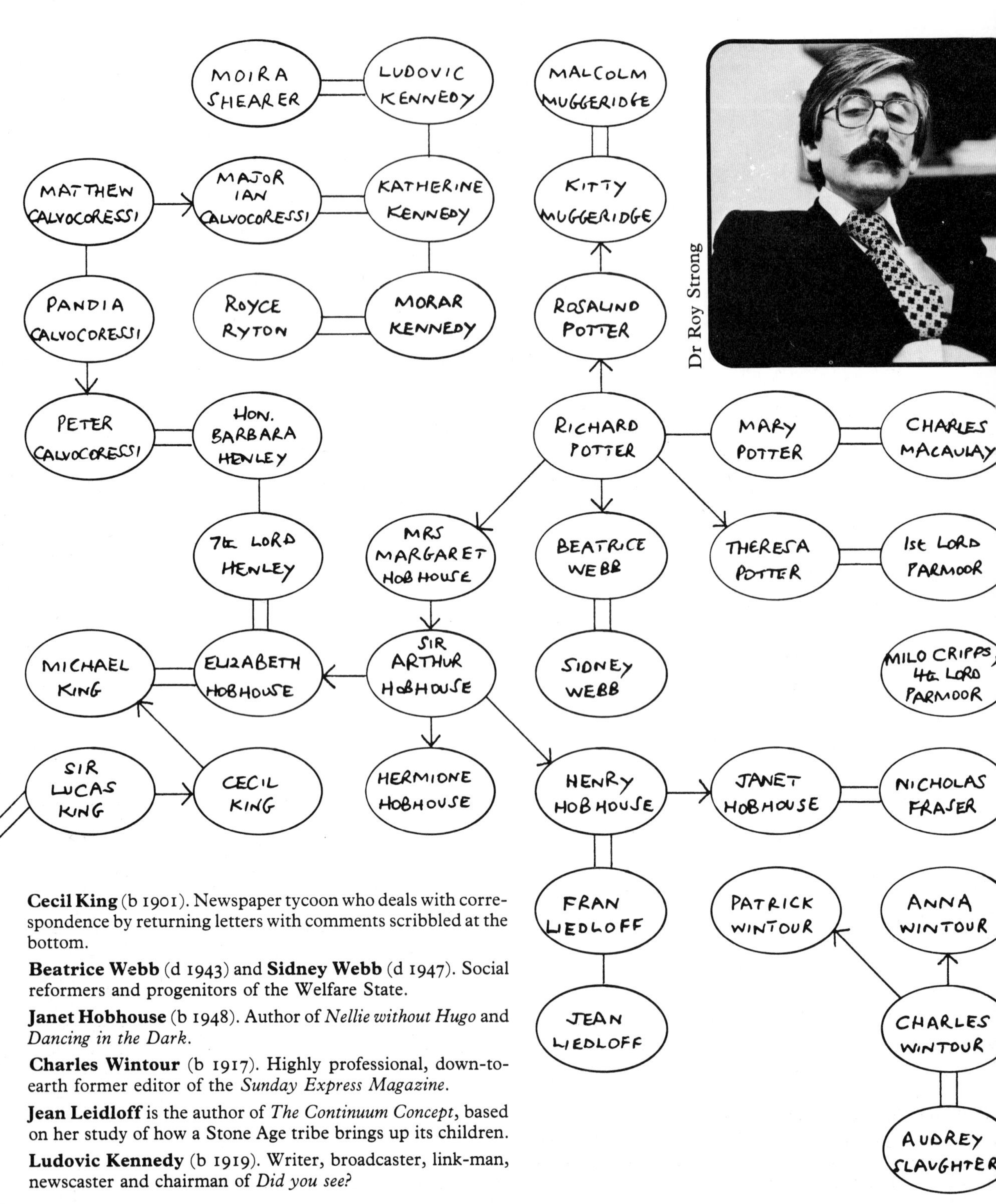

MOIRA SHEARER
LUDOVIC KENNEDY
MALCOLM MUGGERIDGE
MATTHEW CALVOCORESSI
MAJOR IAN CALVOCORESSI
KATHERINE KENNEDY
KITTY MUGGERIDGE
PANDIA CALVOCORESSI
ROYCE RYTON
MORAR KENNEDY
ROSALIND POTTER
PETER CALVOCORESSI
HON. BARBARA HENLEY
RICHARD POTTER
MARY POTTER
CHARLES MACAULAY
7th LORD HENLEY
MRS MARGARET HOBHOUSE
BEATRICE WEBB
THERESA POTTER
1st LORD PARMOOR
MICHAEL KING
ELIZABETH HOBHOUSE
SIR ARTHUR HOBHOUSE
SIDNEY WEBB
MILO CRIPPS, 4th LORD PARMOOR
SIR LUCAS KING
CECIL KING
HERMIONE HOBHOUSE
HENRY HOBHOUSE
JANET HOBHOUSE
NICHOLAS FRASER
FRAN LIEDLOFF
PATRICK WINTOUR
ANNA WINTOUR
JEAN LIEDLOFF
CHARLES WINTOUR
AUDREY SLAUGHTER

Dr Roy Strong

Cecil King (b 1901). Newspaper tycoon who deals with correspondence by returning letters with comments scribbled at the bottom.

Beatrice Webb (d 1943) and **Sidney Webb** (d 1947). Social reformers and progenitors of the Welfare State.

Janet Hobhouse (b 1948). Author of *Nellie without Hugo* and *Dancing in the Dark*.

Charles Wintour (b 1917). Highly professional, down-to-earth former editor of the *Sunday Express Magazine*.

Jean Leidloff is the author of *The Continuum Concept*, based on her study of how a Stone Age tribe brings up its children.

Ludovic Kennedy (b 1919). Writer, broadcaster, link-man, newscaster and chairman of *Did you see?*

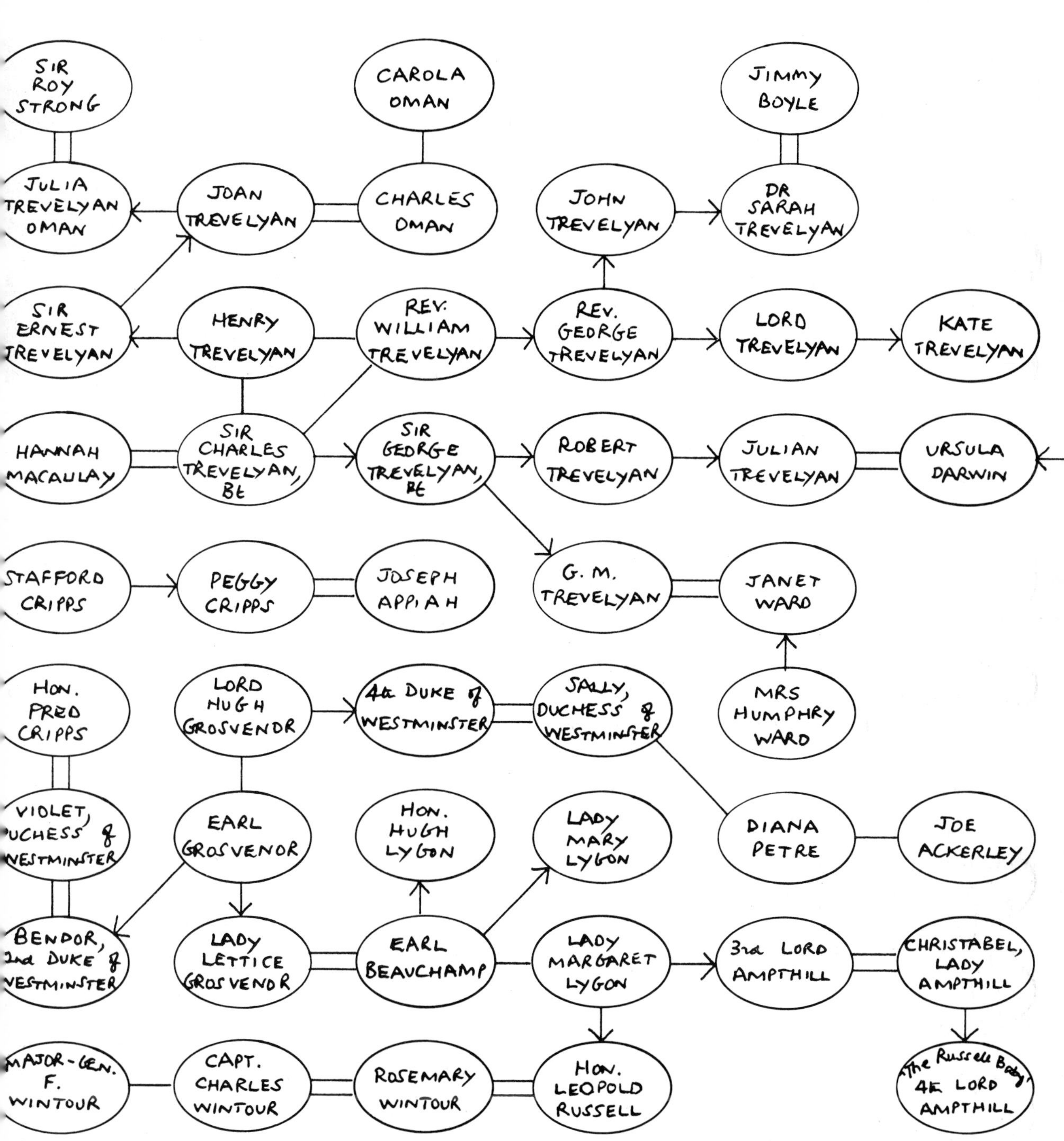
SIR ROY STRONG
CAROLA OMAN
JIMMY BOYLE
JULIA TREVELYAN OMAN
JOAN TREVELYAN
CHARLES OMAN
JOHN TREVELYAN
DR SARAH TREVELYAN
SIR ERNEST TREVELYAN
HENRY TREVELYAN
REV. WILLIAM TREVELYAN
REV. GEORGE TREVELYAN
LORD TREVELYAN
KATE TREVELYAN
HANNAH MACAULAY
SIR CHARLES TREVELYAN, Bt
SIR GEORGE TREVELYAN, Bt
ROBERT TREVELYAN
JULIAN TREVELYAN
URSULA DARWIN
STAFFORD CRIPPS
PEGGY CRIPPS
JOSEPH APPIAH
G. M. TREVELYAN
JANET WARD
HON. FRED CRIPPS
LORD HUGH GROSVENOR
4th DUKE of WESTMINSTER
SALLY, DUCHESS of WESTMINSTER
MRS HUMPHRY WARD
VIOLET, DUCHESS of WESTMINSTER
EARL GROSVENOR
HON. HUGH LYGON
LADY MARY LYGON
DIANA PETRE
JOE ACKERLEY
BENDOR, 2nd DUKE of WESTMINSTER
LADY LETTICE GROSVENOR
EARL BEAUCHAMP
LADY MARGARET LYGON
3rd LORD AMPTHILL
CHRISTABEL, LADY AMPTHILL
MAJOR-GEN. F. WINTOUR
CAPT. CHARLES WINTOUR
ROSEMARY WINTOUR
HON. LEOPOLD RUSSELL
'The Russell Baby', 4th LORD AMPTHILL

nd Duke of Westminster (d 1953) suffered from halitosis.

ady Mary Lygon (d 1982). Owner of a morose and ferocious ekinese named Grainger, who was made a member of the ord's Day Observance Society.

Joseph Appiah (b 1918). Ghana's permanent representative at the United Nations.

Joe Ackerley (d 1967) literary editor of the *Listener*, whose book about his dog Queenie shocked animal-lovers.

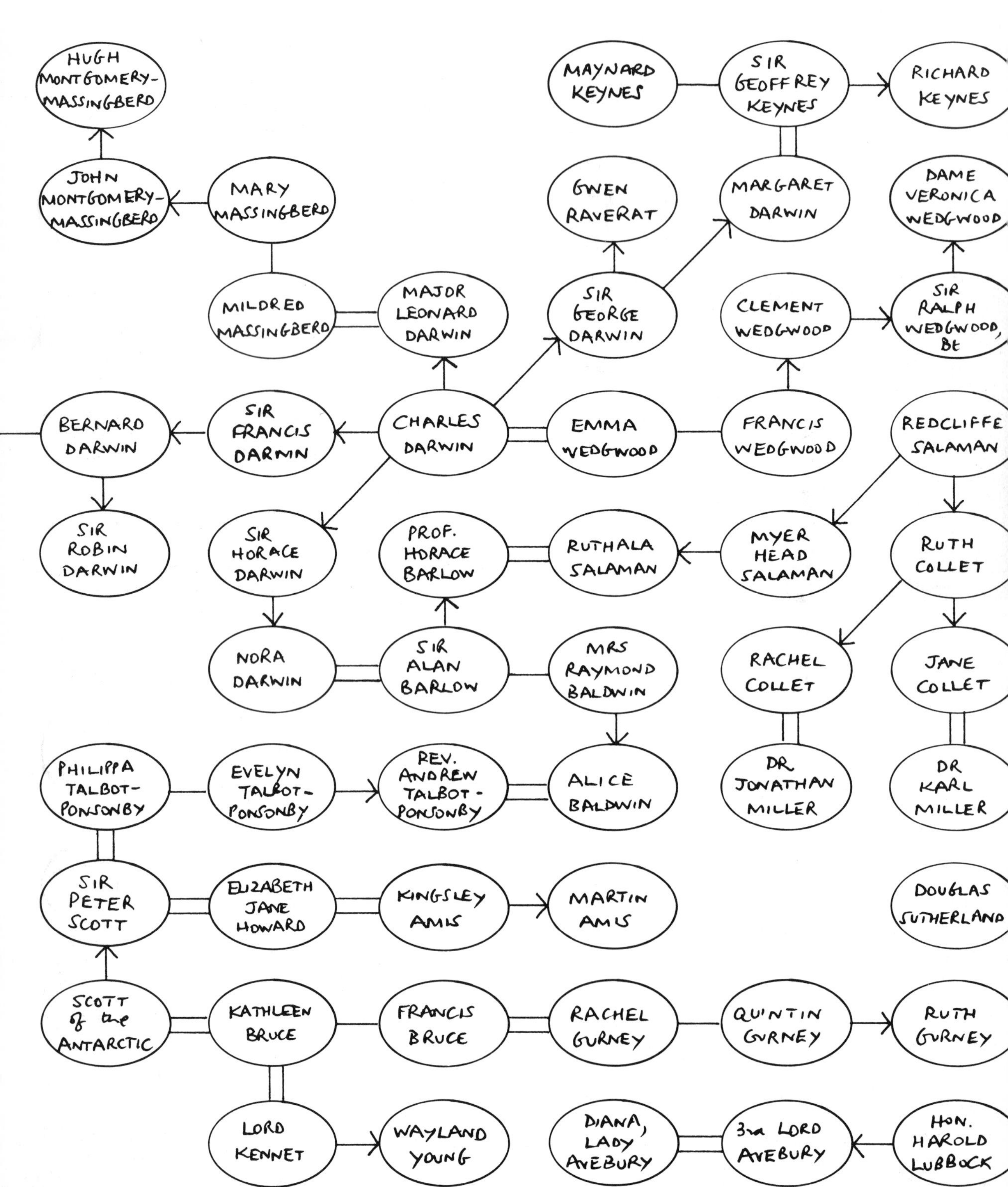
HUGH MONTGOMERY-MASSINGBERD
JOHN MONTGOMERY-MASSINGBERD
MARY MASSINGBERD
MILDRED MASSINGBERD
MAJOR LEONARD DARWIN
MAYNARD KEYNES
SIR GEOFFREY KEYNES
RICHARD KEYNES
GWEN RAVERAT
MARGARET DARWIN
DAME VERONICA WEDGWOOD
SIR GEORGE DARWIN
CLEMENT WEDGWOOD
SIR RALPH WEDGWOOD, Bt
BERNARD DARWIN
SIR FRANCIS DARWIN
CHARLES DARWIN
EMMA WEDGWOOD
FRANCIS WEDGWOOD
REDCLIFFE SALAMAN
SIR ROBIN DARWIN
SIR HORACE DARWIN
PROF. HORACE BARLOW
RUTHALA SALAMAN
MYER HEAD SALAMAN
RUTH COLLET
NORA DARWIN
SIR ALAN BARLOW
MRS RAYMOND BALDWIN
RACHEL COLLET
JANE COLLET
PHILIPPA TALBOT-PONSONBY
EVELYN TALBOT-PONSONBY
REV. ANDREW TALBOT-PONSONBY
ALICE BALDWIN
DR JONATHAN MILLER
DR KARL MILLER
SIR PETER SCOTT
ELIZABETH JANE HOWARD
KINGSLEY AMIS
MARTIN AMIS
DOUGLAS SUTHERLAND
SCOTT of the ANTARCTIC
KATHLEEN BRUCE
FRANCIS BRUCE
RACHEL GURNEY
QUINTIN GURNEY
RUTH GURNEY
LORD KENNET
WAYLAND YOUNG
DIANA, LADY AVEBURY
3rd LORD AVEBURY
HON. HAROLD LUBBOCK

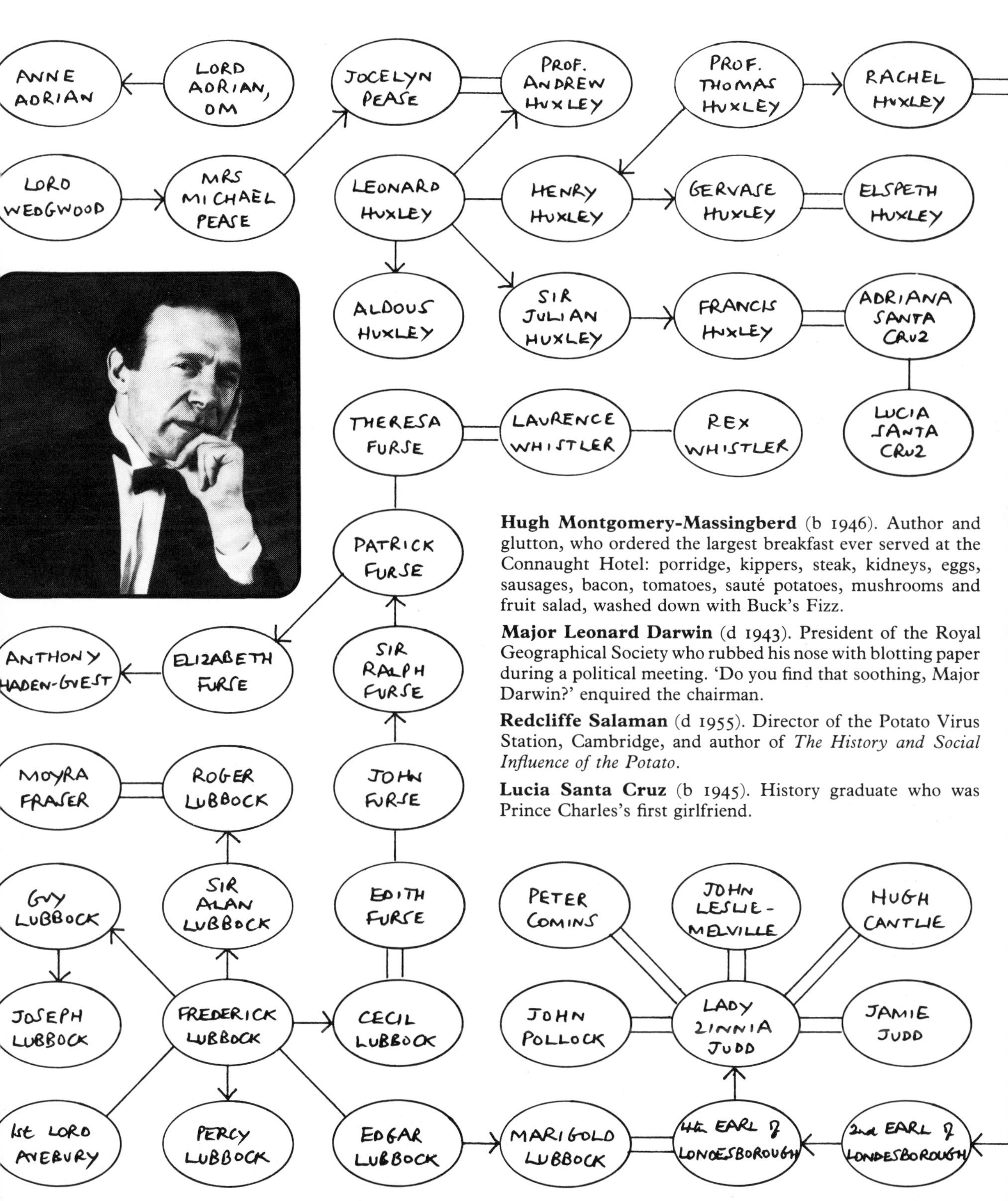
ANNE ADRIAN
LORD ADRIAN, OM
JOCELYN PEASE
PROF. ANDREW HUXLEY
PROF. THOMAS HUXLEY
RACHEL HUXLEY
LORD WEDGWOOD
MRS MICHAEL PEASE
LEONARD HUXLEY
HENRY HUXLEY
GERVASE HUXLEY
ELSPETH HUXLEY
ALDOUS HUXLEY
SIR JULIAN HUXLEY
FRANCIS HUXLEY
ADRIANA SANTA CRUZ
THERESA FURSE
LAURENCE WHISTLER
REX WHISTLER
LUCIA SANTA CRUZ
PATRICK FURSE
ANTHONY HADEN-GUEST
ELIZABETH FURSE
SIR RALPH FURSE
MOYRA FRASER
ROGER LUBBOCK
JOHN FURSE
GUY LUBBOCK
SIR ALAN LUBBOCK
EDITH FURSE
PETER COMINS
JOHN LESLIE-MELVILLE
HUGH CANTLIE
JOSEPH LUBBOCK
FREDERICK LUBBOCK
CECIL LUBBOCK
JOHN POLLOCK
LADY ZINNIA JUDD
JAMIE JUDD
1st LORD AVEBURY
PERCY LUBBOCK
EDGAR LUBBOCK
MARIGOLD LUBBOCK
4th EARL of LONDESBOROUGH
2nd EARL of LONDESBOROUGH

Hugh Montgomery-Massingberd (b 1946). Author and glutton, who ordered the largest breakfast ever served at the Connaught Hotel: porridge, kippers, steak, kidneys, eggs, sausages, bacon, tomatoes, sauté potatoes, mushrooms and fruit salad, washed down with Buck's Fizz.

Major Leonard Darwin (d 1943). President of the Royal Geographical Society who rubbed his nose with blotting paper during a political meeting. 'Do you find that soothing, Major Darwin?' enquired the chairman.

Redcliffe Salaman (d 1955). Director of the Potato Virus Station, Cambridge, and author of *The History and Social Influence of the Potato*.

Lucia Santa Cruz (b 1945). History graduate who was Prince Charles's first girlfriend.

Michael Deakin (b 1939). Director of programmes TV-am.
Sir George Sitwell (d 1943) invented a tiny revolver for killing wasps.

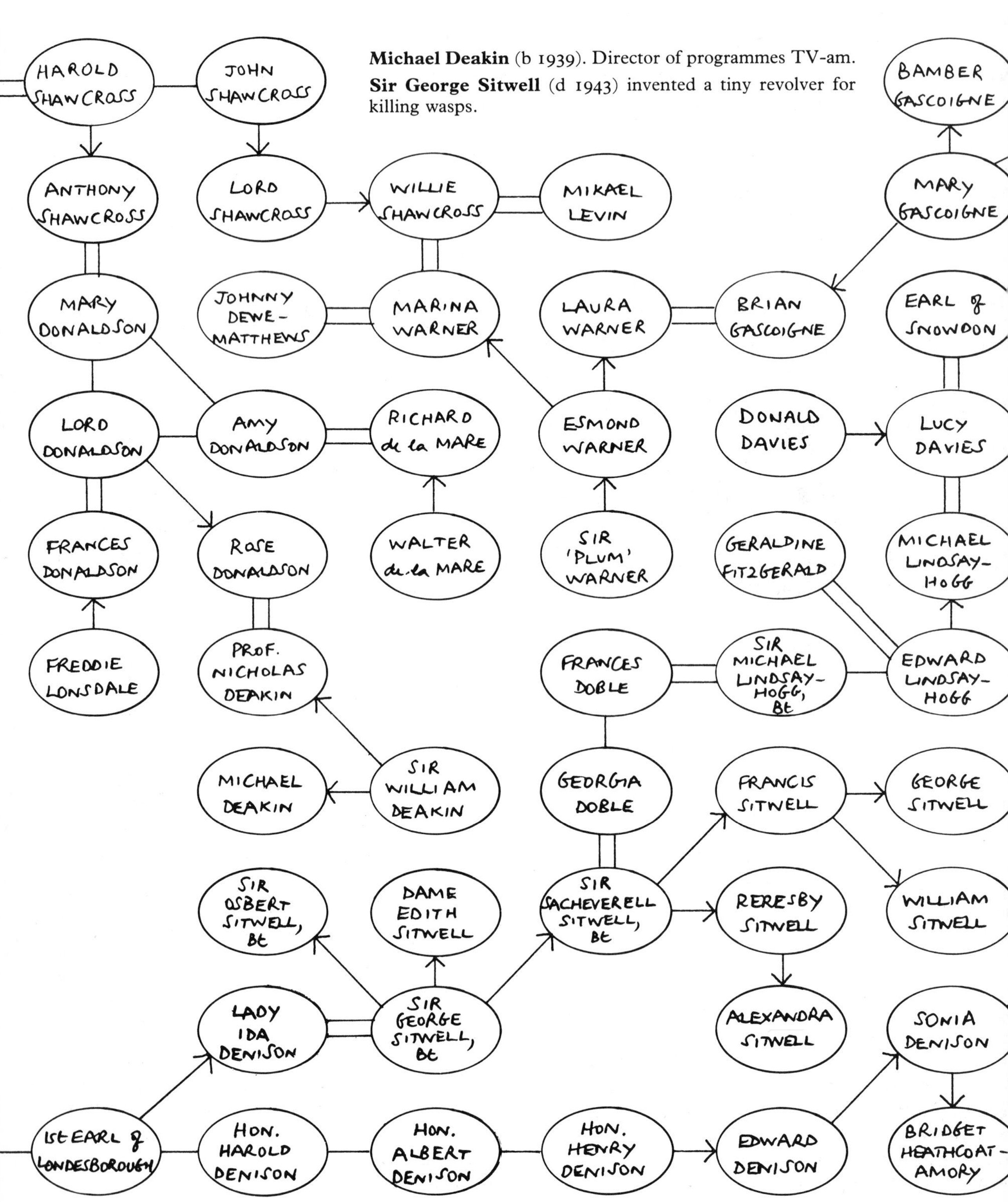

HAROLD SHAWCROSS
JOHN SHAWCROSS
BAMBER GASCOIGNE
ANTHONY SHAWCROSS
LORD SHAWCROSS
WILLIE SHAWCROSS
MIKAEL LEVIN
MARY GASCOIGNE
MARY DONALDSON
JOHNNY DEWE-MATTHEWS
MARINA WARNER
LAURA WARNER
BRIAN GASCOIGNE
EARL of SNOWDON
LORD DONALDSON
AMY DONALDSON
RICHARD de la MARE
ESMOND WARNER
DONALD DAVIES
LUCY DAVIES
FRANCES DONALDSON
ROSE DONALDSON
WALTER de la MARE
SIR 'PLUM' WARNER
GERALDINE FITZGERALD
MICHAEL LINDSAY-HOGG
FREDDIE LONSDALE
PROF. NICHOLAS DEAKIN
FRANCES DOBLE
SIR MICHAEL LINDSAY-HOGG, Bt
EDWARD LINDSAY-HOGG
MICHAEL DEAKIN
SIR WILLIAM DEAKIN
GEORGIA DOBLE
FRANCIS SITWELL
GEORGE SITWELL
SIR OSBERT SITWELL, Bt
DAME EDITH SITWELL
SIR SACHEVERELL SITWELL, Bt
RERESBY SITWELL
WILLIAM SITWELL
LADY IDA DENISON
SIR GEORGE SITWELL, Bt
ALEXANDRA SITWELL
SONIA DENISON
1st EARL of LONDESBOROUGH
HON. HAROLD DENISON
HON. ALBERT DENISON
HON. HENRY DENISON
EDWARD DENISON
BRIDGET HEATHCOAT-AMORY

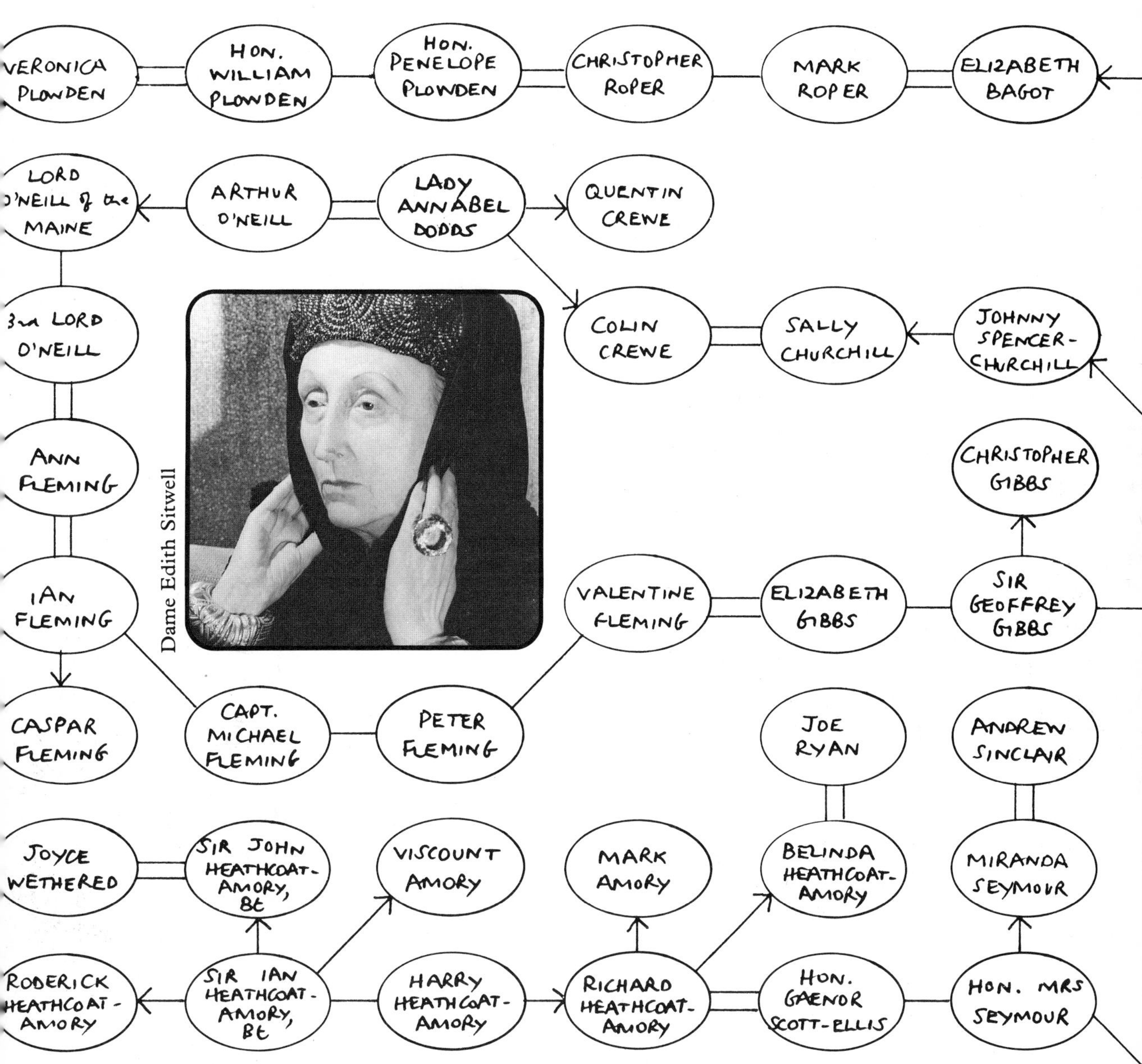
VERONICA PLOWDEN
HON. WILLIAM PLOWDEN
HON. PENELOPE PLOWDEN
CHRISTOPHER ROPER
MARK ROPER
ELIZABETH BAGOT
LORD O'NEILL of the MAINE
ARTHUR O'NEILL
LADY ANNABEL DODDS
QUENTIN CREWE
3rd LORD O'NEILL
COLIN CREWE
SALLY CHURCHILL
JOHNNY SPENCER-CHURCHILL
ANN FLEMING
CHRISTOPHER GIBBS
IAN FLEMING
VALENTINE FLEMING
ELIZABETH GIBBS
SIR GEOFFREY GIBBS
CASPAR FLEMING
CAPT. MICHAEL FLEMING
PETER FLEMING
JOE RYAN
ANDREW SINCLAIR
JOYCE WETHERED
SIR JOHN HEATHCOAT-AMORY, Bt
VISCOUNT AMORY
MARK AMORY
BELINDA HEATHCOAT-AMORY
MIRANDA SEYMOUR
RODERICK HEATHCOAT-AMORY
SIR IAN HEATHCOAT-AMORY, Bt
HARRY HEATHCOAT-AMORY
RICHARD HEATHCOAT-AMORY
HON. GAENOR SCOTT-ELLIS
HON. MRS SEYMOUR
Dame Edith Sitwell

ame Edith Sitwell (d 1964) once disguised herself as an rmchair and was carried upstairs to avoid an unwelcome isitor.

ichael Lindsay-Hogg (b 1940). Film director.

ridget Heathcoat-Amory (b 1952). Business and advertsing manager of the *Literary Review*.

yce Wethered (b 1901). Amateur golfer acknowledged as ne of the finest women players of all time.

Quentin Crewe's famous kipper tie is now preserved in the Victoria and Albert Museum.

Christopher Gibbs (b 1938). Antique dealer who told *Vogue* readers, 'Come in colours and the grey pox will never catch you. Heed only the poets and painters and you'll never go wrong.'

Donald Davies. Manufacturer of hand-loomed Irish tweeds and originator of the shirt dress.

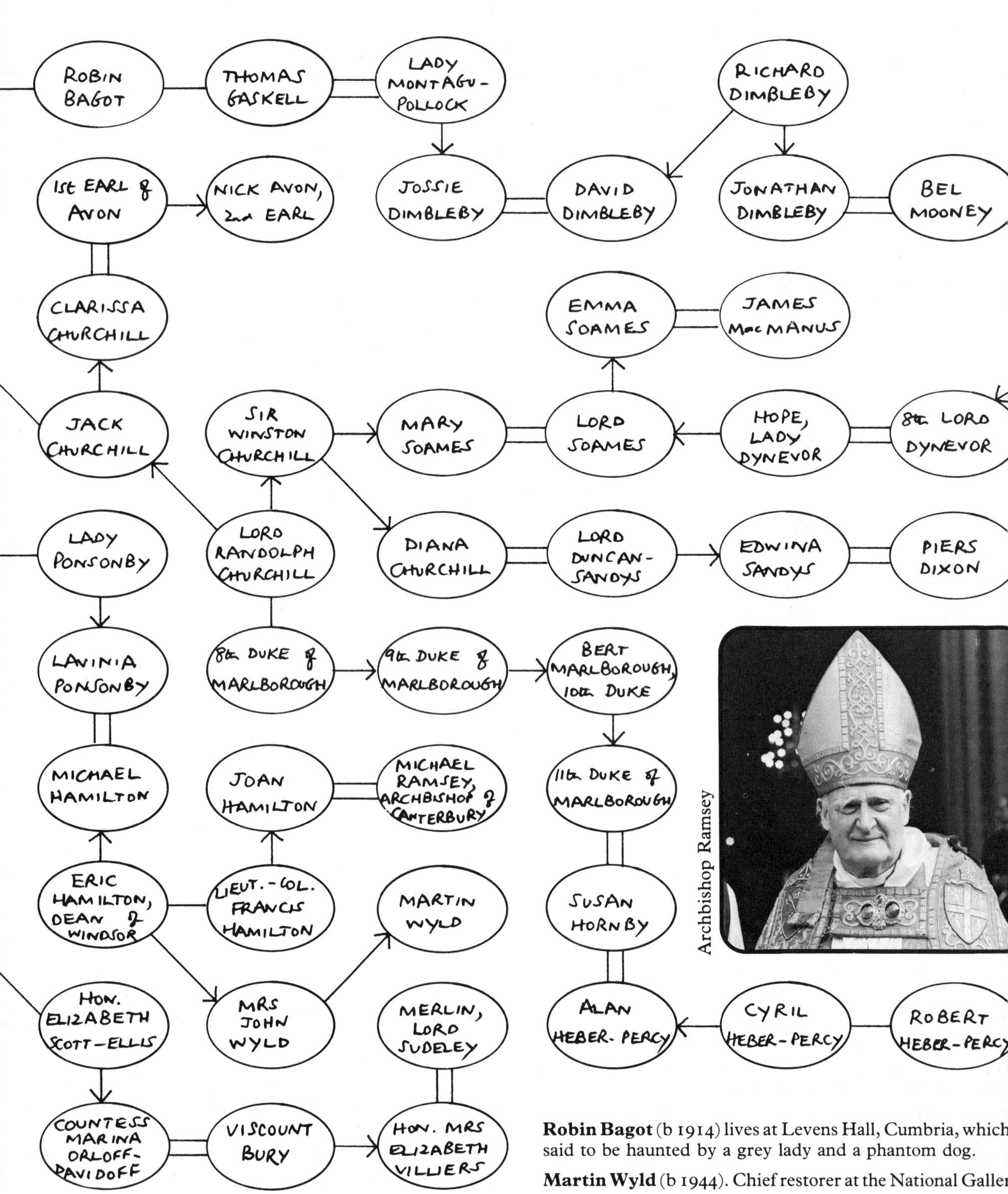
ROBIN BAGOT
THOMAS GASKELL
LADY MONTAGU-POLLOCK
RICHARD DIMBLEBY
1st EARL of AVON
NICK AVON, 2nd EARL
JOSSIE DIMBLEBY
DAVID DIMBLEBY
JONATHAN DIMBLEBY
BEL MOONEY
CLARISSA CHURCHILL
EMMA SOAMES
JAMES MacMANUS
JACK CHURCHILL
SIR WINSTON CHURCHILL
MARY SOAMES
LORD SOAMES
HOPE, LADY DYNEVOR
8th LORD DYNEVOR
LADY PONSONBY
LORD RANDOLPH CHURCHILL
DIANA CHURCHILL
LORD DUNCAN-SANDYS
EDWINA SANDYS
PIERS DIXON
LAVINIA PONSONBY
8th DUKE of MARLBOROUGH
9th DUKE of MARLBOROUGH
BERT MARLBOROUGH, 10th DUKE
MICHAEL HAMILTON
JOAN HAMILTON
MICHAEL RAMSEY, ARCHBISHOP of CANTERBURY
11th DUKE of MARLBOROUGH
ERIC HAMILTON, DEAN of WINDSOR
LIEUT.-COL. FRANCIS HAMILTON
MARTIN WYLD
SUSAN HORNBY
HON. ELIZABETH SCOTT-ELLIS
MRS JOHN WYLD
MERLIN, LORD SUDELEY
ALAN HEBER-PERCY
CYRIL HEBER-PERCY
ROBERT HEBER-PERCY
COUNTESS MARINA ORLOFF-DAVIDOFF
VISCOUNT BURY
HON. MRS ELIZABETH VILLIERS

Archbishop Ramsey

Robin Bagot (b 1914) lives at Levens Hall, Cumbria, which said to be haunted by a grey lady and a phantom dog.

Martin Wyld (b 1944). Chief restorer at the National Galler

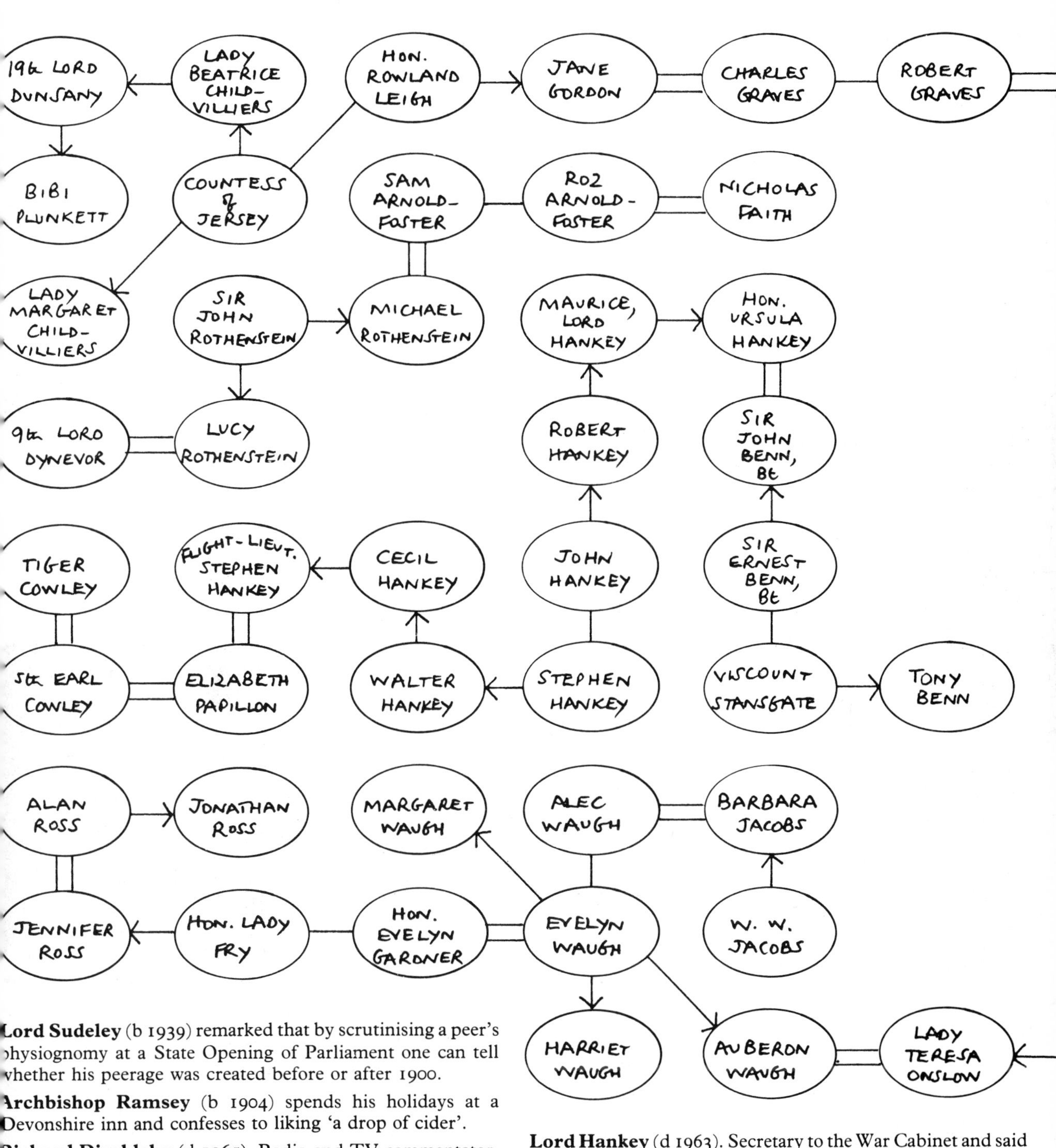
19th LORD DUNSANY
LADY BEATRICE CHILD-VILLIERS
HON. ROWLAND LEIGH
JANE GORDON
CHARLES GRAVES
ROBERT GRAVES
BIBI PLUNKETT
COUNTESS of JERSEY
SAM ARNOLD-FOSTER
ROZ ARNOLD-FOSTER
NICHOLAS FAITH
LADY MARGARET CHILD-VILLIERS
SIR JOHN ROTHENSTEIN
MICHAEL ROTHENSTEIN
MAURICE, LORD HANKEY
HON. URSULA HANKEY
9th LORD DYNEVOR
LUCY ROTHENSTEIN
ROBERT HANKEY
SIR JOHN BENN, Bt
TIGER COWLEY
FLIGHT-LIEUT. STEPHEN HANKEY
CECIL HANKEY
JOHN HANKEY
SIR ERNEST BENN, Bt
5th EARL COWLEY
ELIZABETH PAPILLON
WALTER HANKEY
STEPHEN HANKEY
VISCOUNT STANSGATE
TONY BENN
ALAN ROSS
JONATHAN ROSS
MARGARET WAUGH
ALEC WAUGH
BARBARA JACOBS
JENNIFER ROSS
HON. LADY FRY
HON. EVELYN GARDNER
EVELYN WAUGH
W. W. JACOBS
HARRIET WAUGH
AUBERON WAUGH
LADY TERESA ONSLOW

Lord Sudeley (b 1939) remarked that by scrutinising a peer's physiognomy at a State Opening of Parliament one can tell whether his peerage was created before or after 1900.

Archbishop Ramsey (b 1904) spends his holidays at a Devonshire inn and confesses to liking 'a drop of cider'.

Richard Dimbleby (d 1965). Radio and TV commentator. His first report for the BBC began with an inverted sentence and he was ordered by the Deputy Director General not to broadcast again.

Lord Hankey (d 1963). Secretary to the War Cabinet and said to have 'an unquenchable zest for power behind the scenes'.

Margaret Waugh (b 1942) sucked mercury through a pipette while at school at Ascot.

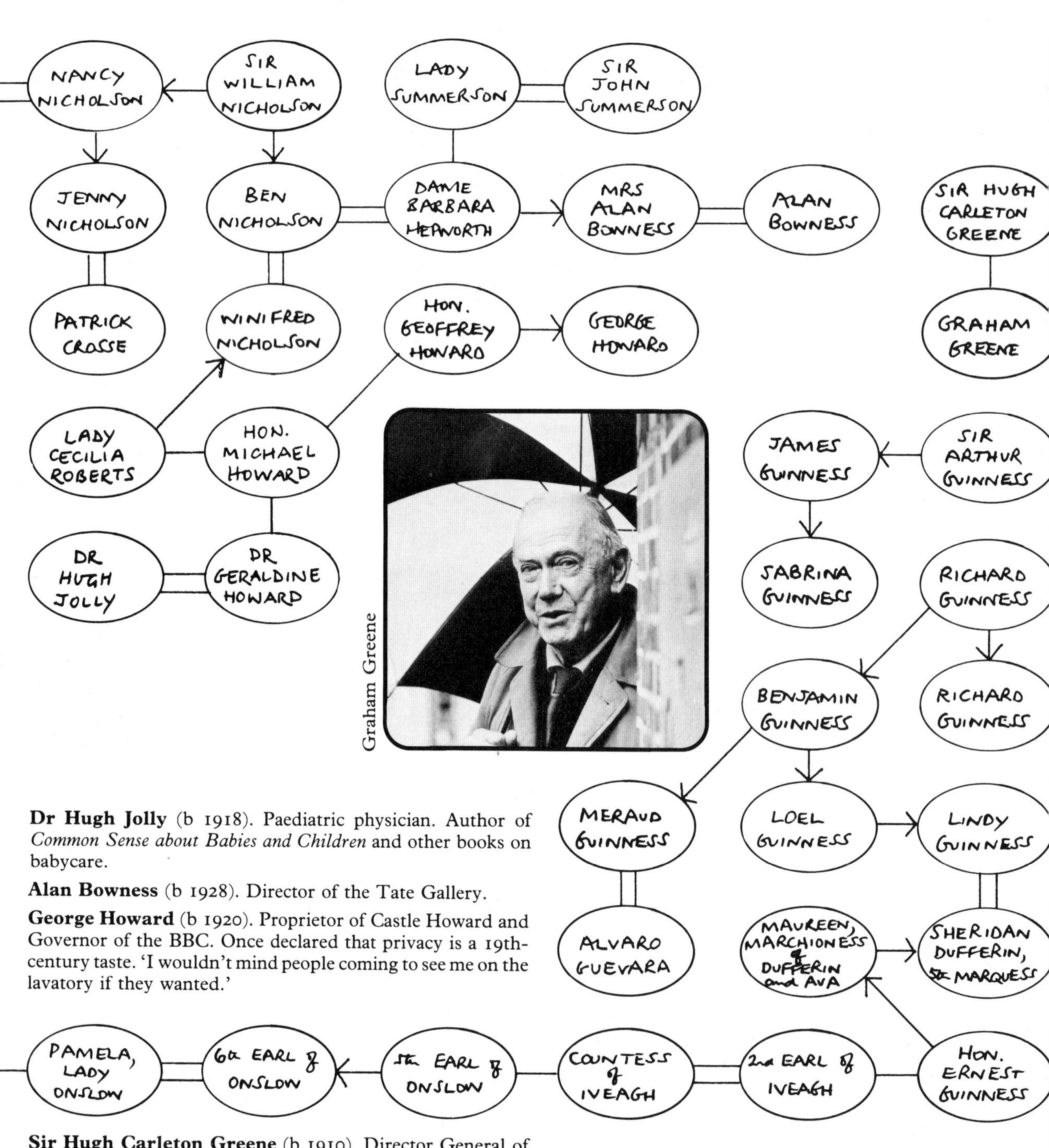
NANCY NICHOLSON
SIR WILLIAM NICHOLSON
LADY SUMMERSON
SIR JOHN SUMMERSON
JENNY NICHOLSON
BEN NICHOLSON
DAME BARBARA HEPWORTH
MRS ALAN BOWNESS
ALAN BOWNESS
SIR HUGH CARLETON GREENE
PATRICK CROSSE
WINIFRED NICHOLSON
HON. GEOFFREY HOWARD
GEORGE HOWARD
GRAHAM GREENE
LADY CECILIA ROBERTS
HON. MICHAEL HOWARD
JAMES GUINNESS
SIR ARTHUR GUINNESS
DR HUGH JOLLY
DR GERALDINE HOWARD
SABRINA GUINNESS
RICHARD GUINNESS
BENJAMIN GUINNESS
RICHARD GUINNESS
MERAUD GUINNESS
LOEL GUINNESS
LINDY GUINNESS
ALVARO GUEVARA
MAUREEN, MARCHIONESS of DUFFERIN and AVA
SHERIDAN DUFFERIN, 5th MARQUESS
PAMELA, LADY ONSLOW
6th EARL of ONSLOW
5th EARL of ONSLOW
COUNTESS of IVEAGH
2nd EARL of IVEAGH
HON. ERNEST GUINNESS

Graham Greene

Dr Hugh Jolly (b 1918). Paediatric physician. Author of *Common Sense about Babies and Children* and other books on babycare.

Alan Bowness (b 1928). Director of the Tate Gallery.

George Howard (b 1920). Proprietor of Castle Howard and Governor of the BBC. Once declared that privacy is a 19th-century taste. 'I wouldn't mind people coming to see me on the lavatory if they wanted.'

Sir Hugh Carleton Greene (b 1910). Director General of the BBC during the satire boom in the 1960s. The late night review *That Was The Week That Was* was partly inspired by the cabaret shows he had seen while working as a journalist in pre-war Berlin.

Tara Browne (d 1966). One of the inventors of Swingin London.

Nicky Haslam (b 1939) was profiled in the *Evening Standar* under the headline 'Who's a party boy, then?'

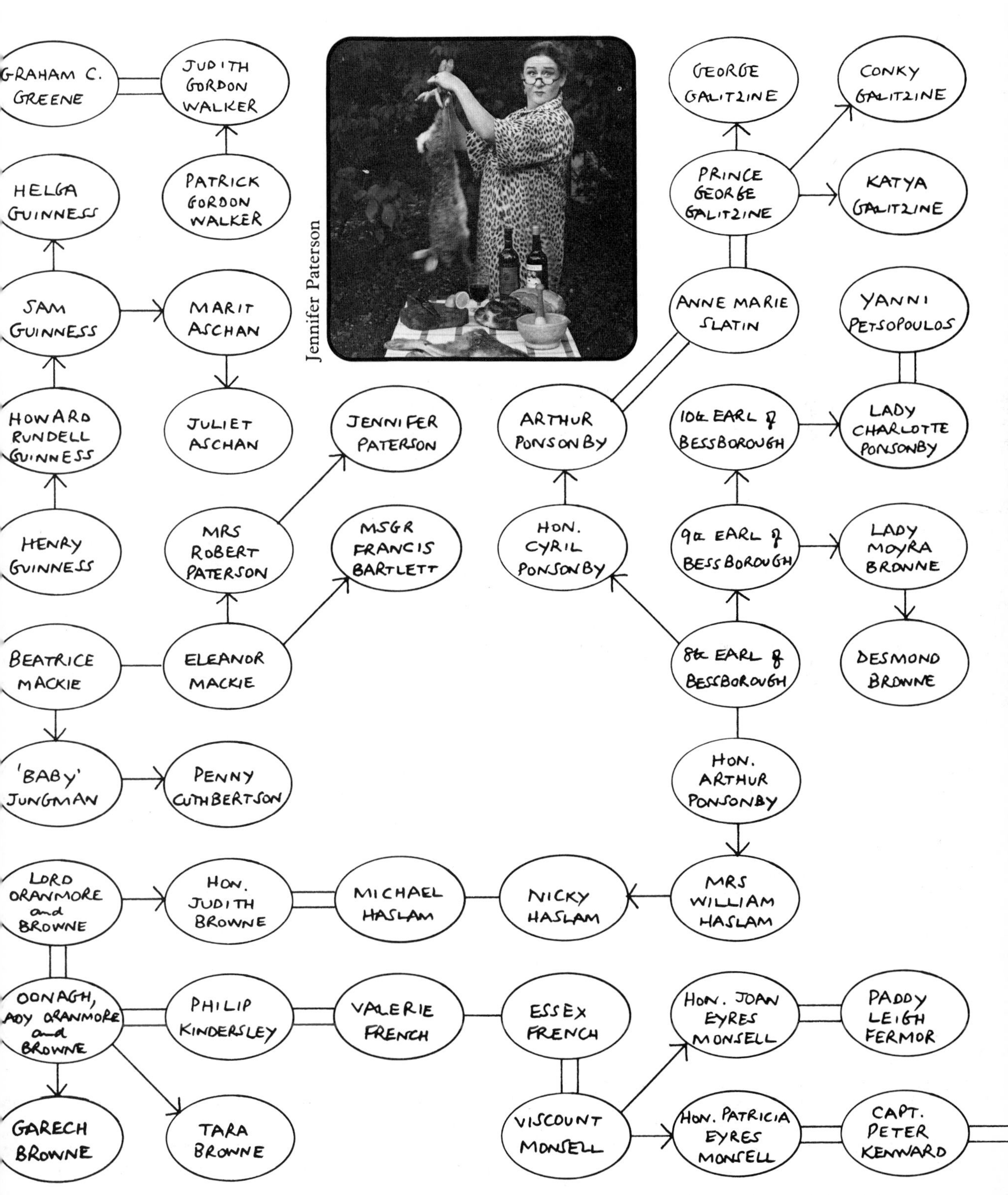
GRAHAM C. GREENE
JUDITH GORDON WALKER
GEORGE GALITZINE
CONKY GALITZINE
HELGA GUINNESS
PATRICK GORDON WALKER
PRINCE GEORGE GALITZINE
KATYA GALITZINE
SAM GUINNESS
MARIT ASCHAN
ANNE MARIE SLATIN
YANNI PETSOPOULOS
HOWARD RUNDELL GUINNESS
JULIET ASCHAN
JENNIFER PATERSON
ARTHUR PONSONBY
10th EARL of BESSBOROUGH
LADY CHARLOTTE PONSONBY
HENRY GUINNESS
MRS ROBERT PATERSON
MSGR FRANCIS BARTLETT
HON. CYRIL PONSONBY
9th EARL of BESSBOROUGH
LADY MOYRA BROWNE
BEATRICE MACKIE
ELEANOR MACKIE
8th EARL of BESSBOROUGH
DESMOND BROWNE
'BABY' JUNGMAN
PENNY CUTHBERTSON
HON. ARTHUR PONSONBY
LORD ORANMORE and BROWNE
HON. JUDITH BROWNE
MICHAEL HASLAM
NICKY HASLAM
MRS WILLIAM HASLAM
OONAGH, LADY ORANMORE and BROWNE
PHILIP KINDERSLEY
VALERIE FRENCH
ESSEX FRENCH
HON. JOAN EYRES MONSELL
PADDY LEIGH FERMOR
GARECH BROWNE
TARA BROWNE
VISCOUNT MONSELL
HON. PATRICIA EYRES MONSELL
CAPT. PETER KENWARD

Jennifer Paterson

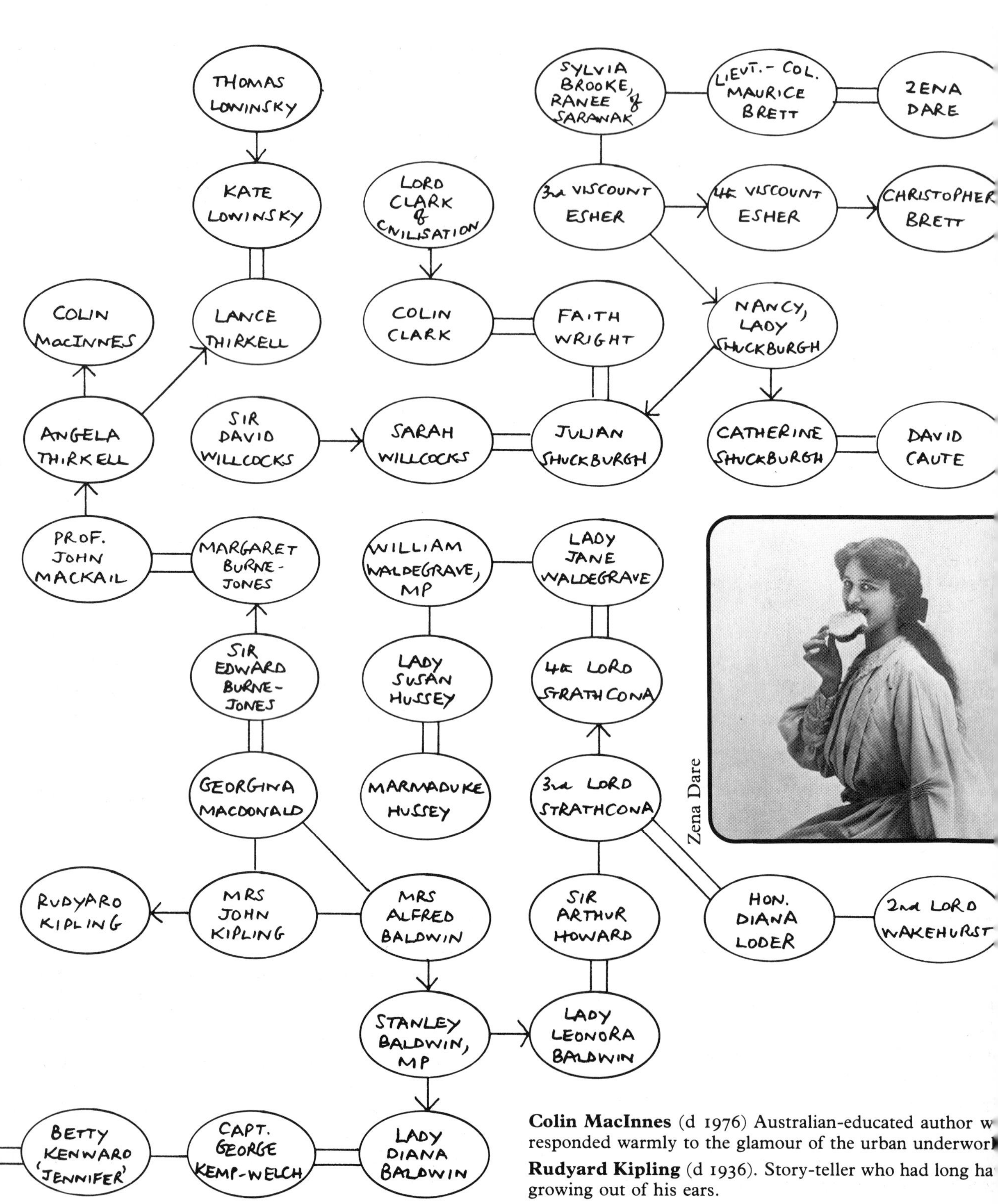
THOMAS LOWINSKY
KATE LOWINSKY
LANCE THIRKELL
COLIN MacINNES
ANGELA THIRKELL
PROF. JOHN MACKAIL
MARGARET BURNE-JONES
SIR EDWARD BURNE-JONES
GEORGINA MACDONALD
RUDYARD KIPLING
MRS JOHN KIPLING
MRS ALFRED BALDWIN
STANLEY BALDWIN, MP
LADY DIANA BALDWIN
CAPT. GEORGE KEMP-WELCH
BETTY KENWARD 'JENNIFER'
LORD CLARK of CIVILISATION
COLIN CLARK
SIR DAVID WILLCOCKS
SARAH WILLCOCKS
WILLIAM WALDEGRAVE, MP
LADY SUSAN HUSSEY
MARMADUKE HUSSEY
SYLVIA BROOKE, RANEE of SARAWAK
LIEUT.-COL. MAURICE BRETT
ZENA DARE
3rd VISCOUNT ESHER
4th VISCOUNT ESHER
CHRISTOPHER BRETT
FAITH WRIGHT
NANCY, LADY SHUCKBURGH
JULIAN SHUCKBURGH
CATHERINE SHUCKBURGH
DAVID CAUTE
LADY JANE WALDEGRAVE
4th LORD STRATHCONA
3rd LORD STRATHCONA
SIR ARTHUR HOWARD
LADY LEONORA BALDWIN
HON. DIANA LODER
2nd LORD WAKEHURST

Zena Dare

Colin MacInnes (d 1976) Australian-educated author w responded warmly to the glamour of the urban underworl

Rudyard Kipling (d 1936). Story-teller who had long ha growing out of his ears.

Zena Dare (d 1975). Former Gaiety girl of legendary beauty, popularised through the medium of cigarette cards. Ended her career with a record-breaking stint as Mrs Higgins in *My Fair Lady* at the Theatre Royal, Drury Lane.

David Caute (b 1936). Author and playwright.

George Orwell (d 1950). Old Etonian author and former police officer who never lost the confidence of his class and school. 'No biographer has yet penetrated the core of his privacy.'

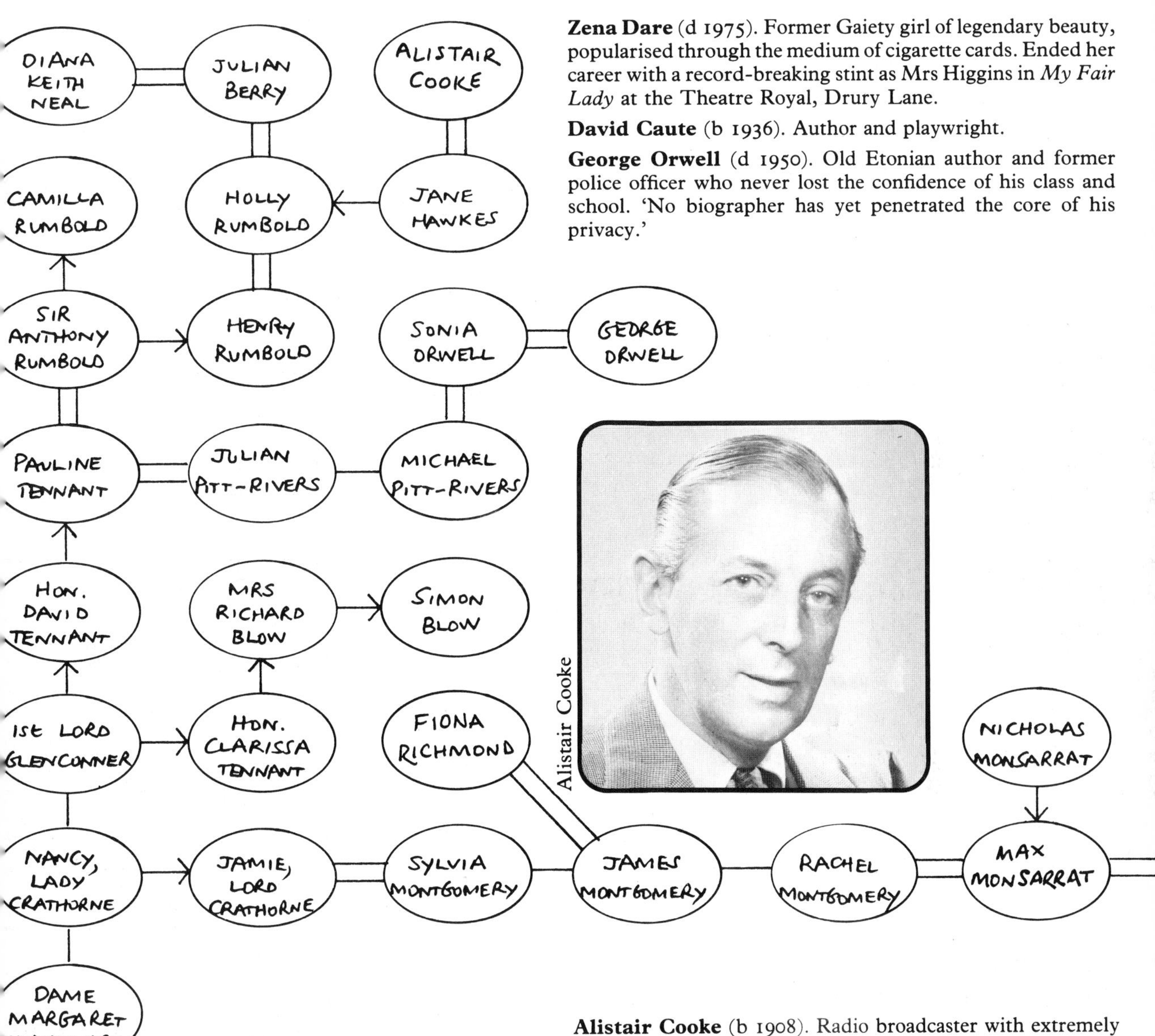
DIANA KEITH NEAL
JULIAN BERRY
ALISTAIR COOKE
CAMILLA RUMBOLD
HOLLY RUMBOLD
JANE HAWKES
SIR ANTHONY RUMBOLD
HENRY RUMBOLD
SONIA ORWELL
GEORGE ORWELL
PAULINE TENNANT
JULIAN PITT-RIVERS
MICHAEL PITT-RIVERS
HON. DAVID TENNANT
MRS RICHARD BLOW
SIMON BLOW
1st LORD GLENCONNER
HON. CLARISSA TENNANT
FIONA RICHMOND
NICHOLAS MONSARRAT
NANCY, LADY CRATHORNE
JAMIE, LORD CRATHORNE
SYLVIA MONTGOMERY
JAMES MONTGOMERY
RACHEL MONTGOMERY
MAX MONSARRAT
DAME MARGARET WAKEHURST
Alistair Cooke

Betty Kenward writes 'Jennifer's Diary' in *Harpers & Queen*.

Stanley Baldwin (d 1947). Conservative Prime Minister who looked like a stalwart old oak.

Sylvia Brooke, the last Ranee of Sarawak (d 1971). As a child, she went to dancing classes at Windsor Castle and in later life recalled Queen Victoria as 'a very aggressive, terrifying old woman . . . She sat in the middle of the dance floor with a big stick, thumping on the ground, screaming at us'.

Alistair Cooke (b 1908). Radio broadcaster with extremely relaxed anecdotal style.

Nicholas Monsarrat (d 1979). As a young man, he slept on the Embankment and in St Martin's crypt. His book *The Cruel Sea,* based on his own experiences in the Battle of the Atlantic later sold over ten million copies.

Lord Clark (d 1983). Former Director of the National Gallery and presenter of the TV series *Civilisation.*

Fiona Richmond starred in *Pyjama Tops* and other Whitehall Theatre productions.

William Waldegrave MP (b 1946) has been heralded as a possible future prime minister.

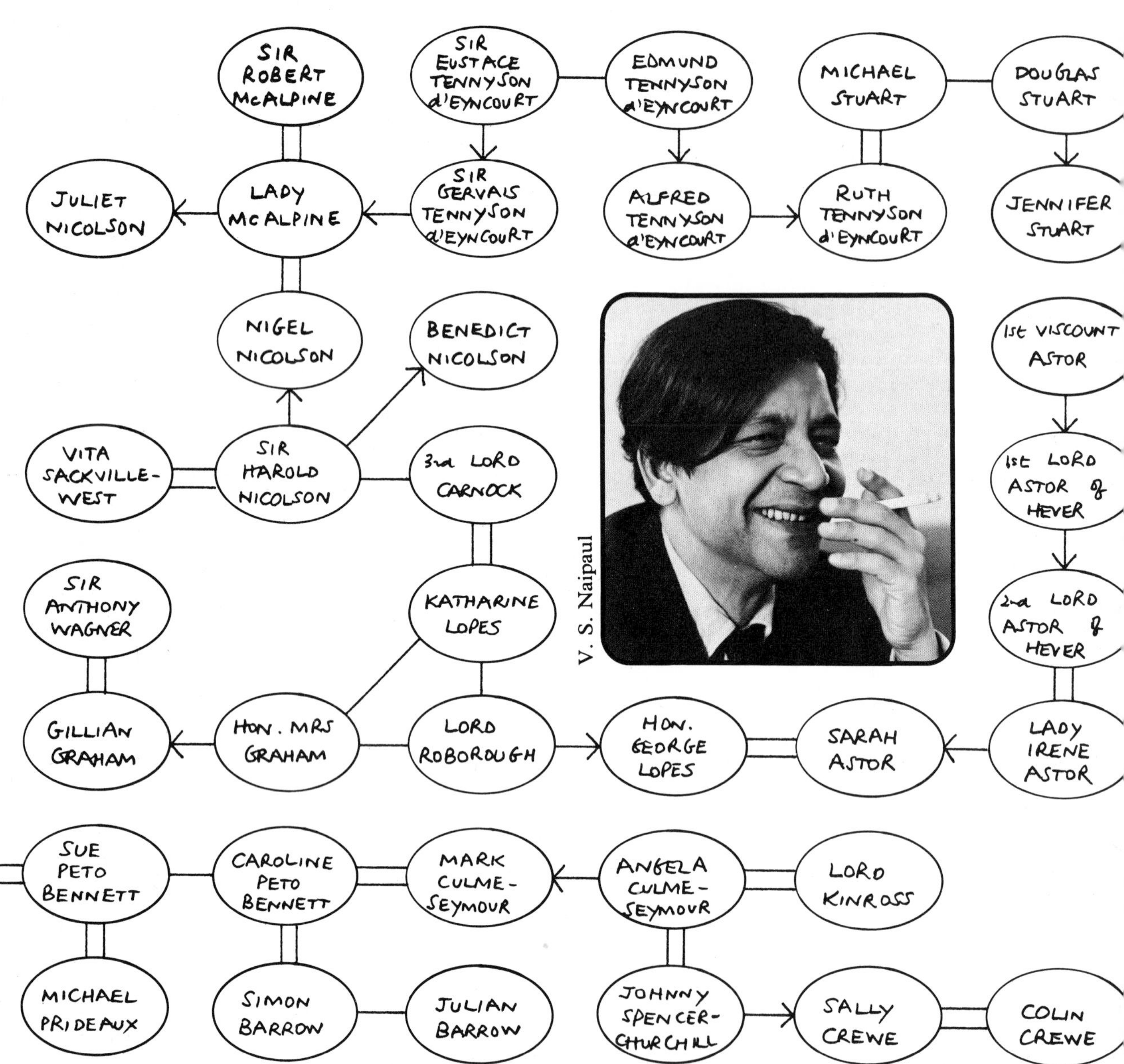
SIR ROBERT McALPINE
SIR EUSTACE TENNYSON d'EYNCOURT
EDMUND TENNYSON d'EYNCOURT
MICHAEL STUART
DOUGLAS STUART
JULIET NICOLSON
LADY McALPINE
SIR GERVAIS TENNYSON d'EYNCOURT
ALFRED TENNYSON d'EYNCOURT
RUTH TENNYSON d'EYNCOURT
JENNIFER STUART
NIGEL NICOLSON
BENEDICT NICOLSON
1st VISCOUNT ASTOR
VITA SACKVILLE-WEST
SIR HAROLD NICOLSON
3rd LORD CARNOCK
1st LORD ASTOR of HEVER
SIR ANTHONY WAGNER
KATHARINE LOPES
2nd LORD ASTOR of HEVER
GILLIAN GRAHAM
HON. MRS GRAHAM
LORD ROBOROUGH
HON. GEORGE LOPES
SARAH ASTOR
LADY IRENE ASTOR
SUE PETO BENNETT
CAROLINE PETO BENNETT
MARK CULME-SEYMOUR
ANGELA CULME-SEYMOUR
LORD KINROSS
MICHAEL PRIDEAUX
SIMON BARROW
JULIAN BARROW
JOHNNY SPENCER-CHURCHILL
SALLY CREWE
COLIN CREWE

V. S. Naipaul

Juliet Nicolson (b 1954). Publicity director, Chatto & Windus.

Sir Anthony Wagner (b 1908). Former Garter King of Arms and author of *English Genealogy*.

Ben Nicolson (d 1978). Writer and editor of the *Burlington Magazine* who regretted not being more dissolute in his youth.

Douglas Stuart (b 1918). BBC radio interviewer and presenter of *The World Tonight*.

Julian Barrow (b 1939). Portrait and landscape painter.

V. S. Naipaul (b 1932). Novelist, historian, social comme tator and autobiographer.

Sir Roderick Jones (d 1962). Chairman of Reuters.

1st Lord Astor of Hever (d 1971) bought *The Times* on t death of Lord Northcliffe and explained that its functi would be 'to lean as far as possible in support of the gover ment of the day'.

2nd Lord Astor of Hever (b 1918) sold *The Times* to Can dian Roy Thomson.

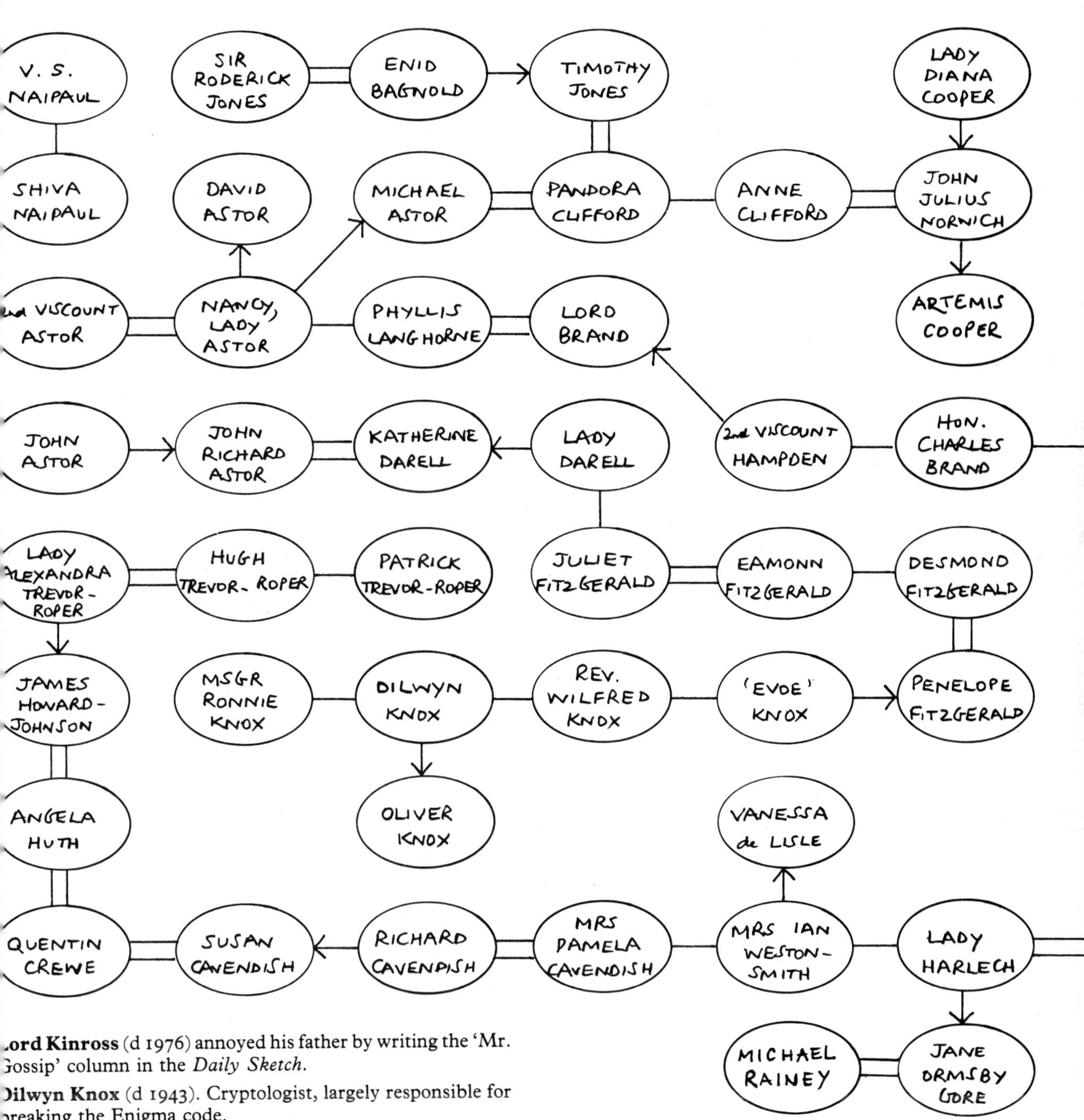
V. S. NAIPAUL
SIR RODERICK JONES
ENID BAGNOLD
TIMOTHY JONES
LADY DIANA COOPER
SHIVA NAIPAUL
DAVID ASTOR
MICHAEL ASTOR
PANDORA CLIFFORD
ANNE CLIFFORD
JOHN JULIUS NORWICH
2nd VISCOUNT ASTOR
NANCY, LADY ASTOR
PHYLLIS LANGHORNE
LORD BRAND
ARTEMIS COOPER
JOHN ASTOR
JOHN RICHARD ASTOR
KATHERINE DARELL
LADY DARELL
2nd VISCOUNT HAMPDEN
HON. CHARLES BRAND
LADY ALEXANDRA TREVOR-ROPER
HUGH TREVOR-ROPER
PATRICK TREVOR-ROPER
JULIET FITZGERALD
EAMONN FITZGERALD
DESMOND FITZGERALD
JAMES HOWARD-JOHNSON
MSGR RONNIE KNOX
DILWYN KNOX
REV. WILFRED KNOX
'EVOE' KNOX
PENELOPE FITZGERALD
ANGELA HUTH
OLIVER KNOX
VANESSA de LISLE
QUENTIN CREWE
SUSAN CAVENDISH
RICHARD CAVENDISH
MRS PAMELA CAVENDISH
MRS IAN WESTON-SMITH
LADY HARLECH
MICHAEL RAINEY
JANE ORMSBY GORE

Lord Kinross (d 1976) annoyed his father by writing the 'Mr. Gossip' column in the *Daily Sketch*.

Dilwyn Knox (d 1943). Cryptologist, largely responsible for breaking the Enigma code.

Enid Bagnold (d 1981) lost her virginity to Frank Harris in an upper room at the Café Royal.

Michael Rainey was one of the inventors of Swinging London and owner of fashionable Chelsea outfitters 'Hung on You' which dressed the Rolling Stones.

Vanessa de Lisle (b 1947). Fashion editor of *Harpers & Queen*.

Michael Astor (b 1916). Author of a book about his family, *Tribal Feeling*, which was hailed as a minor masterpiece.

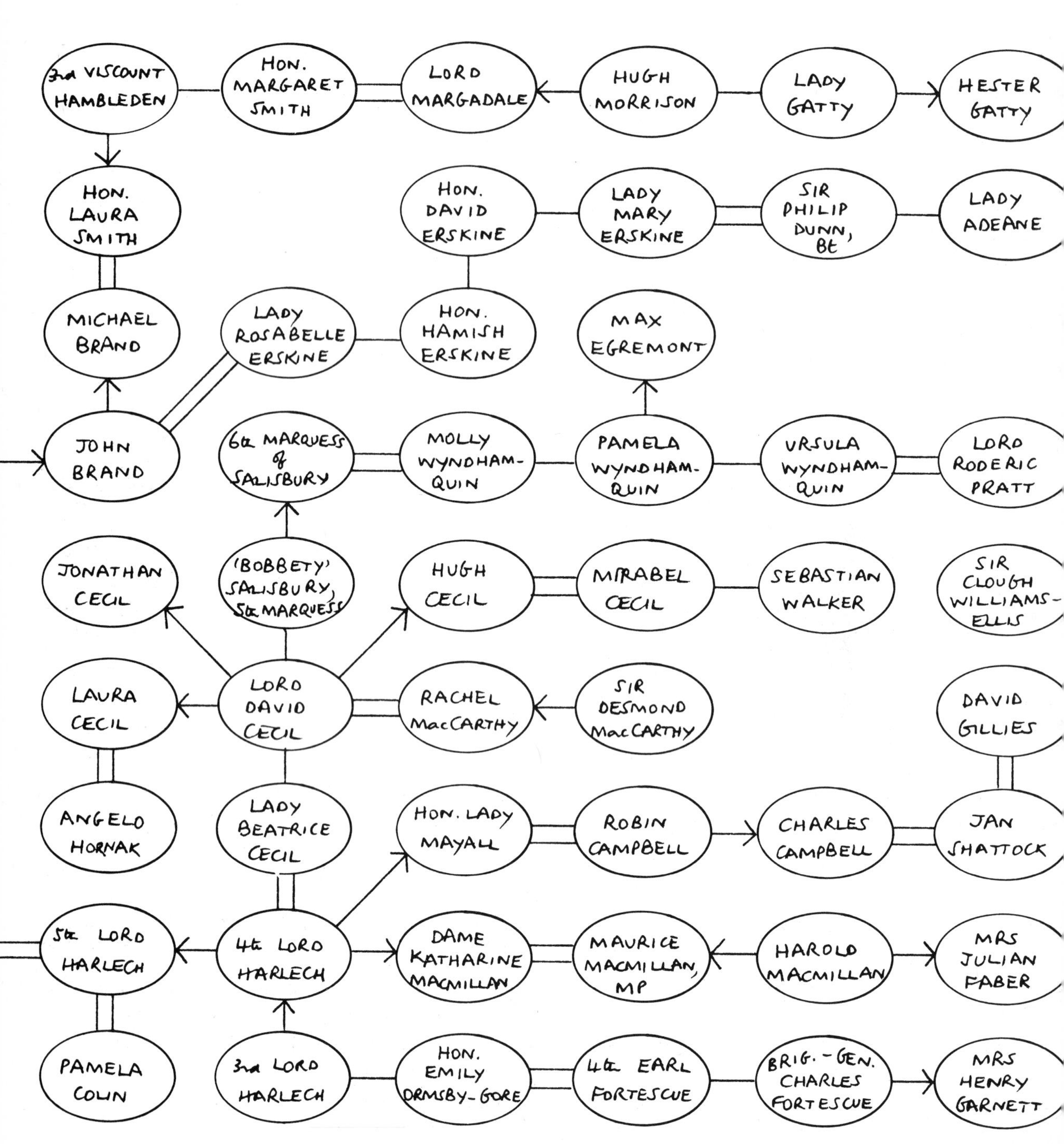
3rd VISCOUNT HAMBLEDEN
HON. MARGARET SMITH
LORD MARGADALE
HUGH MORRISON
LADY GATTY
HESTER GATTY
HON. LAURA SMITH
HON. DAVID ERSKINE
LADY MARY ERSKINE
SIR PHILIP DUNN, Bt
LADY ADEANE
MICHAEL BRAND
LADY ROSABELLE ERSKINE
HON. HAMISH ERSKINE
MAX EGREMONT
JOHN BRAND
6th MARQUESS of SALISBURY
MOLLY WYNDHAM-QUIN
PAMELA WYNDHAM-QUIN
URSULA WYNDHAM-QUIN
LORD RODERIC PRATT
JONATHAN CECIL
('BOBBETY') SALISBURY, 5th MARQUESS
HUGH CECIL
MIRABEL CECIL
SEBASTIAN WALKER
SIR CLOUGH WILLIAMS-ELLIS
LAURA CECIL
LORD DAVID CECIL
RACHEL MacCARTHY
SIR DESMOND MacCARTHY
DAVID GILLIES
ANGELO HORNAK
LADY BEATRICE CECIL
HON. LADY MAYALL
ROBIN CAMPBELL
CHARLES CAMPBELL
JAN SHATTOCK
5th LORD HARLECH
4th LORD HARLECH
DAME KATHARINE MACMILLAN
MAURICE MACMILLAN, MP
HAROLD MACMILLAN
MRS JULIAN FABER
PAMELA COLIN
3rd LORD HARLECH
HON. EMILY ORMSBY-GORE
4th EARL FORTESCUE
BRIG.-GEN. CHARLES FORTESCUE
MRS HENRY GARNETT

3rd Visc. Hambleden (d 1948). A former chairman of W. H. Smith & Son.

Laura Cecil (b 1947). Literary agent specialising in children's books.

The Wyndham-Quin Sisters were photographed by Ce[illegible] Beaton as 'The Three Graces'.

Sebastian Walker publishes picture books for babies a[illegible] toddlers.

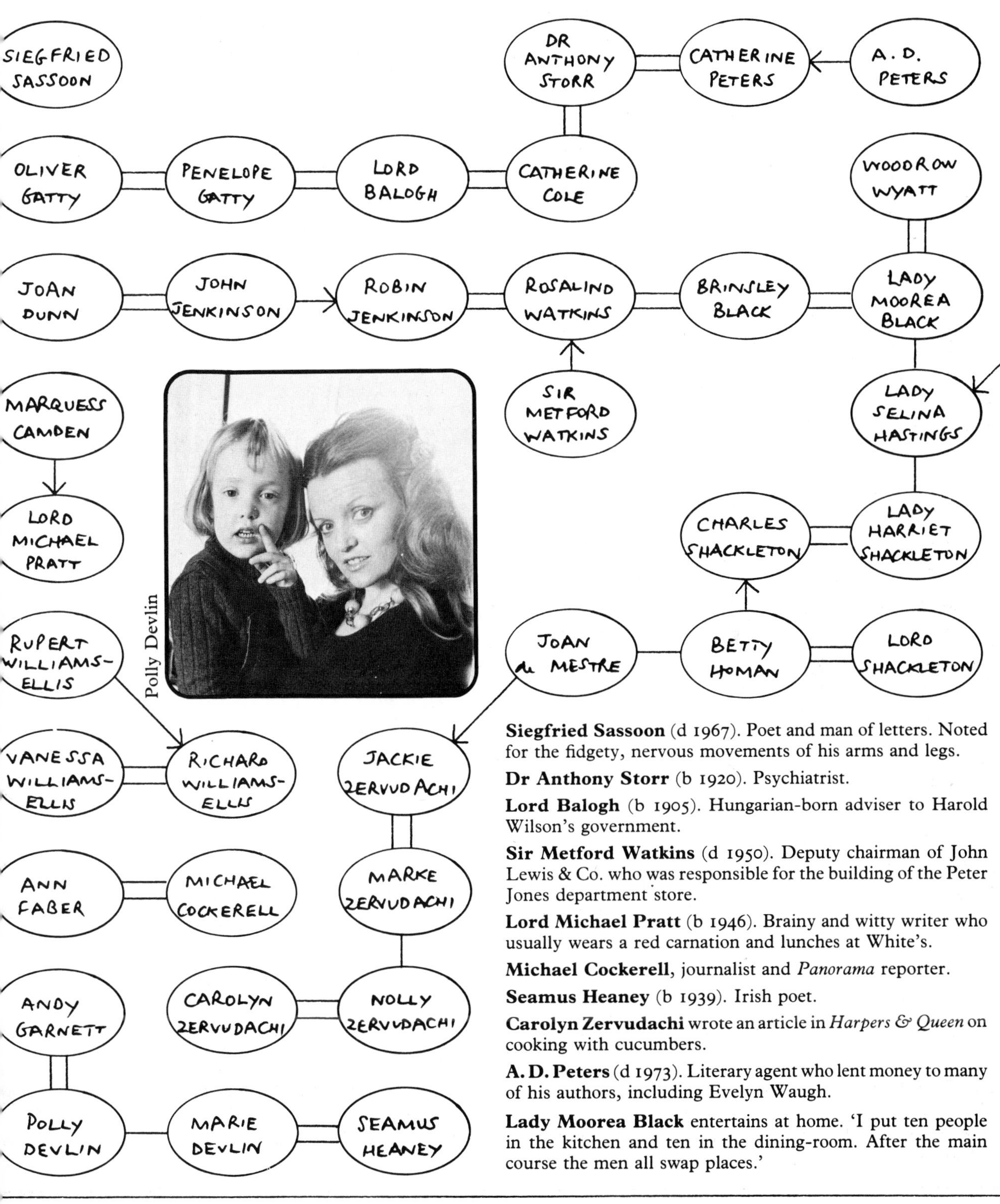
SIEGFRIED SASSOON
DR ANTHONY STORR
CATHERINE PETERS
A. D. PETERS
OLIVER GATTY
PENELOPE GATTY
LORD BALOGH
CATHERINE COLE
WOODROW WYATT
JOAN DUNN
JOHN JENKINSON
ROBIN JENKINSON
ROSALIND WATKINS
BRINSLEY BLACK
LADY MOOREA BLACK
SIR METFORD WATKINS
MARQUESS CAMDEN
LADY SELINA HASTINGS
LORD MICHAEL PRATT
CHARLES SHACKLETON
LADY HARRIET SHACKLETON
RUPERT WILLIAMS-ELLIS
JOAN de MESTRE
BETTY HOMAN
LORD SHACKLETON
VANESSA WILLIAMS-ELLIS
RICHARD WILLIAMS-ELLIS
JACKIE ZERVUDACHI
ANN FABER
MICHAEL COCKERELL
MARKE ZERVUDACHI
ANDY GARNETT
CAROLYN ZERVUDACHI
NOLLY ZERVUDACHI
POLLY DEVLIN
MARIE DEVLIN
SEAMUS HEANEY

Polly Devlin

Siegfried Sassoon (d 1967). Poet and man of letters. Noted for the fidgety, nervous movements of his arms and legs.

Dr Anthony Storr (b 1920). Psychiatrist.

Lord Balogh (b 1905). Hungarian-born adviser to Harold Wilson's government.

Sir Metford Watkins (d 1950). Deputy chairman of John Lewis & Co. who was responsible for the building of the Peter Jones department store.

Lord Michael Pratt (b 1946). Brainy and witty writer who usually wears a red carnation and lunches at White's.

Michael Cockerell, journalist and *Panorama* reporter.

Seamus Heaney (b 1939). Irish poet.

Carolyn Zervudachi wrote an article in *Harpers & Queen* on cooking with cucumbers.

A. D. Peters (d 1973). Literary agent who lent money to many of his authors, including Evelyn Waugh.

Lady Moorea Black entertains at home. 'I put ten people in the kitchen and ten in the dining-room. After the main course the men all swap places.'

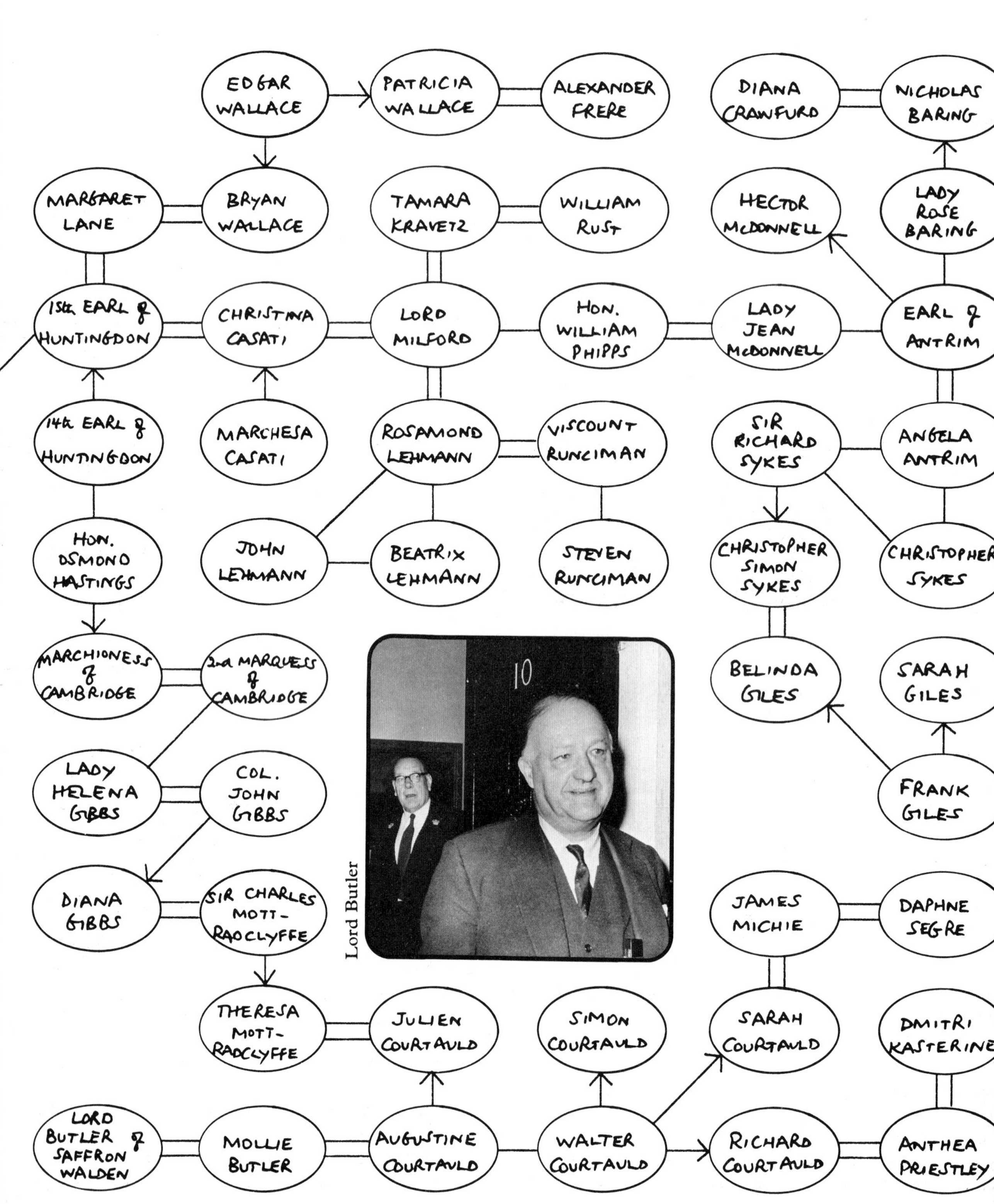
EDGAR WALLACE
PATRICIA WALLACE
ALEXANDER FRERE
DIANA CRAWFURD
NICHOLAS BARING
MARGARET LANE
BRYAN WALLACE
TAMARA KRAVETZ
WILLIAM RUST
HECTOR McDONNELL
LADY ROSE BARING
15th EARL of HUNTINGDON
CHRISTINA CASATI
LORD MILFORD
HON. WILLIAM PHIPPS
LADY JEAN McDONNELL
EARL of ANTRIM
14th EARL of HUNTINGDON
MARCHESA CASATI
ROSAMOND LEHMANN
VISCOUNT RUNCIMAN
SIR RICHARD SYKES
ANGELA ANTRIM
HON. OSMOND HASTINGS
JOHN LEHMANN
BEATRIX LEHMANN
STEVEN RUNCIMAN
CHRISTOPHER SIMON SYKES
CHRISTOPHER SYKES
MARCHIONESS of CAMBRIDGE
2nd MARQUESS of CAMBRIDGE
10
BELINDA GILES
SARAH GILES
LADY HELENA GIBBS
COL. JOHN GIBBS
FRANK GILES
DIANA GIBBS
SIR CHARLES MOTT-RADCLYFFE
JAMES MICHIE
DAPHNE SEGRE
THERESA MOTT-RADCLYFFE
JULIEN COURTAULD
SIMON COURTAULD
SARAH COURTAULD
DMITRI KASTERINE
LORD BUTLER of SAFFRON WALDEN
MOLLIE BUTLER
AUGUSTINE COURTAULD
WALTER COURTAULD
RICHARD COURTAULD
ANTHEA PRIESTLEY

Lord Butler

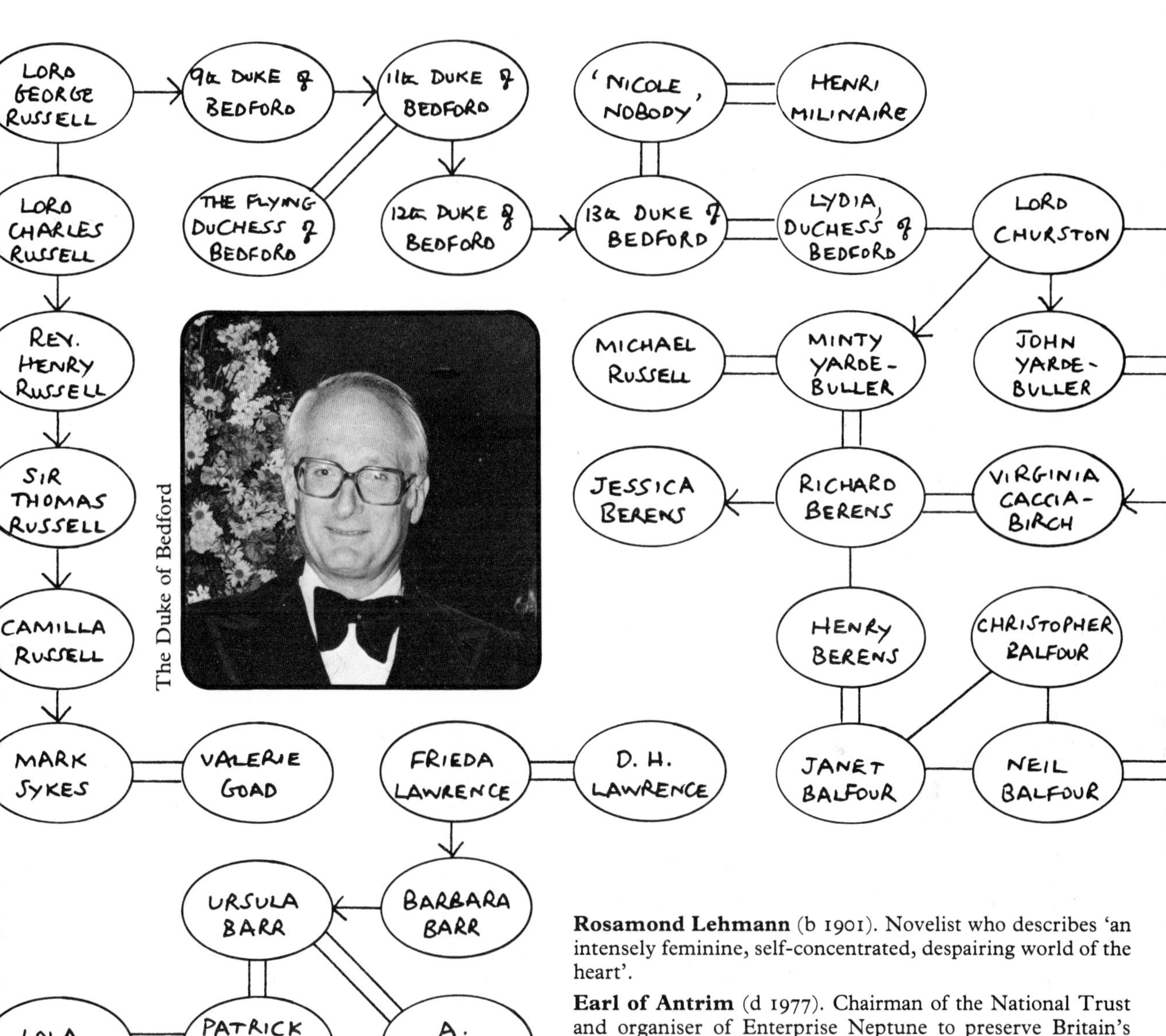
LORD GEORGE RUSSELL
9th DUKE OF BEDFORD
11th DUKE OF BEDFORD
'NICOLE NOBODY'
HENRI MILINAIRE
LORD CHARLES RUSSELL
THE FLYING DUCHESS OF BEDFORD
12th DUKE OF BEDFORD
13th DUKE OF BEDFORD
LYDIA, DUCHESS OF BEDFORD
LORD CHURSTON
REV. HENRY RUSSELL
MICHAEL RUSSELL
MINTY YARDE-BULLER
JOHN YARDE-BULLER
SIR THOMAS RUSSELL
JESSICA BERENS
RICHARD BERENS
VIRGINIA CACCIA-BIRCH
CAMILLA RUSSELL
HENRY BERENS
CHRISTOPHER BALFOUR
MARK SYKES
VALERIE GOAD
FRIEDA LAWRENCE
D. H. LAWRENCE
JANET BALFOUR
NEIL BALFOUR
URSULA BARR
BARBARA BARR
LOLA SEGRE
PATRICK BRASIER-CREAGH
A. ALVAREZ

The Duke of Bedford

Rosamond Lehmann (b 1901). Novelist who describes 'an intensely feminine, self-concentrated, despairing world of the heart'.

Earl of Antrim (d 1977). Chairman of the National Trust and organiser of Enterprise Neptune to preserve Britain's coastline.

9th Duke of Bedford (d 1891) committed suicide in his house in Eaton Square.

12th Duke of Bedford (d 1953). Conscientious objector and active Quaker, who was happiest scrubbing floors or washing up in YMCA canteens.

Michael Russell operates a one man publishing business from his Wiltshire dining-room table.

A. Alvarez (b 1929). Rock-climbing poetry editor and author of a book on suicide.

Richard Berens (b 1933) wrote the William Hickey column.

Jessica Berens (b 1959) is a journalist on the *Standard*.

dgar Wallace (d 1932). Author of 170 books and 17 plays ho died leaving debts of £170,000.

lexander Frere (b 1896). Former chairman of Heinemann td.

ord Milford (b 1902). Farmer, painter and Communist eer.

Villiam Rust (d 1949). Editor of the *Daily Worker*.

ord Butler of Saffron Walden (d 1982) once declared, We have lived too long on old port and over-ripe pheasant.'

Lord Caccia (b 1905). Former British ambassador in Washington and Provost of Eton.

Catherine Oxenberg (b 1961) played the Princess of Wales in an American TV film about the Royal Wedding.

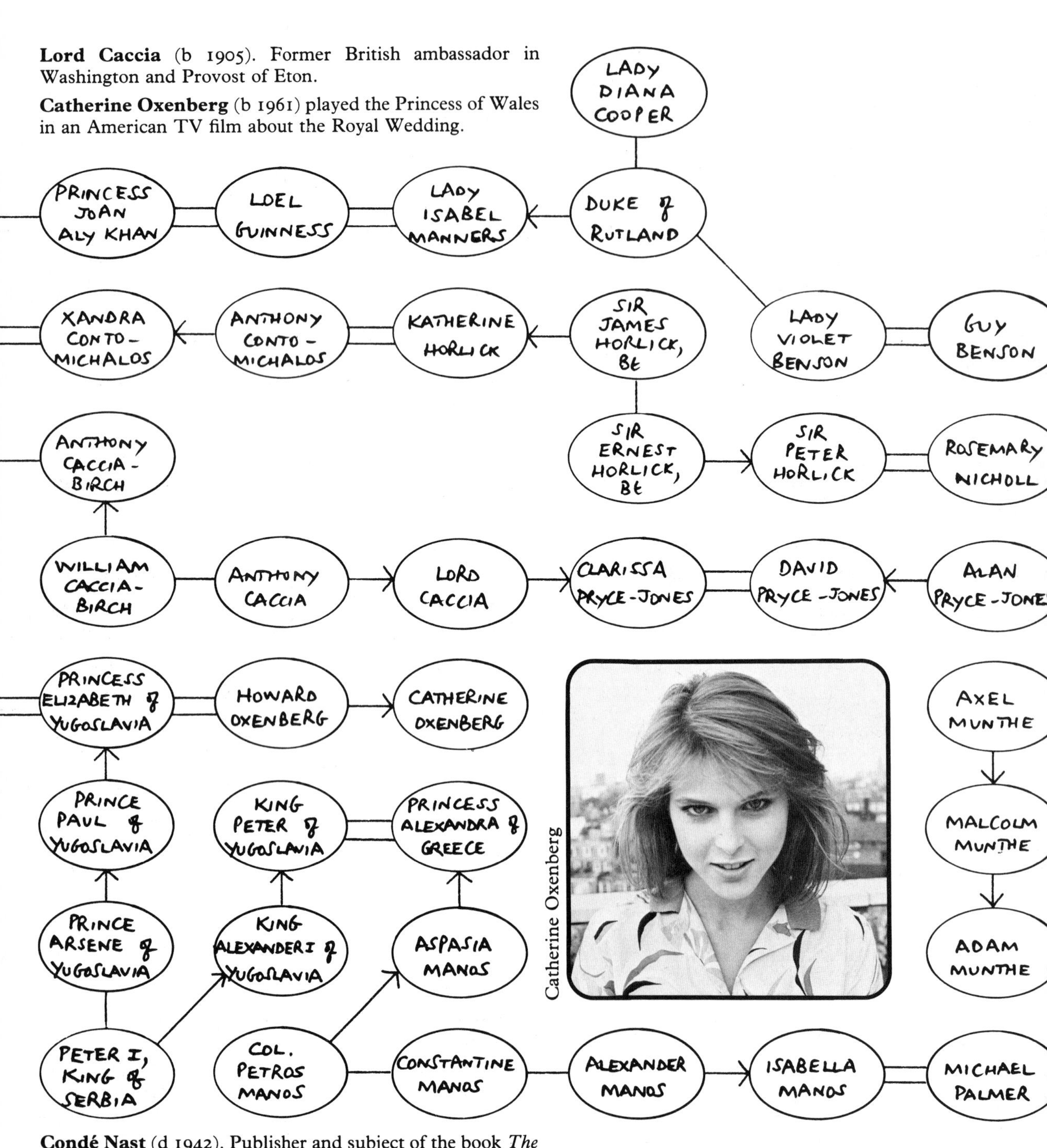

LADY DIANA COOPER
PRINCESS JOAN ALY KHAN
LOEL GUINNESS
LADY ISABEL MANNERS
DUKE OF RUTLAND
XANDRA CONTO-MICHALOS
ANTHONY CONTO-MICHALOS
KATHERINE HORLICK
SIR JAMES HORLICK, Bt
LADY VIOLET BENSON
GUY BENSON
ANTHONY CACCIA-BIRCH
SIR ERNEST HORLICK, Bt
SIR PETER HORLICK
ROSEMARY NICHOLL
WILLIAM CACCIA-BIRCH
ANTHONY CACCIA
LORD CACCIA
CLARISSA PRYCE-JONES
DAVID PRYCE-JONES
ALAN PRYCE-JONES
PRINCESS ELIZABETH OF YUGOSLAVIA
HOWARD OXENBERG
CATHERINE OXENBERG
AXEL MUNTHE
PRINCE PAUL OF YUGOSLAVIA
KING PETER OF YUGOSLAVIA
PRINCESS ALEXANDRA OF GREECE
MALCOLM MUNTHE
PRINCE ARSENE OF YUGOSLAVIA
KING ALEXANDER I OF YUGOSLAVIA
ASPASIA MANOS
ADAM MUNTHE
PETER I, KING OF SERBIA
COL. PETROS MANOS
CONSTANTINE MANOS
ALEXANDER MANOS
ISABELLA MANOS
MICHAEL PALMER

Catherine Oxenberg

Condé Nast (d 1942). Publisher and subject of the book *The Man who was Vogue*.

Sir Rex Benson (d 1968). Captain of the Eton XI and president of Pop who became chairman of his family's merchant bank.

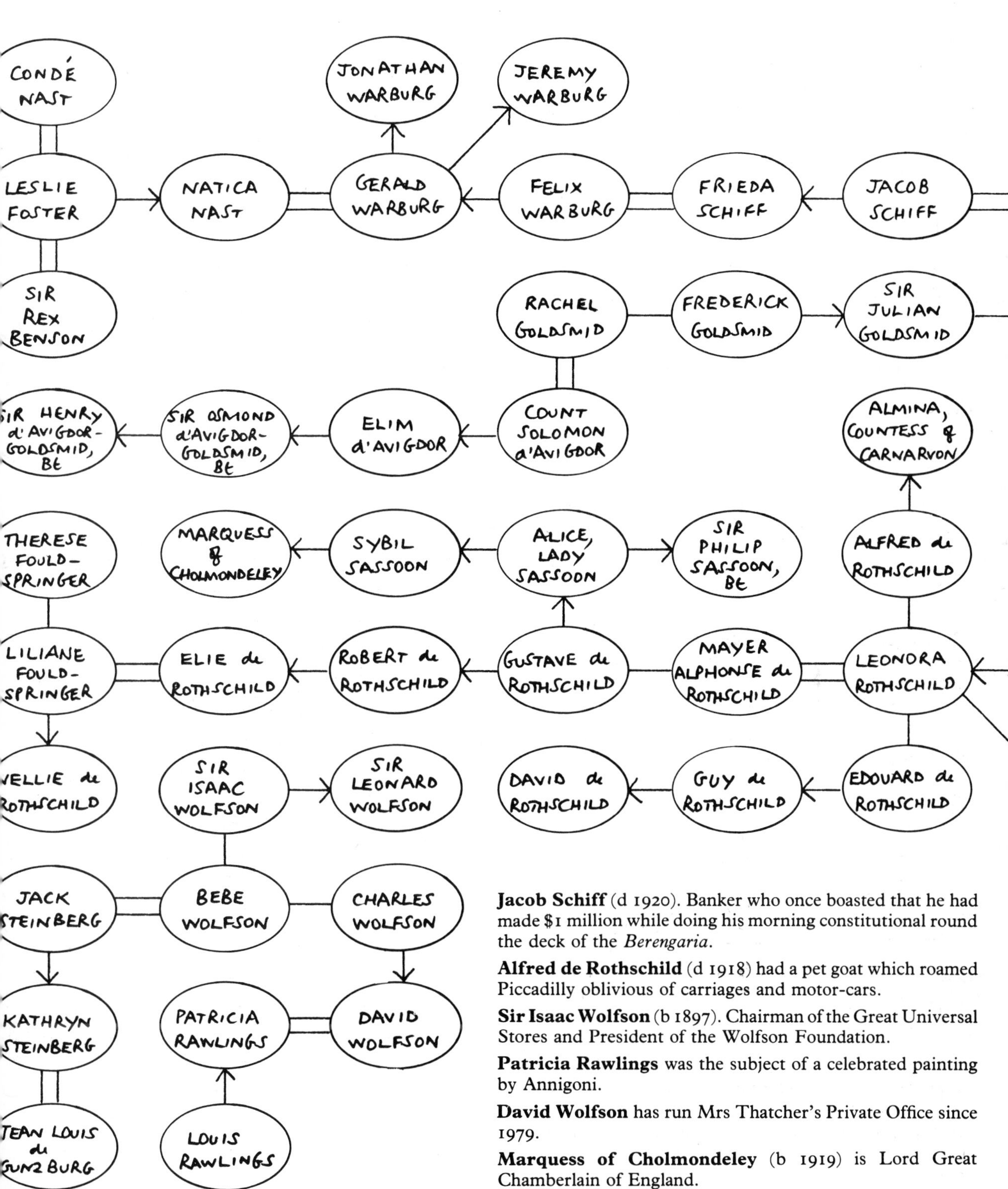
CONDÉ NAST
JONATHAN WARBURG
JEREMY WARBURG
LESLIE FOSTER
NATICA NAST
GERALD WARBURG
FELIX WARBURG
FRIEDA SCHIFF
JACOB SCHIFF
SIR REX BENSON
RACHEL GOLDSMID
FREDERICK GOLDSMID
SIR JULIAN GOLDSMID
SIR HENRY d'AVIGDOR-GOLDSMID, Bt
SIR OSMOND d'AVIGDOR-GOLDSMID, Bt
ELIM d'AVIGDOR
COUNT SOLOMON d'AVIGDOR
ALMINA, COUNTESS of CARNARVON
THERESE FOULD-SPRINGER
MARQUESS of CHOLMONDELEY
SYBIL SASSOON
ALICE, LADY SASSOON
SIR PHILIP SASSOON, Bt
ALFRED de ROTHSCHILD
LILIANE FOULD-SPRINGER
ELIE de ROTHSCHILD
ROBERT de ROTHSCHILD
GUSTAVE de ROTHSCHILD
MAYER ALPHONSE de ROTHSCHILD
LEONORA ROTHSCHILD
NELLIE de ROTHSCHILD
SIR ISAAC WOLFSON
SIR LEONARD WOLFSON
DAVID de ROTHSCHILD
GUY de ROTHSCHILD
EDOUARD de ROTHSCHILD
JACK STEINBERG
BEBE WOLFSON
CHARLES WOLFSON
KATHRYN STEINBERG
PATRICIA RAWLINGS
DAVID WOLFSON
JEAN LOUIS de GUNZBURG
LOUIS RAWLINGS

Jacob Schiff (d 1920). Banker who once boasted that he had made $1 million while doing his morning constitutional round the deck of the *Berengaria*.

Alfred de Rothschild (d 1918) had a pet goat which roamed Piccadilly oblivious of carriages and motor-cars.

Sir Isaac Wolfson (b 1897). Chairman of the Great Universal Stores and President of the Wolfson Foundation.

Patricia Rawlings was the subject of a celebrated painting by Annigoni.

David Wolfson has run Mrs Thatcher's Private Office since 1979.

Marquess of Cholmondeley (b 1919) is Lord Great Chamberlain of England.

Solomon Loeb was a professed agnostic and there were religious observances at his house on East 38th Street.

The Seligmans were the leading Jewish family of Amer noted for their watery, pale blue, heavy lidded eyes. They w said never to talk about money outside business.

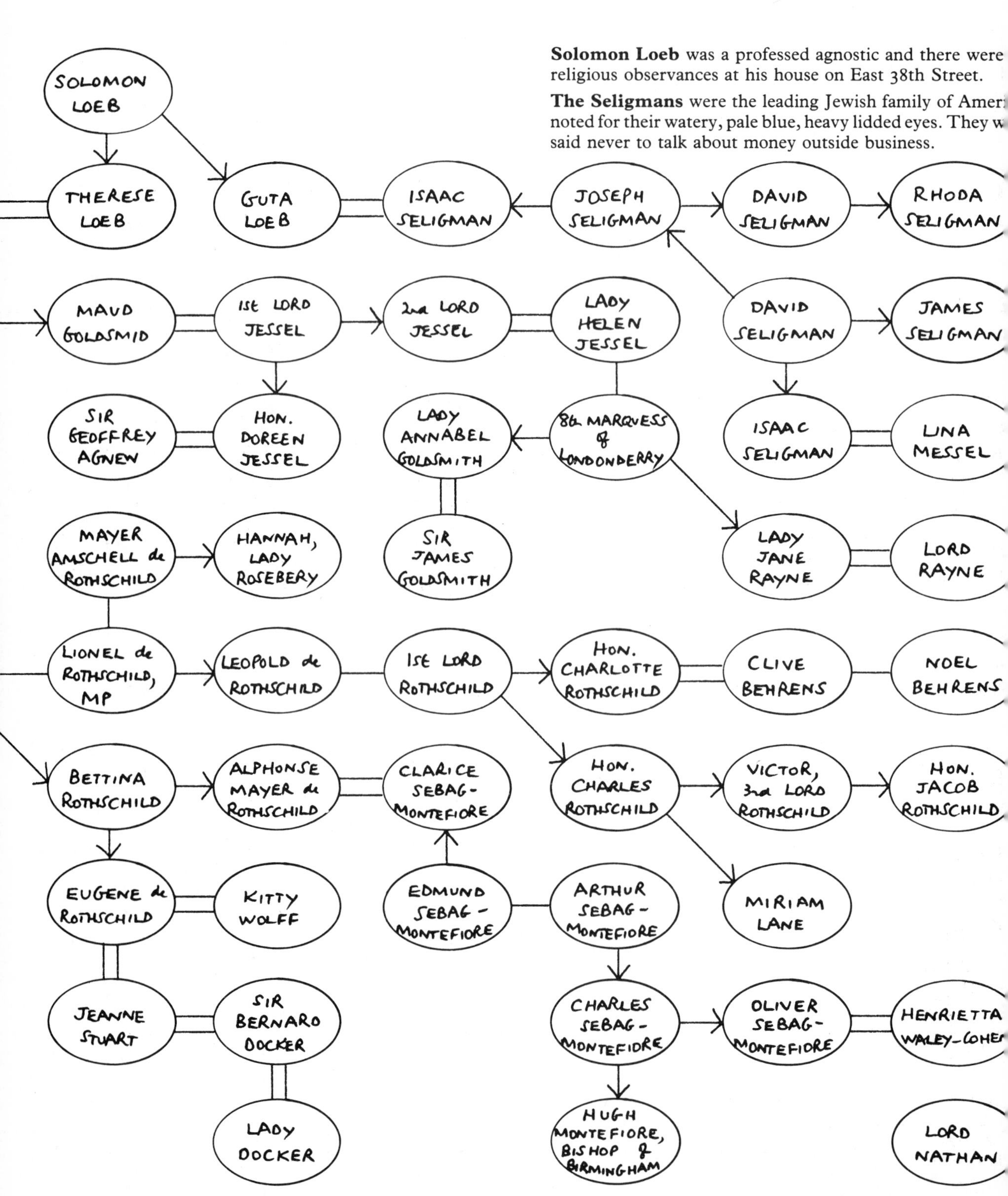
SOLOMON LOEB
THERESE LOEB
GUTA LOEB
ISAAC SELIGMAN
JOSEPH SELIGMAN
DAVID SELIGMAN
RHODA SELIGMAN
MAUD GOLDSMID
1st LORD JESSEL
2nd LORD JESSEL
LADY HELEN JESSEL
DAVID SELIGMAN
JAMES SELIGMAN
SIR GEOFFREY AGNEW
HON. DOREEN JESSEL
LADY ANNABEL GOLDSMITH
8th MARQUESS of LONDONDERRY
ISAAC SELIGMAN
LINA MESSEL
MAYER AMSCHELL de ROTHSCHILD
HANNAH, LADY ROSEBERY
SIR JAMES GOLDSMITH
LADY JANE RAYNE
LORD RAYNE
LIONEL de ROTHSCHILD, MP
LEOPOLD de ROTHSCHILD
1st LORD ROTHSCHILD
HON. CHARLOTTE ROTHSCHILD
CLIVE BEHRENS
NOEL BEHRENS
BETTINA ROTHSCHILD
ALPHONSE MAYER de ROTHSCHILD
CLARICE SEBAG-MONTEFIORE
HON. CHARLES ROTHSCHILD
VICTOR, 3rd LORD ROTHSCHILD
HON. JACOB ROTHSCHILD
EUGENE de ROTHSCHILD
KITTY WOLFF
EDMUND SEBAG-MONTEFIORE
ARTHUR SEBAG-MONTEFIORE
MIRIAM LANE
JEANNE STUART
SIR BERNARD DOCKER
CHARLES SEBAG-MONTEFIORE
OLIVER SEBAG-MONTEFIORE
HENRIETTA WALEY-COHE
LADY DOCKER
HUGH MONTEFIORE, BISHOP of BIRMINGHAM
LORD NATHAN

olph Lewisohn (d 1938). Cooper king, who had an art lery on top of his 5th Avenue house containing works by gas, Cézanne, Renoir, Van Gogh, Monet and Picasso.

n L. Loeb (b 1902). Former Governor of the New York ock Exchange.

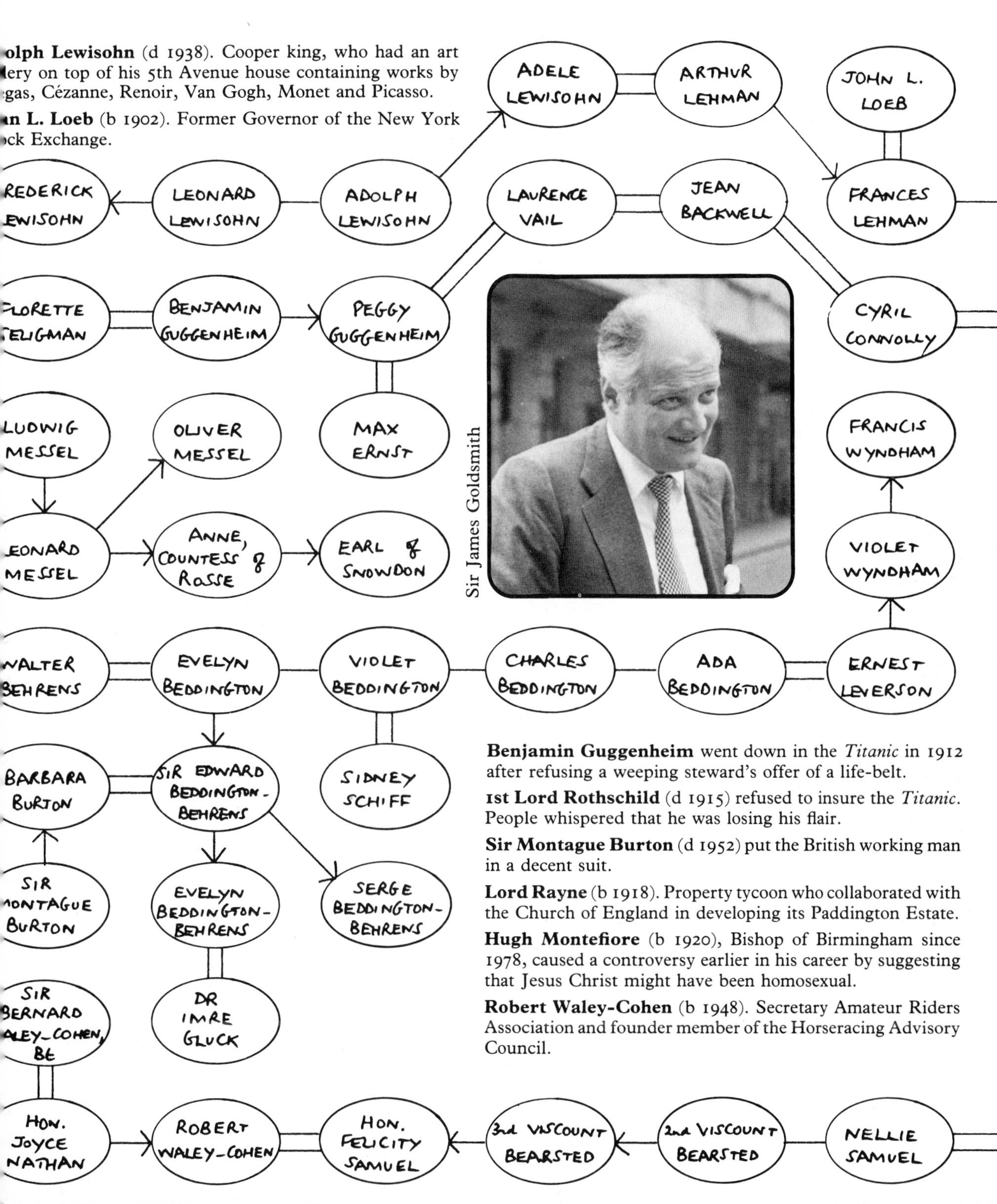
ADELE LEWISOHN
ARTHUR LEHMAN
JOHN L. LOEB
REDERICK EWISOHN
LEONARD LEWISOHN
ADOLPH LEWISOHN
LAURENCE VAIL
JEAN BACKWELL
FRANCES LEHMAN
LORETTE ELIGMAN
BENJAMIN GUGGENHEIM
PEGGY GUGGENHEIM
CYRIL CONNOLLY
LUDWIG MESSEL
OLIVER MESSEL
MAX ERNST
FRANCIS WYNDHAM
EONARD MESSEL
ANNE, COUNTESS of ROSSE
EARL of SNOWDON
VIOLET WYNDHAM
ALTER BEHRENS
EVELYN BEDDINGTON
VIOLET BEDDINGTON
CHARLES BEDDINGTON
ADA BEDDINGTON
ERNEST LEVERSON
BARBARA BURTON
SIR EDWARD BEDDINGTON-BEHRENS
SIDNEY SCHIFF
SIR MONTAGUE BURTON
EVELYN BEDDINGTON-BEHRENS
SERGE BEDDINGTON-BEHRENS
SIR BERNARD ALEY-COHEN, BT
DR IMRE GLUCK
HON. JOYCE NATHAN
ROBERT WALEY-COHEN
HON. FELICITY SAMUEL
3rd VISCOUNT BEARSTED
2nd VISCOUNT BEARSTED
NELLIE SAMUEL

Sir James Goldsmith

Benjamin Guggenheim went down in the *Titanic* in 1912 after refusing a weeping steward's offer of a life-belt.

1st Lord Rothschild (d 1915) refused to insure the *Titanic*. People whispered that he was losing his flair.

Sir Montague Burton (d 1952) put the British working man in a decent suit.

Lord Rayne (b 1918). Property tycoon who collaborated with the Church of England in developing its Paddington Estate.

Hugh Montefiore (b 1920), Bishop of Birmingham since 1978, caused a controversy earlier in his career by suggesting that Jesus Christ might have been homosexual.

Robert Waley-Cohen (b 1948). Secretary Amateur Riders Association and founder member of the Horseracing Advisory Council.

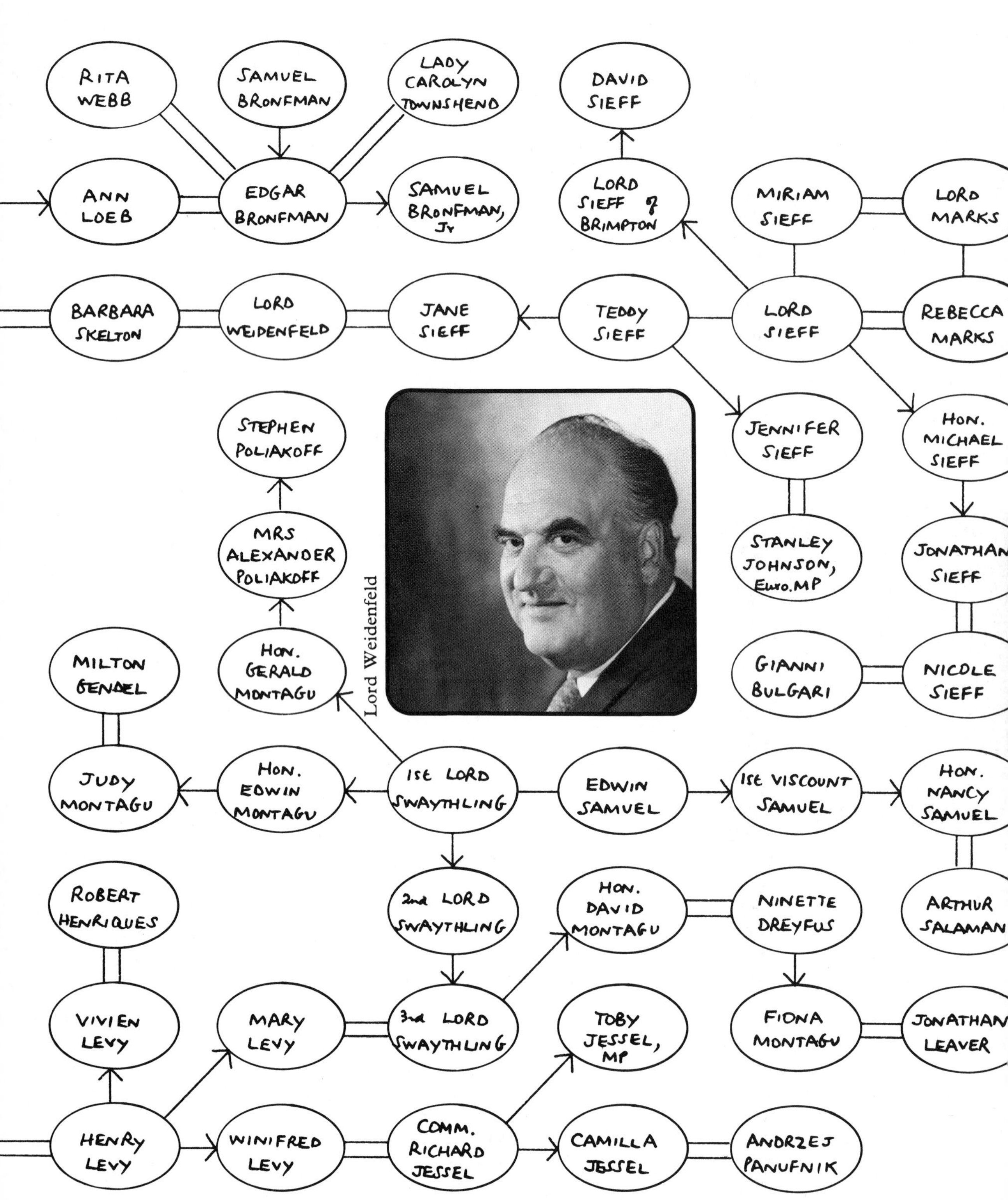
RITA WEBB
SAMUEL BRONFMAN
LADY CAROLYN TOWNSHEND
DAVID SIEFF
ANN LOEB
EDGAR BRONFMAN
SAMUEL BRONFMAN, Jr
LORD SIEFF of BRIMPTON
MIRIAM SIEFF
LORD MARKS
BARBARA SKELTON
LORD WEIDENFELD
JANE SIEFF
TEDDY SIEFF
LORD SIEFF
REBECCA MARKS
STEPHEN POLIAKOFF
JENNIFER SIEFF
HON. MICHAEL SIEFF
MRS ALEXANDER POLIAKOFF
STANLEY JOHNSON, Euro. MP
JONATHAN SIEFF
MILTON GENDEL
HON. GERALD MONTAGU
GIANNI BULGARI
NICOLE SIEFF
JUDY MONTAGU
HON. EDWIN MONTAGU
1st LORD SWAYTHLING
EDWIN SAMUEL
1st VISCOUNT SAMUEL
HON. NANCY SAMUEL
ROBERT HENRIQUES
2nd LORD SWAYTHLING
HON. DAVID MONTAGU
NINETTE DREYFUS
ARTHUR SALAMAN
VIVIEN LEVY
MARY LEVY
3rd LORD SWAYTHLING
TOBY JESSEL, MP
FIONA MONTAGU
JONATHAN LEAVER
HENRY LEVY
WINIFRED LEVY
COMM. RICHARD JESSEL
CAMILLA JESSEL
ANDRZEJ PANUFNIK

Lord Weidenfeld

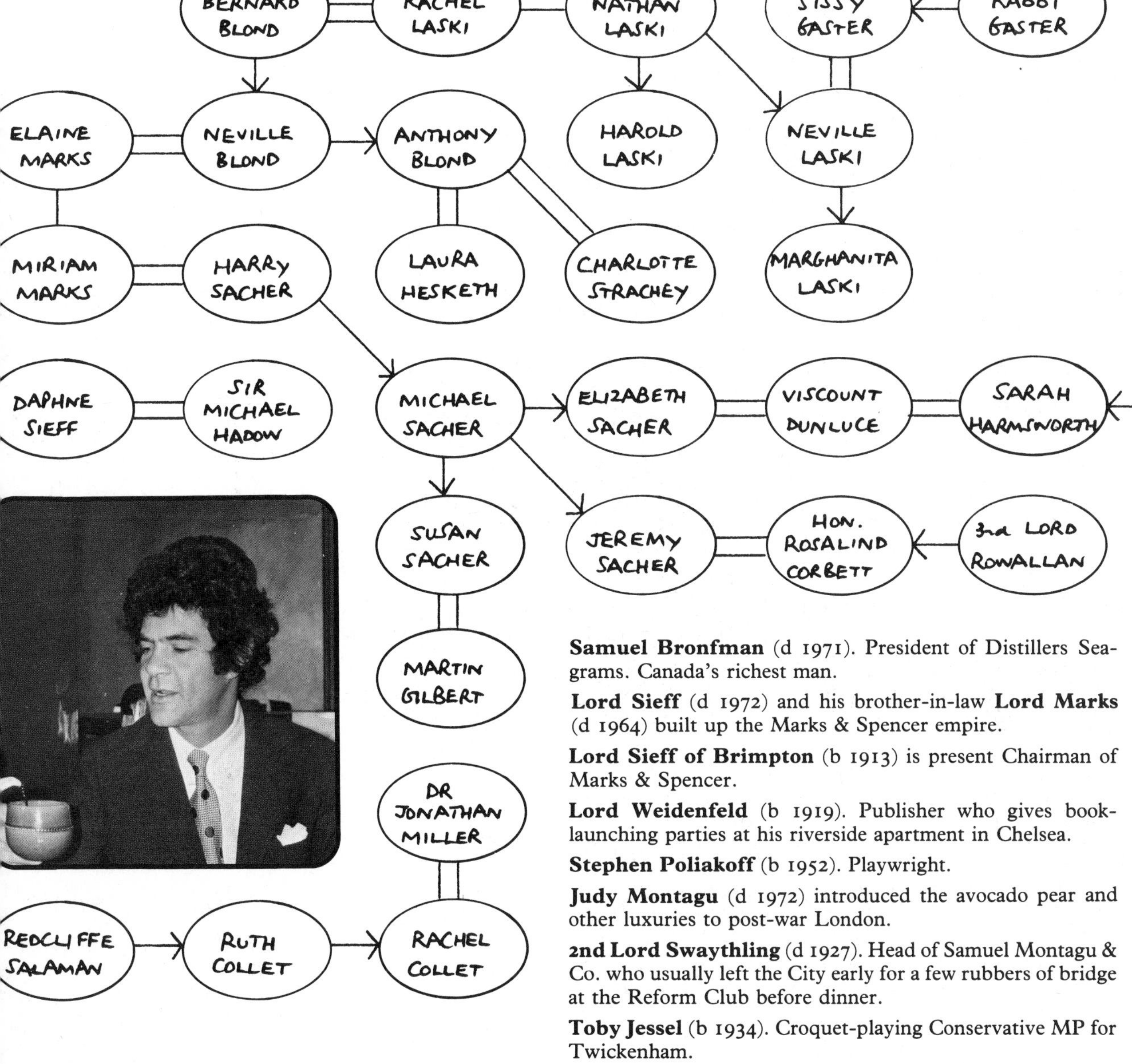
BERNARD BLOND
RACHEL LASKI
NATHAN LASKI
SISSY GASTER
RABBI GASTER
ELAINE MARKS
NEVILLE BLOND
ANTHONY BLOND
HAROLD LASKI
NEVILLE LASKI
MIRIAM MARKS
HARRY SACHER
LAURA HESKETH
CHARLOTTE STRACHEY
MARGHANITA LASKI
DAPHNE SIEFF
SIR MICHAEL HADOW
MICHAEL SACHER
ELIZABETH SACHER
VISCOUNT DUNLUCE
SARAH HARMSWORTH
SUSAN SACHER
JEREMY SACHER
HON. ROSALIND CORBETT
3rd LORD ROWALLAN
MARTIN GILBERT
DR JONATHAN MILLER
REDCLIFFE SALAMAN
RUTH COLLET
RACHEL COLLET

Samuel Bronfman (d 1971). President of Distillers Seagrams. Canada's richest man.

Lord Sieff (d 1972) and his brother-in-law **Lord Marks** (d 1964) built up the Marks & Spencer empire.

Lord Sieff of Brimpton (b 1913) is present Chairman of Marks & Spencer.

Lord Weidenfeld (b 1919). Publisher who gives book-launching parties at his riverside apartment in Chelsea.

Stephen Poliakoff (b 1952). Playwright.

Judy Montagu (d 1972) introduced the avocado pear and other luxuries to post-war London.

2nd Lord Swaythling (d 1927). Head of Samuel Montagu & Co. who usually left the City early for a few rubbers of bridge at the Reform Club before dinner.

Toby Jessel (b 1934). Croquet-playing Conservative MP for Twickenham.

Martin Gilbert (b 1936). Official biographer of Sir Winston Churchill.

Rabbi Gaster (d 1939). Chief Rabbi and most versatile scholar of Anglo-Jewry. As an orator, he could move audiences in half a dozen languages. He died during a car journey from Oxford to Reading.

Dr Jonathan Miller (b 1934). Entertainer, film director and medical man.

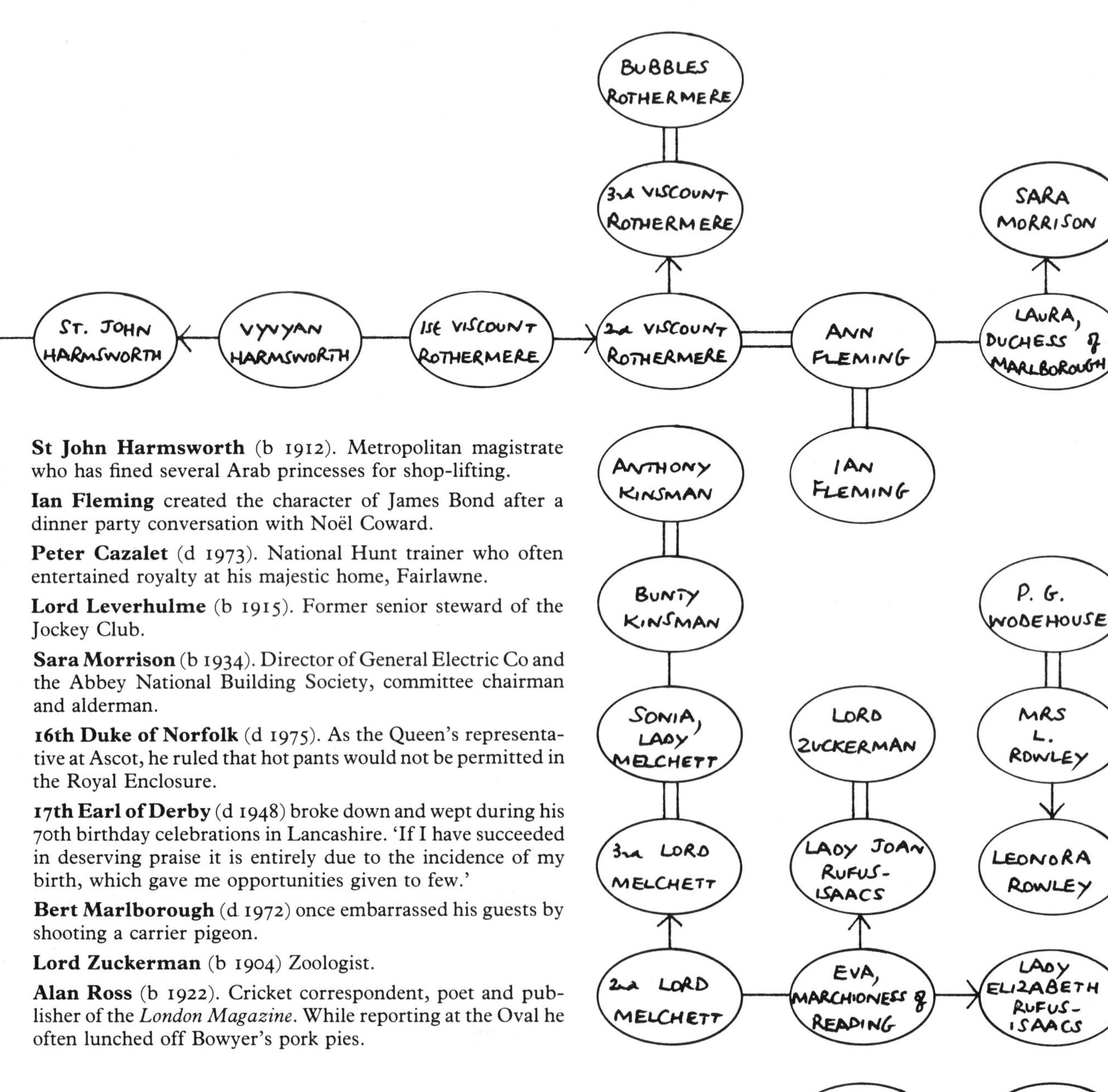
BUBBLES ROTHERMERE
3rd VISCOUNT ROTHERMERE
SARA MORRISON
ST. JOHN HARMSWORTH
VYVYAN HARMSWORTH
1st VISCOUNT ROTHERMERE
2nd VISCOUNT ROTHERMERE
ANN FLEMING
LAURA, DUCHESS of MARLBOROUGH
ANTHONY KINSMAN
IAN FLEMING
BUNTY KINSMAN
P. G. WODEHOUSE
SONIA, LADY MELCHETT
LORD ZUCKERMAN
MRS L. ROWLEY
3rd LORD MELCHETT
LADY JOAN RUFUS-ISAACS
LEONORA ROWLEY
2nd LORD MELCHETT
EVA, MARCHIONESS of READING
LADY ELIZABETH RUFUS-ISAACS
JEREMY MAAS
ATHENA MAAS

St John Harmsworth (b 1912). Metropolitan magistrate who has fined several Arab princesses for shop-lifting.

Ian Fleming created the character of James Bond after a dinner party conversation with Noël Coward.

Peter Cazalet (d 1973). National Hunt trainer who often entertained royalty at his majestic home, Fairlawne.

Lord Leverhulme (b 1915). Former senior steward of the Jockey Club.

Sara Morrison (b 1934). Director of General Electric Co and the Abbey National Building Society, committee chairman and alderman.

16th Duke of Norfolk (d 1975). As the Queen's representative at Ascot, he ruled that hot pants would not be permitted in the Royal Enclosure.

17th Earl of Derby (d 1948) broke down and wept during his 70th birthday celebrations in Lancashire. 'If I have succeeded in deserving praise it is entirely due to the incidence of my birth, which gave me opportunities given to few.'

Bert Marlborough (d 1972) once embarrassed his guests by shooting a carrier pigeon.

Lord Zuckerman (b 1904) Zoologist.

Alan Ross (b 1922). Cricket correspondent, poet and publisher of the *London Magazine*. While reporting at the Oval he often lunched off Bowyer's pork pies.

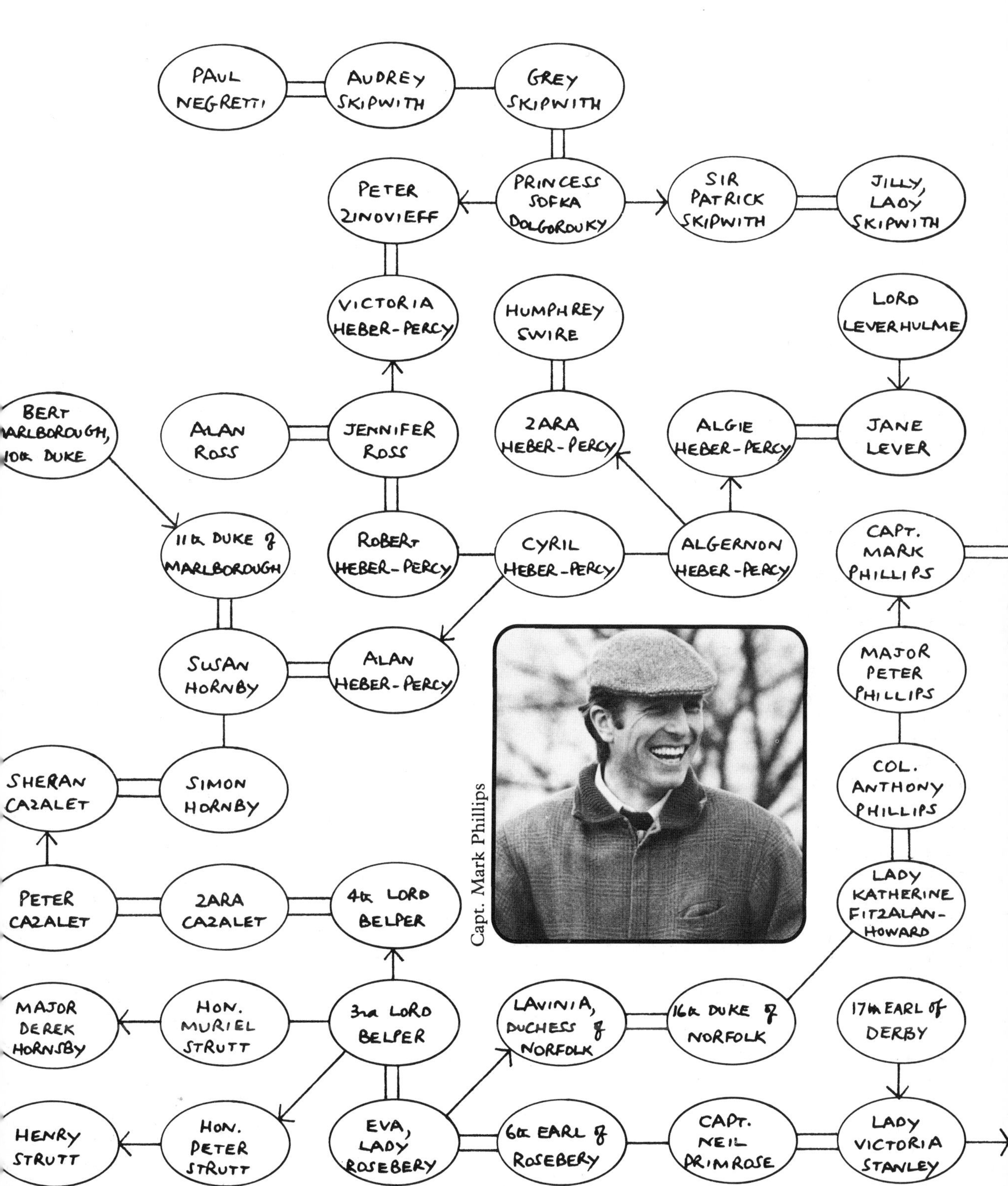
PAUL NEGRETTI
AUDREY SKIPWITH
GREY SKIPWITH
PETER ZINOVIEFF
PRINCESS SOFKA DOLGOROUKY
SIR PATRICK SKIPWITH
JILLY, LADY SKIPWITH
VICTORIA HEBER-PERCY
HUMPHREY SWIRE
LORD LEVERHULME
BERT MARLBOROUGH, 10th DUKE
ALAN ROSS
JENNIFER ROSS
ZARA HEBER-PERCY
ALGIE HEBER-PERCY
JANE LEVER
11th DUKE of MARLBOROUGH
ROBERT HEBER-PERCY
CYRIL HEBER-PERCY
ALGERNON HEBER-PERCY
CAPT. MARK PHILLIPS
SUSAN HORNBY
ALAN HEBER-PERCY
MAJOR PETER PHILLIPS
SHERAN CAZALET
SIMON HORNBY
COL. ANTHONY PHILLIPS
PETER CAZALET
ZARA CAZALET
4th LORD BELPER
LADY KATHERINE FITZALAN-HOWARD
MAJOR DEREK HORNSBY
HON. MURIEL STRUTT
3rd LORD BELPER
LAVINIA, DUCHESS of NORFOLK
16th DUKE of NORFOLK
17th EARL of DERBY
HENRY STRUTT
HON. PETER STRUTT
EVA, LADY ROSEBERY
6th EARL of ROSEBERY
CAPT. NEIL PRIMROSE
LADY VICTORIA STANLEY

Capt. Mark Phillips

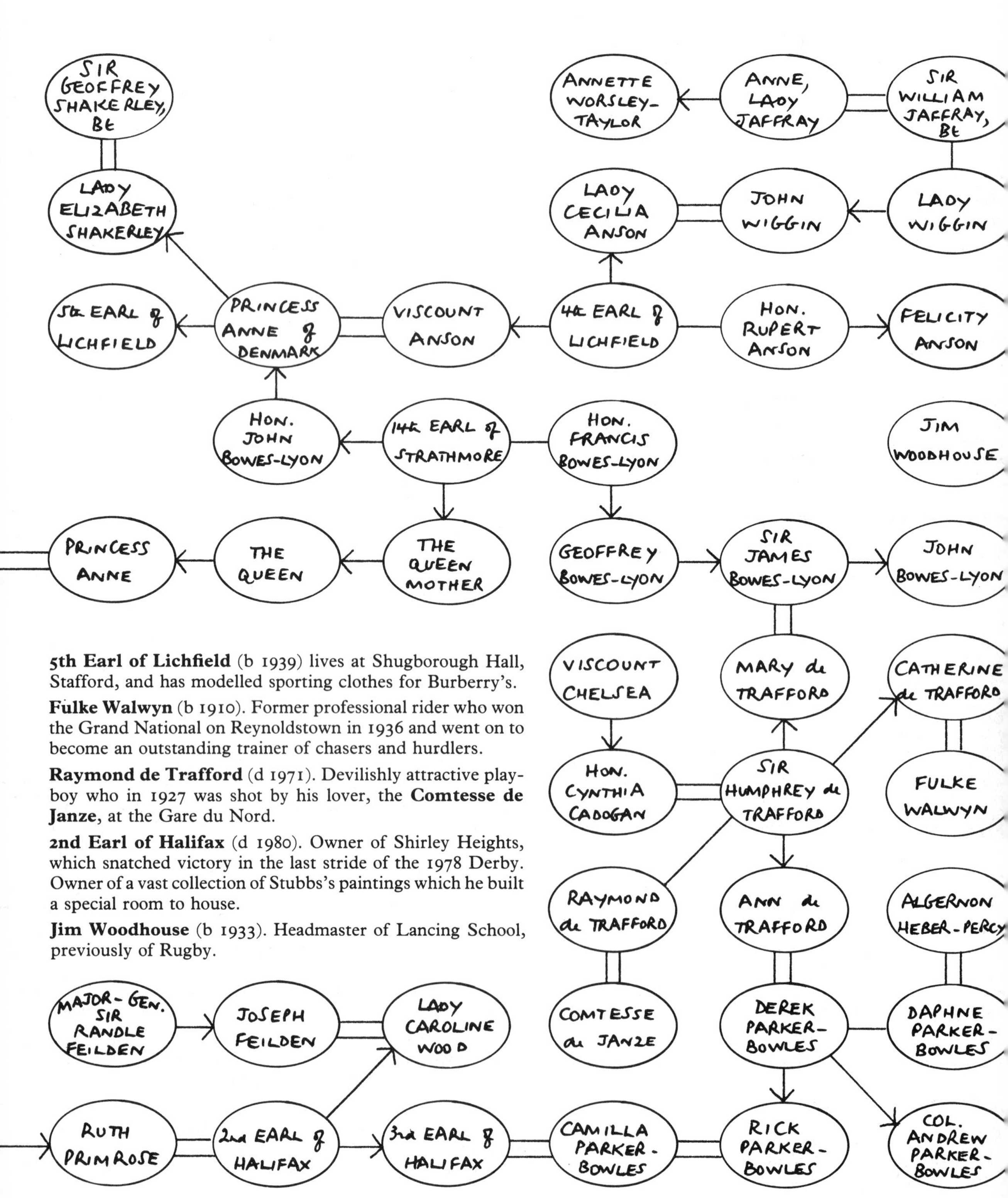
SIR GEOFFREY SHAKERLEY, Bt
ANNETTE WORSLEY-TAYLOR
ANNE, LADY JAFFRAY
SIR WILLIAM JAFFRAY, Bt
LADY ELIZABETH SHAKERLEY
LADY CECILIA ANSON
JOHN WIGGIN
LADY WIGGIN
5th EARL of LICHFIELD
PRINCESS ANNE of DENMARK
VISCOUNT ANSON
4th EARL of LICHFIELD
HON. RUPERT ANSON
FELICITY ANSON
HON. JOHN BOWES-LYON
14th EARL of STRATHMORE
HON. FRANCIS BOWES-LYON
JIM WOODHOUSE
PRINCESS ANNE
THE QUEEN
THE QUEEN MOTHER
GEOFFREY BOWES-LYON
SIR JAMES BOWES-LYON
JOHN BOWES-LYON
VISCOUNT CHELSEA
MARY de TRAFFORD
CATHERINE de TRAFFORD
HON. CYNTHIA CADOGAN
SIR HUMPHREY de TRAFFORD
FULKE WALWYN
RAYMOND de TRAFFORD
ANN de TRAFFORD
ALGERNON HEBER-PERCY
MAJOR-GEN. SIR RANDLE FEILDEN
JOSEPH FEILDEN
LADY CAROLINE WOOD
COMTESSE de JANZE
DEREK PARKER-BOWLES
DAPHNE PARKER-BOWLES
RUTH PRIMROSE
2nd EARL of HALIFAX
3rd EARL of HALIFAX
CAMILLA PARKER-BOWLES
RICK PARKER-BOWLES
COL. ANDREW PARKER-BOWLES

5th Earl of Lichfield (b 1939) lives at Shugborough Hall, Stafford, and has modelled sporting clothes for Burberry's.

Fulke Walwyn (b 1910). Former professional rider who won the Grand National on Reynoldstown in 1936 and went on to become an outstanding trainer of chasers and hurdlers.

Raymond de Trafford (d 1971). Devilishly attractive playboy who in 1927 was shot by his lover, the **Comtesse de Janze**, at the Gare du Nord.

2nd Earl of Halifax (d 1980). Owner of Shirley Heights, which snatched victory in the last stride of the 1978 Derby. Owner of a vast collection of Stubbs's paintings which he built a special room to house.

Jim Woodhouse (b 1933). Headmaster of Lancing School, previously of Rugby.

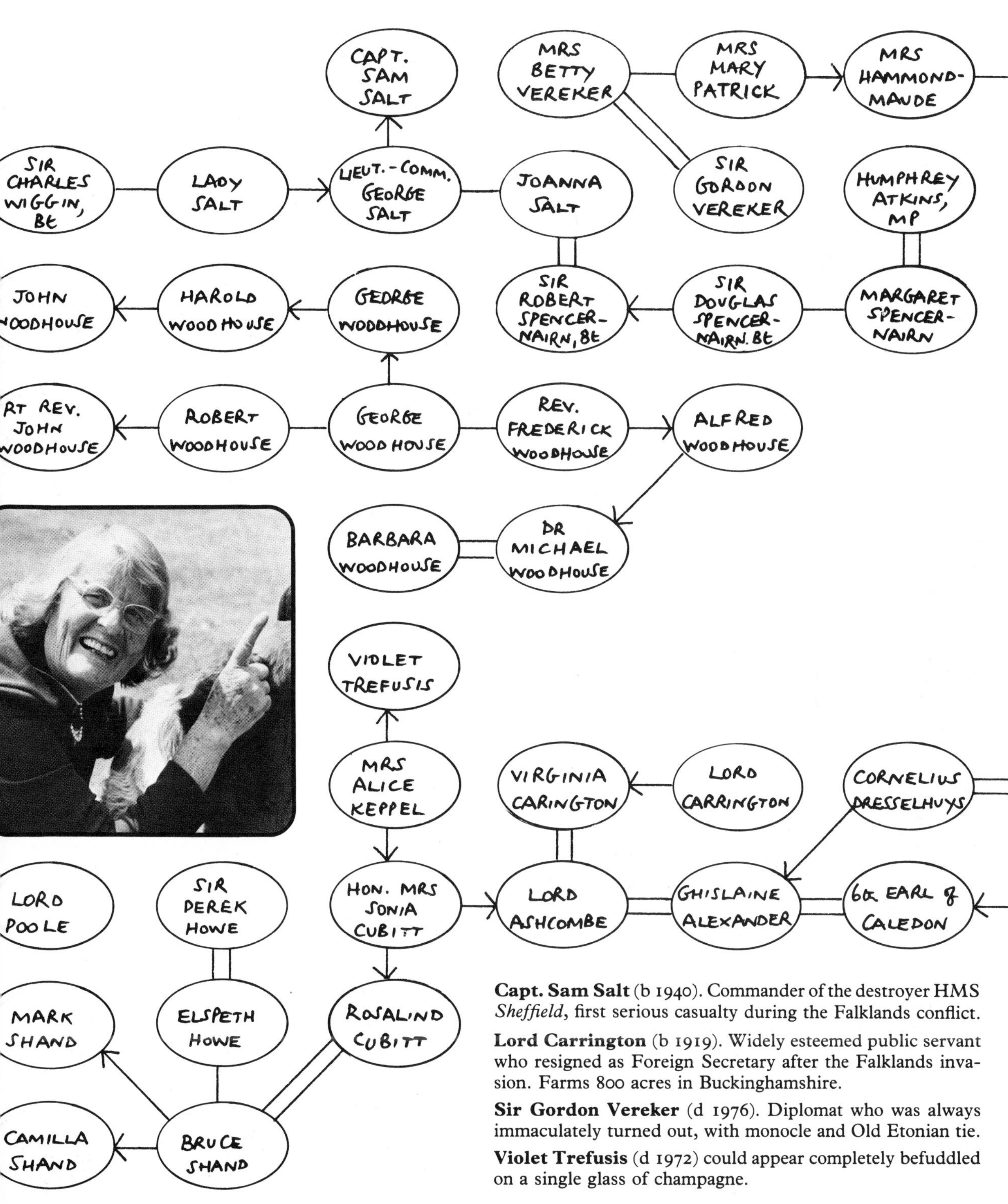
CAPT. SAM SALT
MRS BETTY VEREKER
MRS MARY PATRICK
MRS HAMMOND-MAUDE
SIR CHARLES WIGGIN, Bt
LADY SALT
LIEUT.-COMM. GEORGE SALT
JOANNA SALT
SIR GORDON VEREKER
HUMPHREY ATKINS, MP
JOHN WOODHOUSE
HAROLD WOODHOUSE
GEORGE WOODHOUSE
SIR ROBERT SPENCER-NAIRN, Bt
SIR DOUGLAS SPENCER-NAIRN, Bt
MARGARET SPENCER-NAIRN
RT REV. JOHN WOODHOUSE
ROBERT WOODHOUSE
GEORGE WOODHOUSE
REV. FREDERICK WOODHOUSE
ALFRED WOODHOUSE
BARBARA WOODHOUSE
DR MICHAEL WOODHOUSE
VIOLET TREFUSIS
MRS ALICE KEPPEL
VIRGINIA CARINGTON
LORD CARRINGTON
CORNELIUS DRESSELHUYS
LORD POOLE
SIR DEREK HOWE
HON. MRS SONIA CUBITT
LORD ASHCOMBE
GHISLAINE ALEXANDER
6th EARL of CALEDON
MARK SHAND
ELSPETH HOWE
ROSALIND CUBITT
CAMILLA SHAND
BRUCE SHAND

Capt. Sam Salt (b 1940). Commander of the destroyer HMS *Sheffield*, first serious casualty during the Falklands conflict.

Lord Carrington (b 1919). Widely esteemed public servant who resigned as Foreign Secretary after the Falklands invasion. Farms 800 acres in Buckinghamshire.

Sir Gordon Vereker (d 1976). Diplomat who was always immaculately turned out, with monocle and Old Etonian tie.

Violet Trefusis (d 1972) could appear completely befuddled on a single glass of champagne.

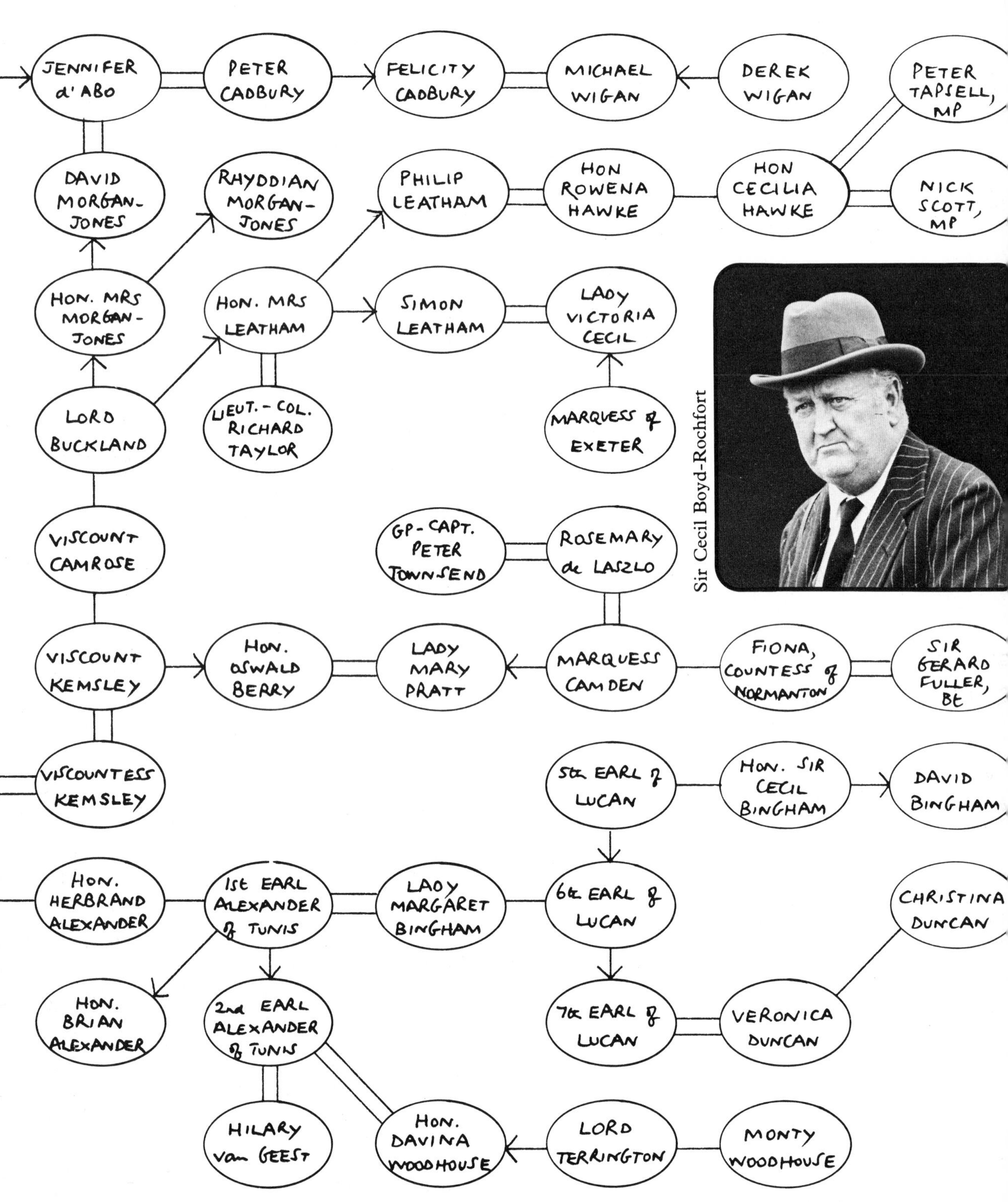
JENNIFER d'ABO
PETER CADBURY
FELICITY CADBURY
MICHAEL WIGAN
DEREK WIGAN
PETER TAPSELL, MP
DAVID MORGAN-JONES
RHYDDIAN MORGAN-JONES
PHILIP LEATHAM
HON ROWENA HAWKE
HON CECILIA HAWKE
NICK SCOTT, MP
HON. MRS MORGAN-JONES
HON. MRS LEATHAM
SIMON LEATHAM
LADY VICTORIA CECIL
LORD BUCKLAND
LIEUT.-COL. RICHARD TAYLOR
MARQUESS of EXETER
VISCOUNT CAMROSE
GP-CAPT. PETER TOWNSEND
ROSEMARY de LASZLO
VISCOUNT KEMSLEY
HON. OSWALD BERRY
LADY MARY PRATT
MARQUESS CAMDEN
FIONA, COUNTESS of NORMANTON
SIR GERARD FULLER, Bt
VISCOUNTESS KEMSLEY
5th EARL of LUCAN
HON. SIR CECIL BINGHAM
DAVID BINGHAM
HON. HERBRAND ALEXANDER
1st EARL ALEXANDER of TUNIS
LADY MARGARET BINGHAM
6th EARL of LUCAN
CHRISTINA DUNCAN
HON. BRIAN ALEXANDER
2nd EARL ALEXANDER of TUNIS
7th EARL of LUCAN
VERONICA DUNCAN
HILARY van GEEST
HON. DAVINA WOODHOUSE
LORD TERRINGTON
MONTY WOODHOUSE
Sir Cecil Boyd-Rochfort

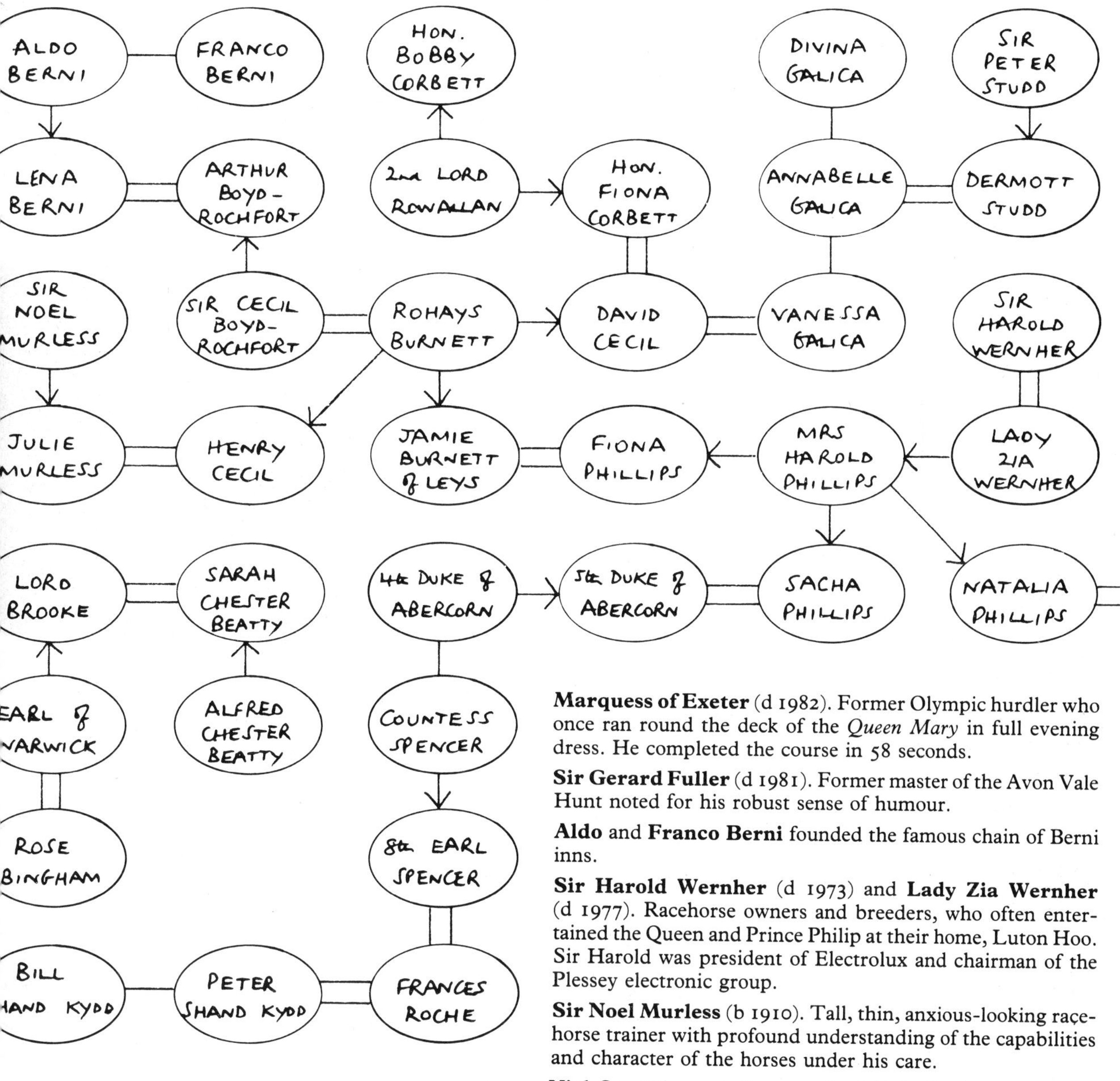
ALDO BERNI
FRANCO BERNI
HON. BOBBY CORBETT
DIVINA GALICA
SIR PETER STUDD
LENA BERNI
ARTHUR BOYD-ROCHFORT
2nd LORD ROWALLAN
HON. FIONA CORBETT
ANNABELLE GALICA
DERMOTT STUDD
SIR NOEL MURLESS
SIR CECIL BOYD-ROCHFORT
ROHAYS BURNETT
DAVID CECIL
VANESSA GALICA
SIR HAROLD WERNHER
JULIE MURLESS
HENRY CECIL
JAMIE BURNETT of LEYS
FIONA PHILLIPS
MRS HAROLD PHILLIPS
LADY ZIA WERNHER
LORD BROOKE
SARAH CHESTER BEATTY
4th DUKE of ABERCORN
5th DUKE of ABERCORN
SACHA PHILLIPS
NATALIA PHILLIPS
EARL of ARWICK
ALFRED CHESTER BEATTY
COUNTESS SPENCER
ROSE BINGHAM
8th EARL SPENCER
BILL HAND KYDD
PETER SHAND KYDD
FRANCES ROCHE

Marquess of Exeter (d 1982). Former Olympic hurdler who once ran round the deck of the *Queen Mary* in full evening dress. He completed the course in 58 seconds.

Sir Gerard Fuller (d 1981). Former master of the Avon Vale Hunt noted for his robust sense of humour.

Aldo and **Franco Berni** founded the famous chain of Berni inns.

Sir Harold Wernher (d 1973) and **Lady Zia Wernher** (d 1977). Racehorse owners and breeders, who often entertained the Queen and Prince Philip at their home, Luton Hoo. Sir Harold was president of Electrolux and chairman of the Plessey electronic group.

Sir Noel Murless (b 1910). Tall, thin, anxious-looking raçehorse trainer with profound understanding of the capabilities and character of the horses under his care.

Nick Scott (b 1933). Conservative MP for Chelsea and golfing and cricket enthusiast.

Divina Galica was captain of the British ski team.

Sir Cecil Boyd-Rochfort (d 1983). Racehorse trainer who stocked up with books at Hatchards before retiring to Ireland.

Lord Brooke (b 1934) distressed some of his relations by selling Warwick Castle and its contents.

Earl of Warwick (b 1911) tried to become a film-star and signed a contract with MGM.

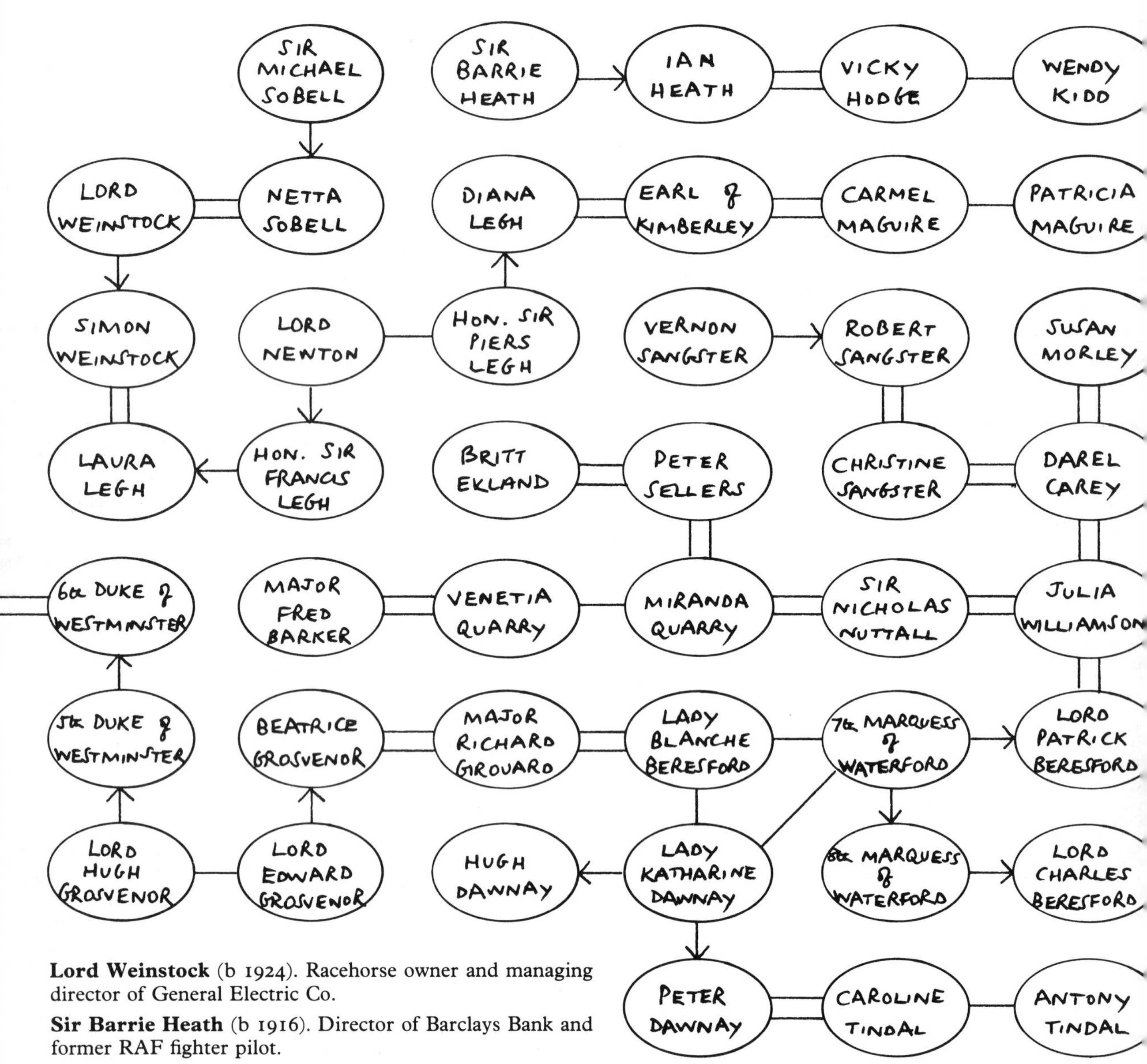
SIR MICHAEL SOBELL
SIR BARRIE HEATH
IAN HEATH
VICKY HODGE
WENDY KIDD
LORD WEINSTOCK
NETTA SOBELL
DIANA LEGH
EARL of KIMBERLEY
CARMEL MAGUIRE
PATRICIA MAGUIRE
SIMON WEINSTOCK
LORD NEWTON
HON. SIR PIERS LEGH
VERNON SANGSTER
ROBERT SANGSTER
SUSAN MORLEY
LAURA LEGH
HON. SIR FRANCIS LEGH
BRITT EKLAND
PETER SELLERS
CHRISTINE SANGSTER
DAREL CAREY
6th DUKE of WESTMINSTER
MAJOR FRED BARKER
VENETIA QUARRY
MIRANDA QUARRY
SIR NICHOLAS NUTTALL
JULIA WILLIAMSON
5th DUKE of WESTMINSTER
BEATRICE GROSVENOR
MAJOR RICHARD GIROUARD
LADY BLANCHE BERESFORD
7th MARQUESS of WATERFORD
LORD PATRICK BERESFORD
LORD HUGH GROSVENOR
LORD EDWARD GROSVENOR
HUGH DAWNAY
LADY KATHARINE DAWNAY
8th MARQUESS of WATERFORD
LORD CHARLES BERESFORD
PETER DAWNAY
CAROLINE TINDAL
ANTONY TINDAL

Lord Weinstock (b 1924). Racehorse owner and managing director of General Electric Co.

Sir Barrie Heath (b 1916). Director of Barclays Bank and former RAF fighter pilot.

Johnny Kidd (b 1944). Show-jumper.

Sir Max Aitken (b 1910) described power-boat-racing as 'like tearing up tenners in a shower'.

Bernard van Cutsem (d 1975). Newmarket trainer whose horses were famous for their general air of well-being and the shine and gloss on their coats.

Edward van Cutsem (b 1972) was a page at the wedding of the Prince and Princess of Wales.

Visc. Boyd of Merton (d 1983) had a collection of over 700 walking sticks.

Henry Clark (b 1929). Former MP for Antrim North w was unseated by the Rev. Ian Paisley.

Wallace Clark (b 1926). Irish linen manufacturer.

Antony Tindal (b 1953) runs two butcher's shops in Lond

Gay Kindersley (b 1930). Amateur steeplechase jockey.

Lady Perdita Blackwood (b 1934). Irish horsebreeder trainer who once remarked, 'I don't miss London and I'm s it doesn't miss me'.

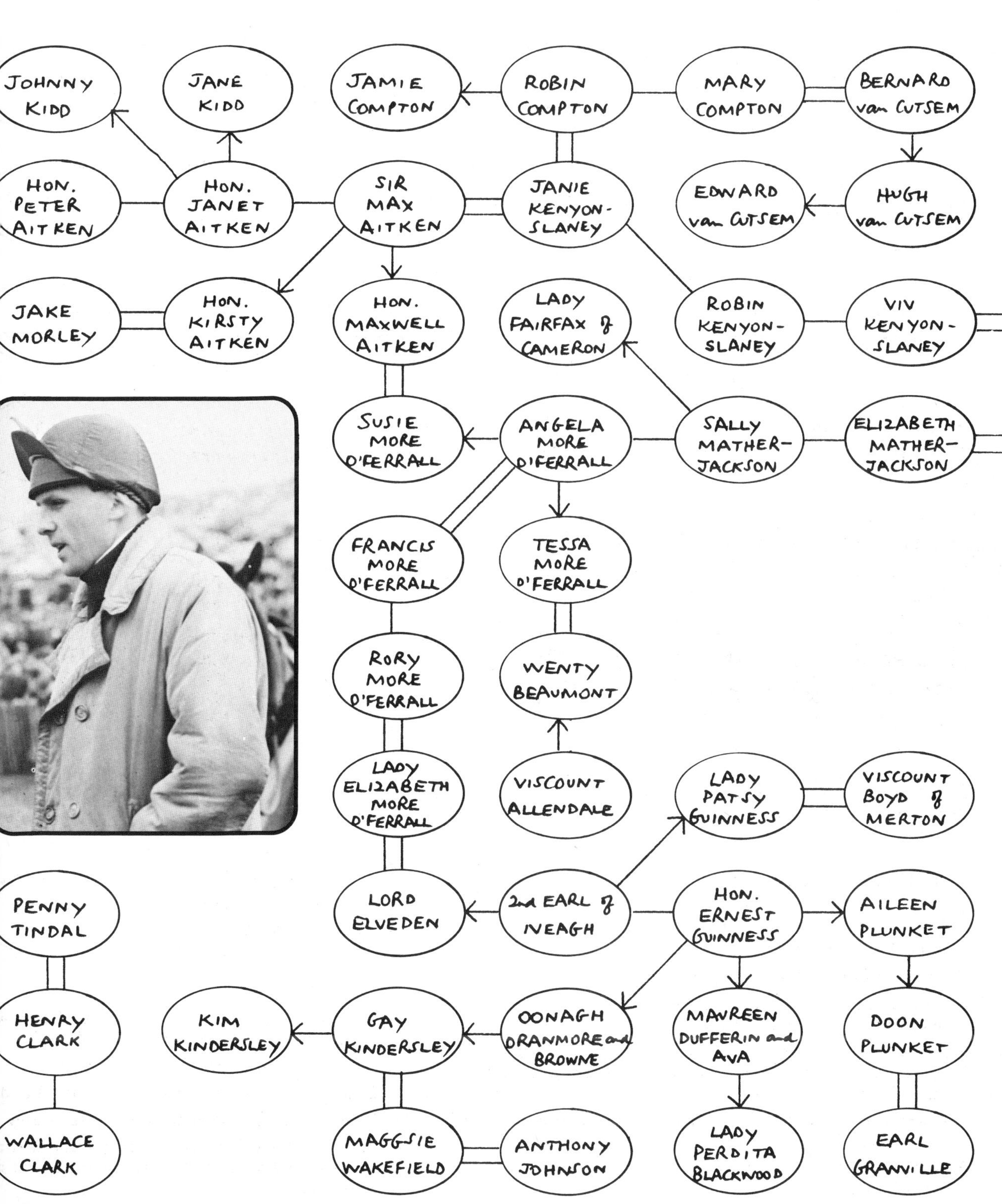
JOHNNY KIDD
JANE KIDD
JAMIE COMPTON
ROBIN COMPTON
MARY COMPTON
BERNARD van CUTSEM
HON. PETER AITKEN
HON. JANET AITKEN
SIR MAX AITKEN
JANIE KENYON-SLANEY
EDWARD van CUTSEM
HUGH van CUTSEM
JAKE MORLEY
HON. KIRSTY AITKEN
HON. MAXWELL AITKEN
LADY FAIRFAX of CAMERON
ROBIN KENYON-SLANEY
VIV KENYON-SLANEY
SUSIE MORE O'FERRALL
ANGELA MORE O'FERRALL
SALLY MATHER-JACKSON
ELIZABETH MATHER-JACKSON
FRANCIS MORE O'FERRALL
TESSA MORE O'FERRALL
RORY MORE O'FERRALL
WENTY BEAUMONT
LADY ELIZABETH MORE O'FERRALL
VISCOUNT ALLENDALE
LADY PATSY GUINNESS
VISCOUNT BOYD of MERTON
PENNY TINDAL
LORD ELVEDEN
2nd EARL of IVEAGH
HON. ERNEST GUINNESS
AILEEN PLUNKET
HENRY CLARK
KIM KINDERSLEY
GAY KINDERSLEY
OONAGH ORANMORE and BROWNE
MAUREEN DUFFERIN and AVA
DOON PLUNKET
WALLACE CLARK
MAGGSIE WAKEFIELD
ANTHONY JOHNSON
LADY PERDITA BLACKWOOD
EARL GRANVILLE

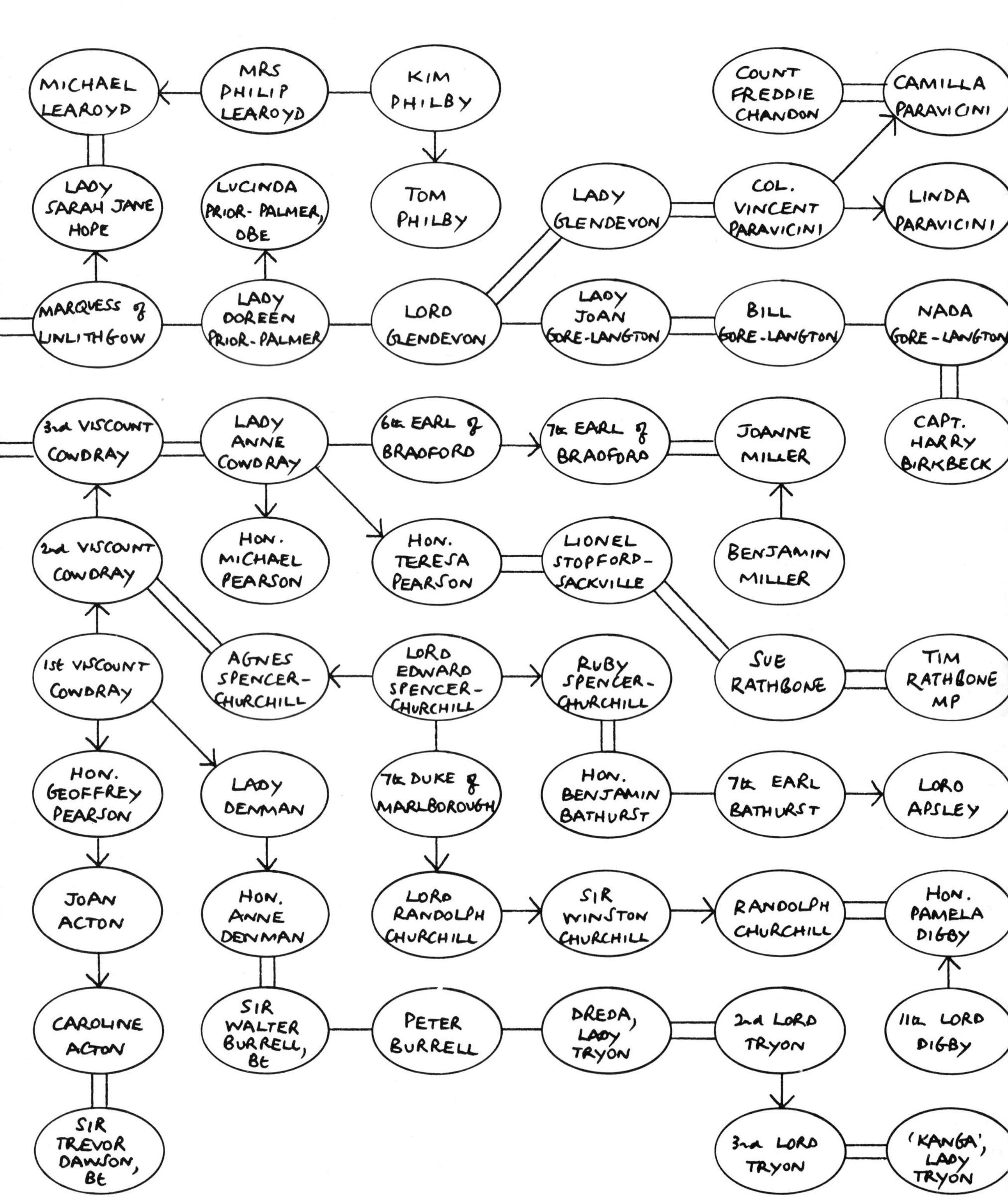
MICHAEL LEAROYD
MRS PHILIP LEAROYD
KIM PHILBY
COUNT FREDDIE CHANDON
CAMILLA PARAVICINI
LADY SARAH JANE HOPE
LUCINDA PRIOR-PALMER, OBE
TOM PHILBY
LADY GLENDEVON
COL. VINCENT PARAVICINI
LINDA PARAVICINI
MARQUESS of LINLITHGOW
LADY DOREEN PRIOR-PALMER
LORD GLENDEVON
LADY JOAN GORE-LANGTON
BILL GORE-LANGTON
NADA GORE-LANGTON
3rd VISCOUNT COWDRAY
LADY ANNE COWDRAY
6th EARL of BRADFORD
7th EARL of BRADFORD
JOANNE MILLER
CAPT. HARRY BIRKBECK
2nd VISCOUNT COWDRAY
HON. MICHAEL PEARSON
HON. TERESA PEARSON
LIONEL STOPFORD-SACKVILLE
BENJAMIN MILLER
1st VISCOUNT COWDRAY
AGNES SPENCER-CHURCHILL
LORD EDWARD SPENCER-CHURCHILL
RUBY SPENCER-CHURCHILL
SUE RATHBONE
TIM RATHBONE MP
HON. GEOFFREY PEARSON
LADY DENMAN
7th DUKE of MARLBOROUGH
HON. BENJAMIN BATHURST
7th EARL BATHURST
LORD APSLEY
JOAN ACTON
HON. ANNE DENMAN
LORD RANDOLPH CHURCHILL
SIR WINSTON CHURCHILL
RANDOLPH CHURCHILL
HON. PAMELA DIGBY
CAROLINE ACTON
SIR WALTER BURRELL, Bt
PETER BURRELL
DREDA, LADY TRYON
2nd LORD TRYON
11th LORD DIGBY
SIR TREVOR DAWSON, Bt
3rd LORD TRYON
'KANGA', LADY TRYON

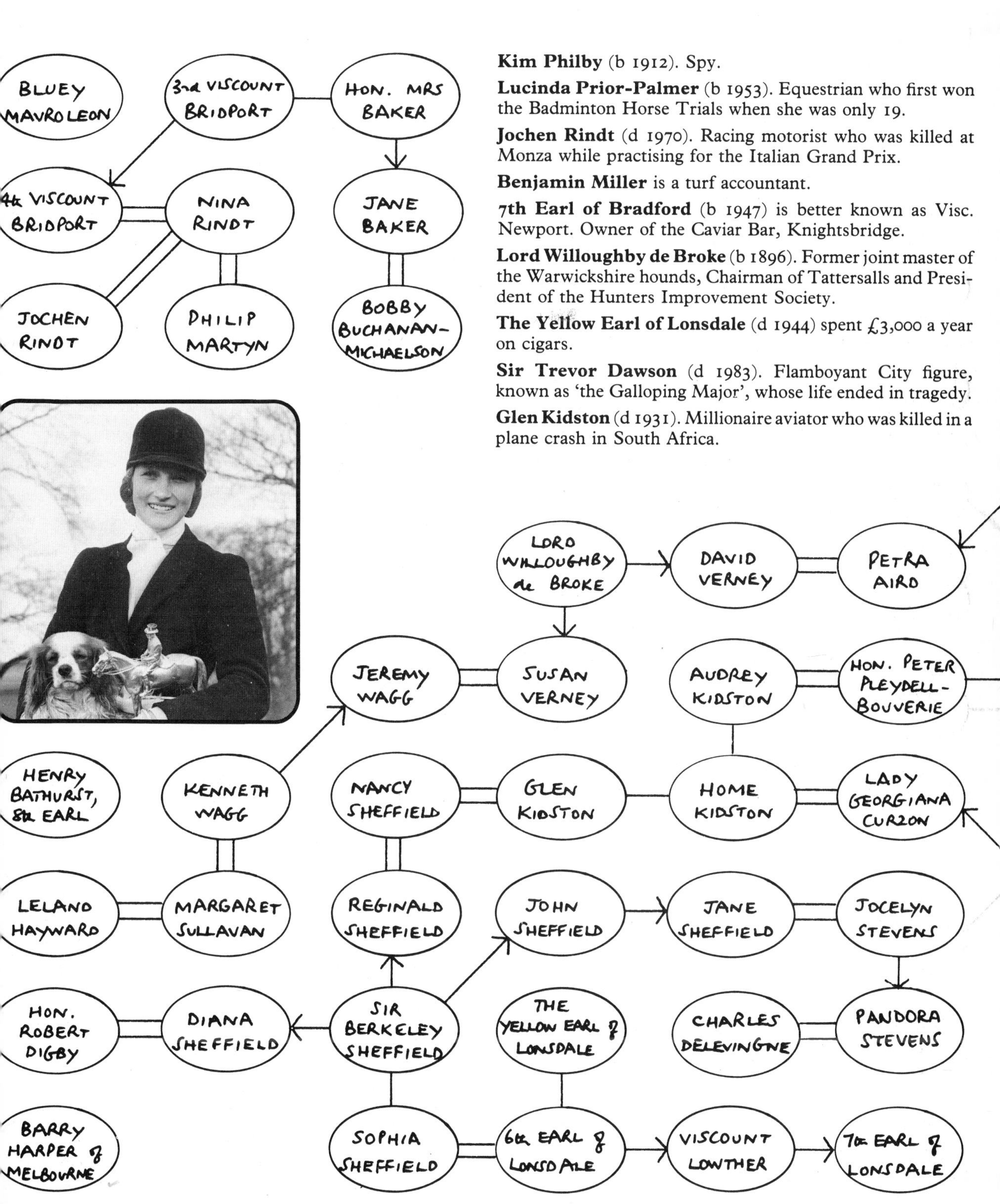
BLUEY MAVROLEON
3rd VISCOUNT BRIDPORT
HON. MRS BAKER
4th VISCOUNT BRIDPORT
NINA RINDT
JANE BAKER
JOCHEN RINDT
PHILIP MARTYN
BOBBY BUCHANAN-MICHAELSON
LORD WILLOUGHBY de BROKE
DAVID VERNEY
PETRA AIRD
JEREMY WAGG
SUSAN VERNEY
AUDREY KIDSTON
HON. PETER PLEYDELL-BOUVERIE
HENRY BATHURST, 8th EARL
KENNETH WAGG
NANCY SHEFFIELD
GLEN KIDSTON
HOME KIDSTON
LADY GEORGIANA CURZON
LELAND HAYWARD
MARGARET SULLAVAN
REGINALD SHEFFIELD
JOHN SHEFFIELD
JANE SHEFFIELD
JOCELYN STEVENS
HON. ROBERT DIGBY
DIANA SHEFFIELD
SIR BERKELEY SHEFFIELD
THE YELLOW EARL of LONSDALE
CHARLES DELEVINGNE
PANDORA STEVENS
BARRY HARPER of MELBOURNE
SOPHIA SHEFFIELD
6th EARL of LONSDALE
VISCOUNT LOWTHER
7th EARL of LONSDALE

Kim Philby (b 1912). Spy.

Lucinda Prior-Palmer (b 1953). Equestrian who first won the Badminton Horse Trials when she was only 19.

Jochen Rindt (d 1970). Racing motorist who was killed at Monza while practising for the Italian Grand Prix.

Benjamin Miller is a turf accountant.

7th Earl of Bradford (b 1947) is better known as Visc. Newport. Owner of the Caviar Bar, Knightsbridge.

Lord Willoughby de Broke (b 1896). Former joint master of the Warwickshire hounds, Chairman of Tattersalls and President of the Hunters Improvement Society.

The Yellow Earl of Lonsdale (d 1944) spent £3,000 a year on cigars.

Sir Trevor Dawson (d 1983). Flamboyant City figure, known as 'the Galloping Major', whose life ended in tragedy.

Glen Kidston (d 1931). Millionaire aviator who was killed in a plane crash in South Africa.

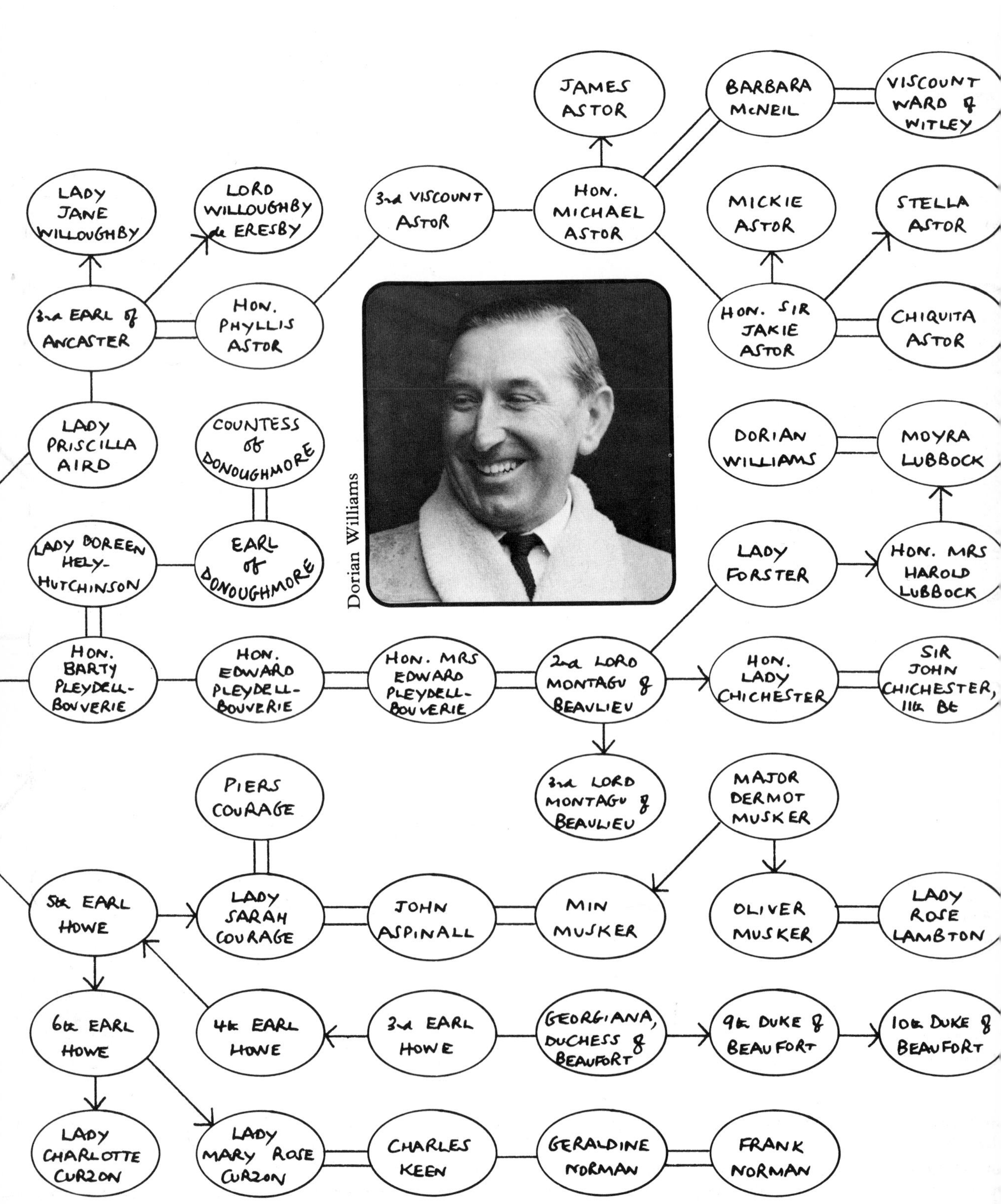
JAMES ASTOR
BARBARA McNEIL
VISCOUNT WARD of WITLEY
LADY JANE WILLOUGHBY
LORD WILLOUGHBY de ERESBY
3rd VISCOUNT ASTOR
HON. MICHAEL ASTOR
MICKIE ASTOR
STELLA ASTOR
3rd EARL of ANCASTER
HON. PHYLLIS ASTOR
HON. SIR JAKIE ASTOR
CHIQUITA ASTOR
LADY PRISCILLA AIRD
COUNTESS of DONOUGHMORE
DORIAN WILLIAMS
MOYRA LUBBOCK
LADY DOREEN HELY-HUTCHINSON
EARL of DONOUGHMORE
LADY FORSTER
HON. MRS HAROLD LUBBOCK
HON. BARTY PLEYDELL-BOUVERIE
HON. EDWARD PLEYDELL-BOUVERIE
HON. MRS EDWARD PLEYDELL-BOUVERIE
2nd LORD MONTAGU of BEAULIEU
HON. LADY CHICHESTER
SIR JOHN CHICHESTER, 11th Bt
PIERS COURAGE
3rd LORD MONTAGU of BEAULIEU
MAJOR DERMOT MUSKER
5th EARL HOWE
LADY SARAH COURAGE
JOHN ASPINALL
MIN MUSKER
OLIVER MUSKER
LADY ROSE LAMBTON
6th EARL HOWE
4th EARL HOWE
3rd EARL HOWE
GEORGIANA, DUCHESS of BEAUFORT
9th DUKE of BEAUFORT
10th DUKE of BEAUFORT
LADY CHARLOTTE CURZON
LADY MARY ROSE CURZON
CHARLES KEEN
GERALDINE NORMAN
FRANK NORMAN

Dorian Williams

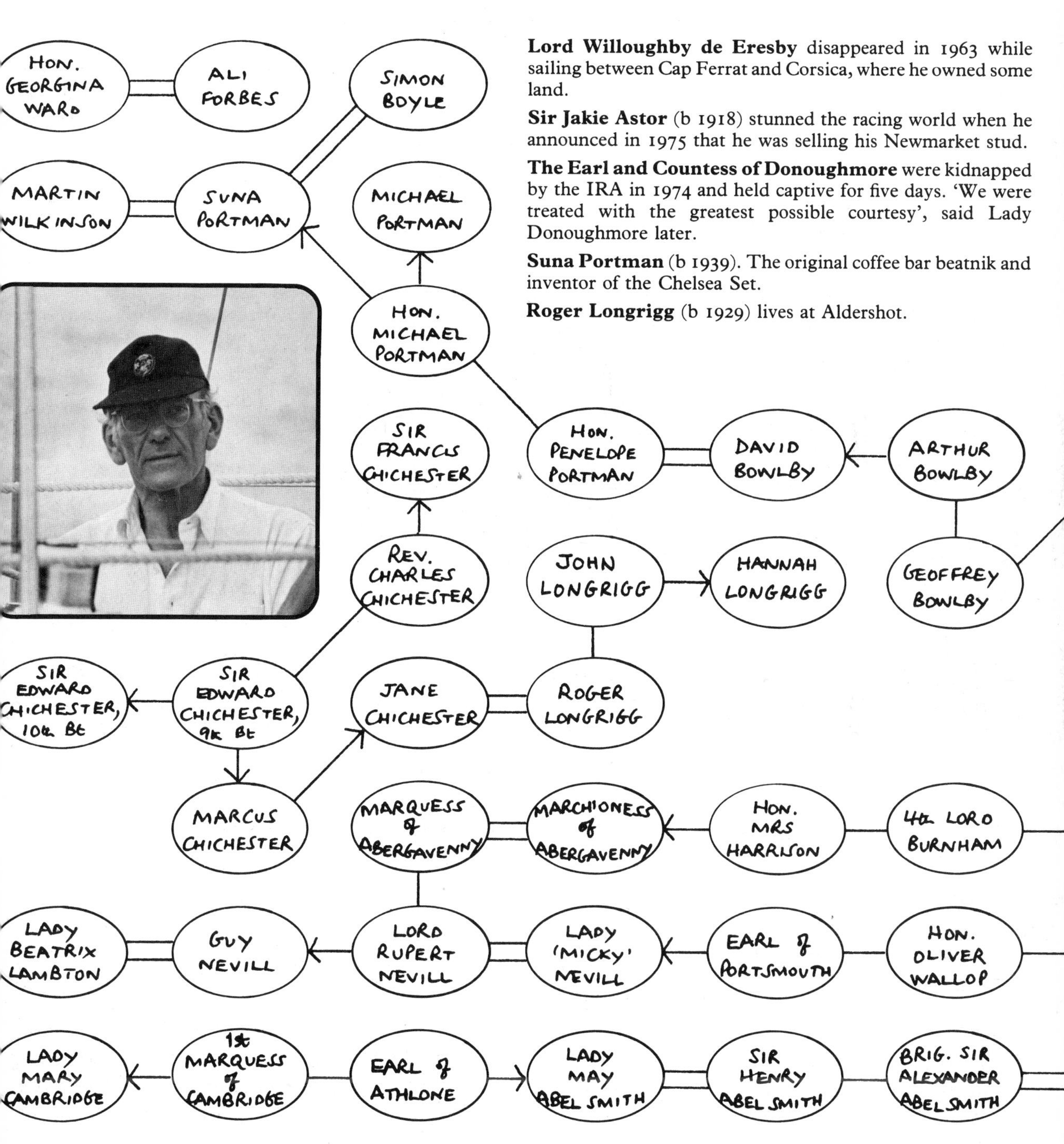
HON. GEORGINA WARD
ALI FORBES
SIMON BOYLE
MARTIN WILKINSON
SUNA PORTMAN
MICHAEL PORTMAN
HON. MICHAEL PORTMAN
SIR FRANCIS CHICHESTER
HON. PENELOPE PORTMAN
DAVID BOWLBY
ARTHUR BOWLBY
REV. CHARLES CHICHESTER
JOHN LONGRIGG
HANNAH LONGRIGG
GEOFFREY BOWLBY
SIR EDWARD CHICHESTER, 10th Bt
SIR EDWARD CHICHESTER, 9th Bt
JANE CHICHESTER
ROGER LONGRIGG
MARCUS CHICHESTER
MARQUESS of ABERGAVENNY
MARCHIONESS of ABERGAVENNY
HON. MRS HARRISON
4th LORD BURNHAM
LADY BEATRIX LAMBTON
GUY NEVILL
LORD RUPERT NEVILL
LADY 'MICKY' NEVILL
EARL of PORTSMOUTH
HON. OLIVER WALLOP
LADY MARY CAMBRIDGE
1st MARQUESS of CAMBRIDGE
EARL of ATHLONE
LADY MAY ABEL SMITH
SIR HENRY ABEL SMITH
BRIG. SIR ALEXANDER ABEL SMITH

Lord Willoughby de Eresby disappeared in 1963 while sailing between Cap Ferrat and Corsica, where he owned some land.

Sir Jakie Astor (b 1918) stunned the racing world when he announced in 1975 that he was selling his Newmarket stud.

The Earl and Countess of Donoughmore were kidnapped by the IRA in 1974 and held captive for five days. 'We were treated with the greatest possible courtesy', said Lady Donoughmore later.

Suna Portman (b 1939). The original coffee bar beatnik and inventor of the Chelsea Set.

Roger Longrigg (b 1929) lives at Aldershot.

.ord Montagu of Beaulieu (b 1926) is President of the how Biz Car Club.

oth Duke of Beaufort (b 1900) protested that the M4 motor-'ay would ruin some of the best hunting country in the world.

Frank Norman (d 1980). Novelist, playwright, Soho boozer and former Borstal boy best known for the script of the musical *Fings Ain't What They Used To Be*.

Sir Henry Abel Smith (b 1900). Polo enthusiast.

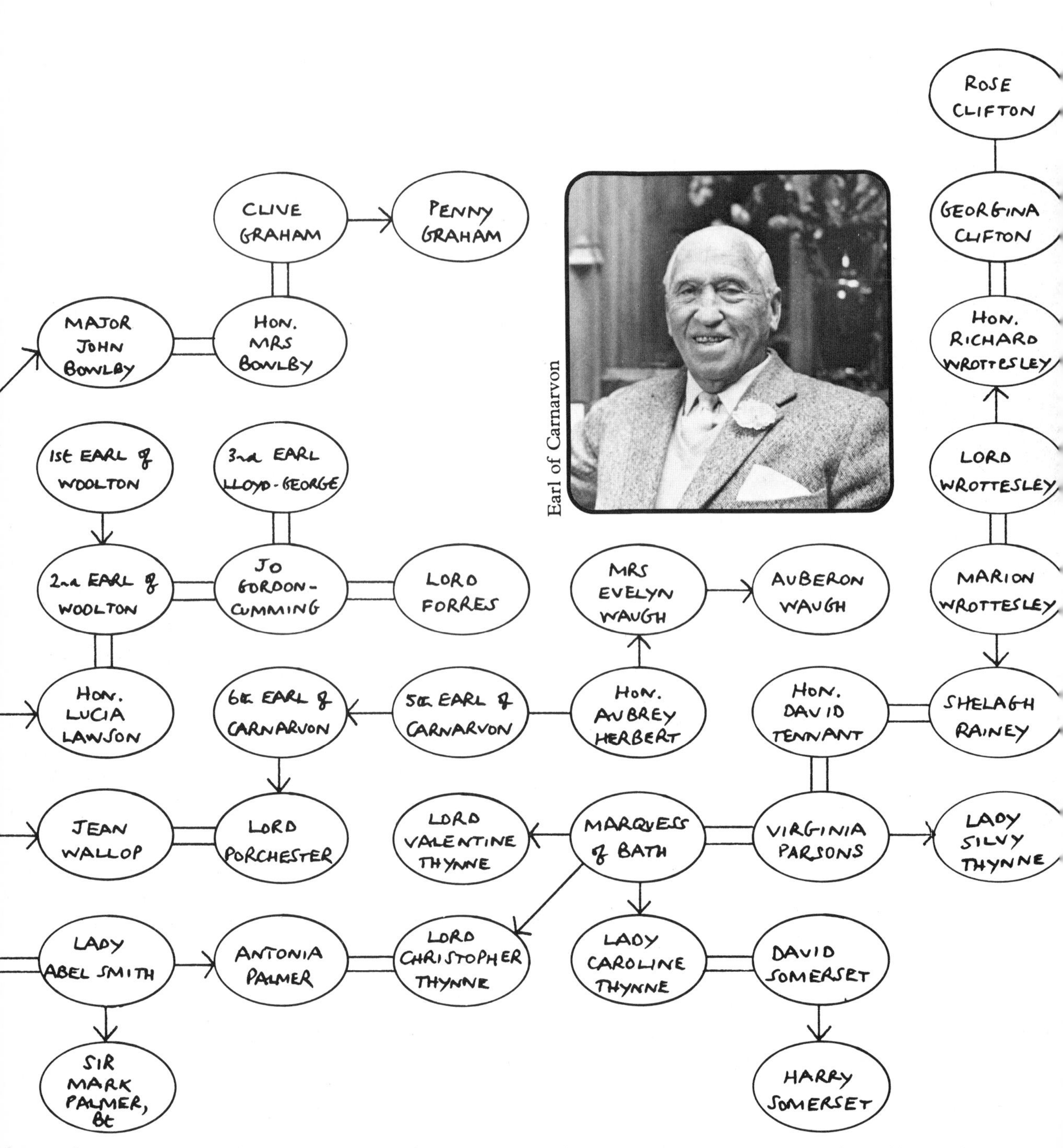
ROSE CLIFTON
GEORGINA CLIFTON
HON. RICHARD WROTTESLEY
LORD WROTTESLEY
MARION WROTTESLEY
SHELAGH RAINEY
CLIVE GRAHAM
PENNY GRAHAM
MAJOR JOHN BOWLBY
HON. MRS BOWLBY
1st EARL of WOOLTON
3rd EARL LLOYD-GEORGE
2nd EARL of WOOLTON
JO GORDON-CUMMING
LORD FORRES
MRS EVELYN WAUGH
AUBERON WAUGH
HON. LUCIA LAWSON
6th EARL of CARNARVON
5th EARL of CARNARVON
HON. AUBREY HERBERT
HON. DAVID TENNANT
JEAN WALLOP
LORD PORCHESTER
LORD VALENTINE THYNNE
MARQUESS of BATH
VIRGINIA PARSONS
LADY SILVY THYNNE
LADY ABEL SMITH
ANTONIA PALMER
LORD CHRISTOPHER THYNNE
LADY CAROLINE THYNNE
DAVID SOMERSET
SIR MARK PALMER, Bt
HARRY SOMERSET
Earl of Carnarvon

MARK VESTEY
LORD VESTEY
ANTHONY GILBEY
QUINTIN GILBEY
MICHAEL RAINEY
JOHN PACKE-DRURY-LOWE
ROSEMARY HOPE-VERE
JANE ORMSBY-GORE
PATRICK DRURY-LOWE
SIR NAPOLEON BRINCKMAN
5th LORD HARLECH
HON. LADY MAYALL
THEADORA BRINCKMAN
CHARLES CAMPBELL
GERARD CAMPBELL

Clive Graham (d 1974). *Daily Express* racing correspondent better known as 'The Scout'.

Hon. Richard Wrottesley (d 1970). Bob-sleigh champion and darling of the gossip columns in the 1960s.

1st Earl of Woolton (d 1964). Minister of Food who fought the 2nd World War 'on the kitchen front'. Inventor of the meatless Woolton Pie.

Auberon Waugh (b 1939). Dog-lovers' Party candidate at the 1979 General Election.

Marquess of Bath (b 1905). Snuff-taker and ballroom dancer.

Lord Valentine Thynne (d 1979). 'The Prince of the Beatniks'.

Quintin Gilbey was a racing journalist and author of *Fun Was My Living*.

Charles Campbell (b 1939). Schoolboy boxer and former manager of the Neal Street Restaurant, Covent Garden.

Anthony Gilbey (b 1933). Manufacturer of sporting trophies, replicas and heraldic memorabilia.

Index